Why Read PAVEL FLORENSKY?

Why Read?

JOHN P. BURGESS

Why Read PAVEL FLORENSKY?

Foreword by Andrew Louth

THE CATHOLIC UNIVERSITY OF AMERICA PRESS
Washington, D.C.

The paper used in this publication meets the minimum
requirements of American National Standards for
Information Science—Permanence of Paper for Printed
Library Materials, ANSI Z39.48-1992.
∞

Cataloging-in-Publication Data is available
from the Library of Congress

ISBN: 978-0-8132-3868-5
eISBN: 978-0-8132-3869-2

To theological colleagues and friends
in Belgorod and Moscow

TABLE OF CONTENTS

ILLUSTRATIONS

FOREWORD

In the chapter in *Modern Orthodox Thinkers* on Fr. Pavel Florensky, I concluded what I described as a "possibly idiosyncratic introduction" by saying: "I am increasingly coming to regard him as the greatest Orthodox thinker of recent times, one whose ideas have been preserved in an inevitably fragmented way, but who provides so many insights that we need to develop today."[1] It was about ten years ago that I wrote that, and all I have read, mainly by but also about, Florensky since then has only confirmed and deepened that conviction. Florensky had a mind so full of ideas, so able to make connexions across disciplines, and with a vision of Orthodoxy so profound and all-embracing, that we need to hear his voice. And for that we need John P. Burgess's book, *Why Read Florensky?*—a book that morphs into *How to Read Florensky?*, for the "why" and the "how" are intimately linked.

Why read Florensky? This is a question that can be asked of any author for many reasons, but in the case of Pavel Florensky the question seems especially acute. To ask it at all is to suggest that there is a problem or difficulty. And indeed there are a host of difficulties. His Russian is difficult, with long tangled sentences seeking to express complex thoughts, often of great originality. His learning was prodigious: As a priest, his theological vision was

1. *Modern Orthodox Thinkers: From the* Philokalia *to the Present* (2015), 41.

central to his thought, but he had mastered many other aspects of learning—philosophy, psychology, comparative linguistics, history, and phenomenology. He was fascinated by etymology, he acquired early on a knowledge of several modern languages, as well as classical languages, like Greek, Latin, and Hebrew. But he was also a scientist, his interest in the natural world, nurtured by his father from childhood, from flowers and plants to trees and the landscape of the natural world, running from botany, through biology, to geology. He began his university studies in mathematics, just as mathematics was advancing into new worlds of imaginary and complex numbers and challenging traditional notions of space and time, reaching back to Euclid, providing mathematical ways of understanding that enabled the coming ideas of relativity and quantum mechanics to be expressed and nurtured. He was on the point of embarking on a career as a mathematician when he abandoned that path and enrolled in the Spiritual Academy of Moscow to study theology. His learning was not just diverse; he saw *connexions*: connexions that linked the natural and human world, connexions conveyed by the etymology of names and words, connexions that lay beneath the words and syntax of different languages, connexions that linked the forgotten learning of the past with the astonishing progress of science since the Enlightenment and sought to bring to light what had been forgotten in the process. His first major work, *The Pillar and Ground of the Truth*, makes severe demands on the reader of the history of philosophy and theology, but also expects competence (at least) in the symbolic logic that undergirded Whitehead and Russell's *Principia Mathematica*, published only a few years before Florensky's book. So straightforward difficulties posed by diverse regions of learning, building bridges over the divide that had become something of a gulf during the nineteenth century between humane learning in art, literature, history, philosophy, and theology, on the one hand, and the world of the empirical sciences and mathematics, on the other.

So approaching Florensky is to set out on a course littered with difficulties. But that is only the beginning: To read Florensky is to encounter further difficulties—associated with the nature of what he has written. Some of these difficulties are intrinsic to Florensky, difficulties bound up with the genres in which he wrote. Further difficulties are due to the turbulent times in which he lived, for after the Bolshevik Revolution he remained in Russia, his scientific expertise being of value to the Soviet authorities. This placed limitations both on what he could write and, more explicitly, on what he could publish.

His writing and thinking falls into two groups separated by the caesura of the Russian Revolution: Before the Revolution his thinking consists, for the most part, of tributaries that converge on the themes of his first major work (the only one to be completed), *The Pillar and Ground of the Truth*. After the Revolution it seems that he saw his intellectual interests as components of a complex work to be called *On the Watersheds of Thought*. These intellectual enterprises were conceived of as complementary: The first, "an essay in Orthodox theodicy," that is the "justification of God," and the second concerned with "anthropodicy," "the justification of man." Both enterprises raise further difficulties. *The Pillar and Ground of the Truth*, though submitted as a master's thesis, manifests its academic credentials mainly in the sixteen appendices and 1,056 endnotes, the body of the thesis consisting of twelve letters, with a prologue and an afterword, continuously enumerated as fourteen chapters. To present the body of the thesis in letters is unusual, to say the least. Some of the letters, in part at least, seem to be to Sergei Troitsky, his fellow student at the Spiritual Academy, with whom he had a brief, but passionate friendship—which adds a further twist to the question of what we are reading in this work. The problems with *On the Watersheds of Thought* are bound up with the conditions under which its components were written: After the Revolution, when Florensky was employed on scientific projects for the Soviet state, and maybe later on, while imprisoned or in penal exile. These conditions severely limited his time and concentration. It is not entirely clear which of the works that survive would have belonged to *On the Watersheds* or how they are related one to another. There is a group of writings on art historical or art critical interests, sparked off by his involvement in the fate of the Trinity–St Sergii Monastery and its icons, relics, and other sacred items. An essay on "The Trinity–St Sergii Monastery and Russia" was published, but most of the rest of his profoundly interesting reflections on the nature of the icon, and especially its use of "reverse perspective," in contrast with linear perspective of most Western painting (though increasingly challenged by Florensky's contemporaries), had to wait decades to be published. A substantial work destined for *On the Watersheds* is *The Philosophy of Cult (?Worship)*, the structure and much of the content of which has been assembled by his grandson, Igumen Andronik. Another component is *Names*—consisting of essays on the inner significance of the Christian names we bear—which draws on an understanding of language, in which words have intrinsic significance, and which also underlies his passionate defence of the "Name-glorifying" monks, for whom "the name of God is God," who practised the Jesus prayer and alarmed the Russian Orthodox hierarchy—and attracted the defence of other intellectuals including Bulgakov and Losev. The collections of memoirs, *For my Children*, may also have been destined for inclusion. A later collection of letters to his wife, Anna, and his family, *All my Thoughts are of You*, can hardly have been intended by Florensky for *On the Watersheds of Thought*.

Clearly, the difficulties of reading Florensky pile up, to which one can add a final one, which applies especially to *On the Watersheds of Thought*, namely that he was writing for no clear audience, and when his works were eventually (and even then slowly) published, they were read in a context that Florensky himself could have hardly envisaged. A parallel to this might be the case of

Gerard Manley Hopkins, whose poems were written with no hope of publication and, when eventually published—by his friend, Robert Bridges, a very different poet from himself, in 1918—were greeted with some astonishment, his first biographer seeing in his œuvre "poetic idiosyncrasy."

In this book, John Burgess does not pile up the difficulties, as I have done, but takes us on a gentler course, placing his writings in the context of his life, and taking as a guide his letters, especially *For my Children* and *All my Thoughts are of You*. The difficulties with reading Florensky are not so much analysed—which could well be too discouraging—as illuminated as he takes the reader through his ideas, thus giving to the reader an initial grasp of some of Florensky's ideas, which provides signposts that will assist the reader, as and when he makes his own way through the dense thicket of Florensky's reflections. His presentation, for instance, of the nature of Orthodox worship in *The Philosophy of Cult* will inspire the reader with some Russian to tackle the fragments of Florensky's text, and perhaps even inspire someone to embark on translating that key work of Florensky's. The way in which Burgess admits the reader to his own search for Florensky—the places he visited, the people he met—will also be an encouragement to the reader. Burgess convinces us that we should indeed read Florensky, and helps us to embark on the endeavour: He not only puts future readers of Florensky in his debt, but will encourage many to embark on a daunting but nevertheless deeply worthwhile task.

Andrew Louth

PREFACE

This book offers an introduction to the life and thought of Fr. Pavel Florensky, a prominent religious philosopher of Russia's Silver Age at the beginning of the twentieth century. Florensky, an Orthodox priest, died in Stalin's gulag in 1937. His writings were long suppressed in the Soviet Union, and Western Protestant and Catholic theologians have known little about him. It is time to give Florensky his due. His worldview is as important today as it was during his lifetime: his deep sensitivity to the beauty of the natural world; his conviction that the religious cult—acts of worship and ritual—makes human culture possible; and his understanding of Christian faith as, above all, a way of seeing God's glorious presence in all of creation.

I write as a Protestant theologian, yet as one who has immersed himself deeply in Russia and its Orthodoxy. Between 2004 and 2019, I spent three sabbatical years in Russia, made numerous shorter trips in between, and was able to visit a number of the places associated with Florensky. Moreover, my experience, even as an outsider, of Orthodox worship and practice—its liturgical cycles, iconography, seasons of fasting and feasting, and monasteries and holy sites—has enabled me to understand Florensky's admonition that one must enter into Orthodoxy in order to understand it (and his) thinking.

The flow of the book corresponds roughly to the chronological sequence of Florensky's life and writings. I have not tried to be comprehensive. Rather, my goal has been to offer a close reading of several of Florensky's most important texts. I have studied them in the original Russian, and the translations are my own, unless I indicate otherwise. Where English translations are available, I have provided the corresponding page numbers in the notes. My quotations of Scripture are from the Revised Standard Version.

Florensky wrote prodigiously, and the scholarly literature about him is immense (although mostly from historians and philosophers, not theologians). I have consulted important parts of this literature but have not directly interacted with it. Nevertheless, I trust that my work will satisfy Florensky experts. Readers who wish to learn more may refer to the bibliography at the end of the book.

Research for this book began during a sabbatical year (2018–19) at the State University in Belgorod, Russia, where I was supported by a Fulbright fellowship and hosted by the social work-theological faculty. My thanks to Prof. Tamara Lipich, head of the faculty, for her commitment to making my stay productive and enjoyable. Prof. Pavel Ol'khov guided me into Florensky's works and became an invaluable conversation partner. With his support, I was able to publish two short pieces (in Russian) on Florensky in the university's online humanities journal, *Nauchnyi resul'tat* [Scientific Result]. Some of that material appears here in a different form.

Many other persons have given me encouragement during the writing of this book. I drafted the first chapters at the Orthodox Monastery of the Transfiguration in Ellwood City, Pennsylvania, where the abbess, Mother Christophora, and other members of the community welcomed me into their worship and fellowship. I am grateful to a group of former Pittsburgh Seminary students, led by the Rev. Garrett Yates, and to the Rev. Joseph D. Small for allowing me to introduce them to Florensky's writings, and they commented insightfully on early drafts of several of my chapters. Colleagues in the Society of Christian Ethics made extensive suggestions for revising a paper on Florensky that I delivered at an annual meeting and subsequently published in the Society's journal. In this case, too, I draw on previous material while framing it differently.

Two important scholars of Silver Age Russian religious philosophy, Dr. Paul Valliere and Dr. Christoph Schneider, generously agreed to read the manuscript in its entirety. Their suggestions for additional clarification and nuance have been tremendously helpful. Any errors that remain are my responsibility alone.

My special thanks goes to Dr. Michael Root and Dr. Bruce Marshall, editors of this *Why Read . . . ?* series, for inviting my contribution. Their confidence in my work has helped bring it across the finish line. In addition, I am grateful to John Martino and his staff at The Catholic University of America Press for guiding me through the production process.

My wife Deborah L. Burgess has carefully read and commented on each chapter and on the book as a whole. Her eye for detail, her familiarity with Orthodoxy and Russia, and her assistance in tracking down references and citations have been invaluable. I would not be able to do what I do without her love, loyalty, and expertise.

A Note about Transliteration

I have generally followed the standard (modified Library of Congress) system for transliterating Cyrillic. However, in the case of Florensky's own name—and of people and places well known in the West—I have retained anglicized forms. Readers will forgive me if I have not been rigorously consistent.

Why Read PAVEL FLORENSKY?

Introduction

WHY READ PAVEL FLORENSKY?

"Blessed are the dead who die in the Lord."

The way to the ancient monastery on the island of Solovki in Russia's far north is arduous. Before the days of modern travel, pilgrims made their way on foot, sometimes for hundreds of miles, through dense birch and pine forests to the towns of Kem' or Archangelsk on the shores of the White Sea. There they might wait for days until they found a boatman willing to transport them to the island.

The trip across the deep, dangerous waters took two days or longer. Only in the brief summer did one risk the journey. Storms could come up suddenly. But when the skies cleared and the sea calmed, the voyage was glorious. Seagulls accompanied the boat overhead, while seals swam alongside it. As the island drew closer, the white towers and glistening golden crosses of the monastery churches rose magically out of the sea's deep blue waters. Soon, thick, high walls that appeared to extend from one end of the island to the other came into view.

Solovki—historically a monastery, a fortress, and sometimes a prison for the tsar's or the patriarch's enemies—became, after 1924, one of the Soviet Union's first concentration camps. In the days of religious veneration, Solovki had been the trip of a lifetime, never to be repeated. Most pilgrims would remain only three days, before making the long journey back home. In contrast, some of the Bolsheviks' prisoners would never leave.

In the winter, the sun barely rose above the horizon; the wind was cold and raw. In the summer, night never came. Uncooperative prisoners were stripped naked, tied to trees, and left to be devoured by mosquitos. Those who contracted typhoid were sent to small wooden churches on other parts of the island, where at night they slept on the bare floorboards, packed together like sardines.

In its first years, the Solovki camp nevertheless had a rich cultural life. Among the prisoners were bishops and priests, intellectuals and artists. They were able to organize a theater, an orchestra, and even a newspaper. In the 1930s, things began to change. Hardened criminals and political prisoners were grouped together; all were expected to provide economically productive labor.

Toward the end of the decade, conditions grew even worse. Stalin, seeking to renew the fervor of the 1917 Revolution and to consolidate his power over the party and the state, unleashed the Great Terror. People of foreign heritage, members of the intelligentsia, government officials, and religious believers were especially vulnerable. Hastily organized courts, the troikas, condemned thousands of people to death.

In November 1937, Pavel Florensky was among a group of prisoners transferred from Solovki to the mainland, somewhere north of Leningrad. Later that month (December 8), he was sentenced and shot. His remains have never been found.

After Solovki, beyond Death

Florensky's work was largely forgotten in the Soviet Union until the late 1960s, when individual essays were republished or published for the first time. His work on religious philosophy and on art won interest from Soviet intellectuals who were disenchanted with Marxist-Leninist ideology. Today, Florensky is regarded as one of the most significant Russian thinkers of the early twentieth century. Because of his intellectual achievements in a wide variety of fields, including physics and electrical engineering, he has been called Russia's Leonardo da Vinci or Blaise Pascal.

Florensky is not well known in the English-speaking world, however. Translations of several key works did not appear until the late 1990s; only in 2010 was a major English biography published. Much of his correspondence remains available only in Russian. Reading and understanding Florensky are further complicated by a writing style that sometimes seems deliberately convoluted and obscure. Moreover, some of his ideas, such as his "Sophiology" or his privileging same-sex friendship over male-female marriage, have proven highly controversial. Indeed, in many Orthodox circles in Russia, he has been and continues to be regarded with suspicion. Scholars in the West have been especially troubled by evidence that he was anti-Semitic and that he glorified absolutist political rule.

Why, then, read Pavel Florensky? In an era in which pressing concerns of this world—political, social, technological, and material—so easily become all-consuming, Florensky directs us to the "other"—heavenly, divine—world that is always near us and around us but that we so easily miss. As he probes the mystical depth of all that exists, he teaches us to attend also to the "otherness" of the people and things with which we share "this" world—to enter into their unique existence, where we will rediscover ourselves. We will learn to treat the created order with reverence, to live in right relation with one another, and to open ourselves to a transcendent dimension of life.

Florensky can be approached from many angles—philosophical, historical, artistic, and scientific. This book focuses on his contributions to Christian theology. It is important from the outset to note that, for Florensky, Christianity, particularly as guarded by the Orthodox Church, expresses what is true for humans of every time and place. His Christianity helped him make sense of insights that he had gained over a lifetime both from personal experience and from the many different cultures, philosophies, and religions that he had studied.

In our time, which some call "postmodern," when we are so aware of human difference, we are skeptical about claims to universal truth. Florensky offers us a way beyond our impasse. He challenges us to conceive of a multiplicity that is also a unity, and vice versa. What appears as contradictory to instrumental reason is nevertheless true according to the reasoning that characterizes Christian faith: there can be no difference without oneness, and there can be no oneness without difference.

After years of pursuing truth through mathematics, the natural sciences, Greek antiquity, ancient religions, and Western idealist philosophy, Florensky embraced Orthodox Christianity, eventually becoming a priest. Many times, as he participated in the liturgy, he would have proclaimed, "Father, Son, and Holy Spirit—the Trinity one in essence and undivided." Here, for him, is the primal expression of a multiplicity that is also a unity. The Trinity is the truth that is Truth as inscribed in all of existence.

Florensky sought to understand that truth-Truth, to experience it as a living presence, and to witness to it, until the henchmen of the gulag took his life. May the Lord have mercy on Fr. Pavel Florensky. "Blessed are the dead who die in the Lord" (Rev. 14:13).

I

FLORENSKY'S LIFE AND DEATH

"Never forget God ... never forget your past."

A major theme in Florensky's life and work is memory and memorializing. Florensky is convinced that we will know ourselves and our purpose in life only if we remember where we have come from. We will attend both to our family heritage and to our society's history. To be sure, the past does not wholly determine the present: we freely decide how to relate to what we have been given. Nevertheless, we can exercise our freedom rightly only within parameters that we have inherited. As Florensky remembers his own past, he reconstructs the patterns of interdependence that existed between himself and the people, places, and events that had shaped him.[1]

1. Much of the information in this chapter comes from Sviashchennik Pavel Florenskii, *Detiam moim* [To my children] (Moscow: Moskovskii rabochii, 1992). The most complete biography of Florensky in English is Avril Pyman, *Pavel Florensky: A Quiet Genius* (New York: Continuum, 2010). Pyman writes beautifully, covering in detail each period of Florensky's

As an adult, Florensky lamented that his parents had told their children little about their family heritage. He came to believe that this break with the past had left him and his siblings without necessary life orientation as they grew up: "To live without a sense of a living connection to grandparents and great-grandparents—that is to be deprived of a point of support in history."[2] To correct this deficit, he carefully researched his family genealogy; dedicated a last "Testament" (1917–23) to his children, in which he identified specific spiritual and moral values that he believed had been entrusted to him and to them; and composed a memoir (1916–25) of his own childhood.

Florensky's first entry in his "Testament" is dated April 11, 1917. Florensky already senses that Russia's growing social and political turmoil, which later in that year would culminate in the Bolsheviks' October Revolution, threatens his life. He tells his children that he has prepared the "Testament" in the event of his death: "The most important thing, what I am asking of you is, above all, that you commemorate the Lord and walk before him.... Everything else ... is secondary. Never forget this. And do not forget your family heritage, your past. Learn about your grandparents and great-grandparents. Make the effort to secure them in your memory."[3]

Over the next years, Florensky would dedicate himself to memorializing not only his family heritage but also Russia's past. He would work to protect the country's natural beauty and religious heritage against the onslaughts of Bolshevik revolution, industrialization, and political repression. For Florensky, humans are most fully human when they remember, commemorate, and

life. Also helpful are: Nicoletta Misler, "Pavel Florensky: A Biographical Sketch," in Pavel Florensky, *Beyond Vision: Essays on the Perception of Art*, ed. Nicoletta Misler, trans. Wendy Salmond (London: Reaktion Books, 2002), 13–28; and Donald Sheehan, "Introduction," in Pavel Florensky, *Iconostasis* (Crestwood, NY: St. Vladimir's Seminary Press, 1996), 5–29.

2. Florenskii, *Detiam moim*, 26.

3. Pavel Florenskii, "Zaveshchanie" [Testament], in Sviashchennik Pavel Florenskii, *Vse Dumy—o Vas* [All my thoughts are about you] (St. Petersburg: Satis'/Derzhava, 2004), 23–24.

memorialize the precious inheritance that they have received from God and from their ancestors.

Growing Up

Florensky's father, a Russian, worked as a survey engineer for the imperial railroads in the Caucasus, where Florensky was born in 1882 in what is now Azerbaijan. Florensky's mother came from a wealthy Armenian family that had settled in the Caucasus. Her family roots may have gone back to Asia Minor and even North Africa. Although neither parent was interested in the family ancestry, Florensky came to believe that their different lineages had connected him to the ancient cultures of both East and West. The "antinomies" (a term that becomes central to his philosophical and religious thinking) between these two worlds shaped his life and enriched his work.

By Florensky's account, he was especially close to his father, who taught him skills of scientific observation and rationality. By contrast, his mother seemed to him hardly a real person but rather an abstract representation of the primal forces of nature. Florensky inherited both ways of relating to the world, and as he grew older, they struggled within him for dominance, until he reached a point of crisis.

Although having had their infant children baptized, as was the established social custom of the time, neither parent was formally religious. Indeed, both rejected the church. A paternal great-grandfather had been an Orthodox priest (from a line of poor but educated country priests), but his son (Florensky's grandfather) had abandoned seminary studies for a medical education and career, and Florensky's father had inherited his father's secular, scientific outlook. Florensky's mother observed some of the traditional folk customs associated with Orthodox holy days (such as dying eggs and preparing special foods for Easter) but like her husband never attended religious services or showed interest in praying or fasting.

Instead, Florensky's parents idolized their children and sought to create a refuge for them away from the world's trials and temptations. Home life was to be a "little self-enclosed world," a "heaven." Intrusions from or into the surrounding society could only spoil it.[4] Florensky later asserted that this experiment failed miserably: "You can't even imagine the incredible, almost superhuman efforts that my dear father made to create a genuine, strong, unbreakable family. But already in his lifetime … the family somehow … fell apart, even though this made all of us unhappy."[5]

Not until Florensky was seven years old did his parents decide that he needed to learn something about religion—although, even then, just for practical reasons. They were preparing to move to Tbilisi, where he would begin school, and the program would include religious observance and education. His aunt Iuliia, his father's sister, taught him to cross himself and say simple prayers, prepared him for confession and communion, and took him to church to become familiar with the Divine Liturgy.

Notwithstanding his parents' distance from the church, Florensky had a profound sense of otherworldly powers, as he grew up. In his memoirs, he writes about a day when as a little boy he wandered through the courtyard next to the family's apartment building. What he saw overwhelmed him: an unearthly creature was standing over a mysterious projectile out of which rained streams of sparks. When he ran back home, someone told him that it was just a man sharpening knives. But Florensky was convinced that he had penetrated beyond the external and empirical world to its inner, mystical meaning. As he would tell his children, he had for the first time encountered "the living power of the mysterious forces of nature"—what, he said, Jakob Böhme had called the *Urgrund*, or what Goethe in his *Faust* had ascribed to the "Mothers," "the creative matrix of all things."[6]

4. Florenskii, *Detiam moim*, 25.

5. Pavel Florenskii to V. V. Rozanov, November 15, 1909, in V. V. Rozanov, *Literaturnye izgnanniki* [Literary exiles], vol. 2 (Moscow: Respublika, 2010), 38.

6. Florenskii, *Detiam moim*, 32; for Goethe's "Mothers" scene, see Heinrich Henel,

Florensky's father often took him on scientific expeditions into the Caucasus, teaching him to identify and categorize its plants and animals. But while his father was interested in understanding their "mechanical processes," Florensky sensed something else in them: what he called the mystery or secret that "lies in the depths of what is physical."[7] He sometimes felt as though a "concealed essence lifted the curtain of its mystery" to him, such that he found himself "looking eye to eye ... into the face of Nature."[8]

As Florensky grew older, the logical, analytical approach to the world that he had inherited from his father increasingly supplanted his childhood sense of wonder at the creation's inner mystery. In school, he proved to be a brilliant pupil, and before graduating in 1899, academic journals had published several of his scientific discoveries. Nevertheless, an intellectual, spiritual crisis was brewing in him. As he concluded school at age seventeen, at the top of his class, and contemplated his future, his suppressed sense of the mystical dimension of all reality dramatically reasserted itself.

"Pavel, Pavel"

One night, while in a deep sleep, Florensky dreamt that he had been cast into utter darkness and was being buried alive. All of his scientific interests suddenly meant nothing to him. As he lay numb in bed, the word "God" came to him, and he sensed that his very existence now depended on this name. A new insight, as though a divine revelation, came to him: that although a threatening realm of darkness and death truly exists, God's salvation of humans takes place precisely there. Florensky awoke and cried out words that seemed to come from beyond himself, "No, it's impossible to live without God."

Several weeks later he was awakened, as though by a jolt of

---

review of "The Mothers in 'Faust': The Myth of Time and Creativity by Harold Jantz," *Modern Philology* 69, no. 2 (November 1971): 175–78.

7. Florenskii, *Detiam moim*, 175.

8. Florenskii, *Detiam moim*, 88. For "face," Florensky uses the Russian word *litso*, which also refers to a person's face.

electricity, out of another deep sleep. He got up and ran into the courtyard below. A small but bright moon was shining, and he heard a voice calling to him, "Pavel, Pavel." As earlier, Florensky felt the presence of mysterious spiritual powers. He was convinced that what he was experiencing was not simply a mental projection; rather, it was an ontological reality.

Florensky first recorded these memories twenty-five years later. Like anyone remembering the past, he interprets these events in light of where life has in the meantime brought him, including a seminary education and priestly service. Although he does not mention Scripture, the first experience—darkness, yet salvation—seems to allude to Jesus on the cross ("there was darkness over all the earth," Mt. 27:45), and the second has clear parallels with the conversion of the apostle Paul on the road to Damascus ("Saul, Saul," Acts 9:4). Florensky, it seems, had begun to connect his childhood wonder at creation with his faith in the God of Jesus Christ, each experience illuminating the other.

At the time, however, the two dreams-visions did not give Florensky clarity about what to do with his life. In search of a truth by which he could live, he began reading Tolstoy's religious writings, the biblical book of Ecclesiastes, and collections of Buddhist sayings. He did not find what he was looking for. But, here, another antinomy appeared: next to his continuing hopelessness about finding truth was a conviction that he would eventually find it. Ready to broaden his intellectual horizons, he decided to study mathematics at the renowned Moscow University.

The next four years in Moscow proved crucially important to his intellectual development. The mathematics professor at the university, Nikolai Bugaev, introduced Florensky to the idea of "discontinuity" in space and time, thereby liberating Florensky from the mechanical determinism that he had learned from his father. Florensky also became interested in non-Euclidian geometry, for which space is curved and irregular, rather than flat and divisible by parallel lines. He would later argue that Orthodox iconography is based on non-Euclidian principles and, therefore, is not subject to the demands of traditional visual perspective, for which parallel lines move toward each other as they approach the horizon.

Although deeply engaged in his university studies, Florensky found time to get acquainted with Moscow's leading circles of artists and thinkers. During these years, Russia was undergoing intense intellectual and political turmoil, and its intelligentsia was exploring a wide variety of philosophies, religious ideas, and political loyalties. Especially important to Florensky was a close friendship with Bugaev's son, Andrei Bely, a poet and literary critic who was part of a group known as the Symbolists. Florensky, remembering his childhood experiences of a mysterious, other world, was interested in their efforts to interpret worldly phenomena as symbols pointing to hidden spiritual realities.

Through Bely, Florensky also got to know Antonii (Florensov), an Orthodox bishop in retirement in Moscow's Donskoi Monastery (later, a center of church resistance to the Bolsheviks). Antonii was highly educated in several academic disciplines, including art, literature, and mathematics. A number of Moscow's religious intellectuals—among them, friends of Florensky from his school days in Georgia—had sought him out for spiritual counsel, as now did Florensky himself.

In his single-minded pursuit of truth and meaning for his life—and perhaps inspired by Antonii's example—Florensky resolved to become a monk. The fact that since adolescence he had had a number of emotionally intense same-sex friendships seemed to make monastic life all the more attractive. But when he asked Antonii to bless his intentions, Antonii refused. Florensky, he said, was not ready for the monastic life; he still hardly knew anything about the church's life and teaching.

Moreover, Antonii sensed that an ascetic life would deaden Florensky's extraordinary intellectual creativity. He advised him instead to enter the Moscow Theological Academy in the renowned Holy Trinity–St. Sergius Monastery (also known as a lavra, the highest status that a monastery can achieve) in Sergiev Posad. When Florensky completed his mathematical studies in 1904, he heeded Antonii, declined a teaching post in mathematics at the university, and moved to Sergiev Posad.

Encountering Christ

Florensky proved to be as talented in theology and philosophy as he had been in mathematics. By the time that he had graduated in 1908, he had written much of what would later become his great work, *The Pillar and Ground of the Truth*. The mathematical ideas that he had explored under Bugaev now gave him insight into how humans can relate to God. What was needed, Florensky believed, was a different kind of thinking from that of scientific, instrumental rationality. The search for the truth that is God requires one to transcend oneself, and that can happen only by God's grace. A person must be grasped by the life-power that Christians worship as Father, Son, and Holy Spirit.

For this reason, Florensky in a 1906 essay criticized the church's dogmatic system: "[It] is so boring that people do not even take the time to polemicize with it."[9] "Dogmatics," he complained, "has been replaced by dogmatism.... In the contemporary consciousness dogmatics has lost its connection with living feelings and living perceptions."[10] Florensky argued that what was needed, instead, was a dogmatics based on "direct experience" of God, grounded in Scripture and the Church Fathers and as realized by Jesus of Nazareth.[11]

Florensky's insight was surely indebted to his relationship

9. Pavel Florensky, "Dogmatics and Dogmatism," in Pavel Florensky, *Early Religious Writings, 1902–1909,* trans. Boris Jakim (Grand Rapids, MI: Eerdmans, 2017), 127. For the Russian, see Pavel Florenskii, "Dogmatizm i dogmatika," in P. A. Florenskii, *Bogoslovskie trudy, 1902–1909* [Theological works, 1902–1909], ed. N. N. Pavliuchenkov (Moscow: St. Tikhon's University Press, 2018), 226.

10. Florensky, "Dogmatics" 129. See Florenskii, "Dogmatizm," 228.

11. Florensky, "Dogmatics," 136–37. See Florenskii, "Dogmatizm," 235–36.

at this time with Fr. Isidore (Kozin), a member of a small, semi-hermetic monastic community, the Gethsemane Skete, on the outskirts of Sergiev Posad. Fr. Isidore was formally uneducated and culturally unsophisticated, but he had a spiritual depth and freedom for which Florensky longed. In the tradition of Orthodoxy's holy elders, Fr. Isidore seemed to live above the world even as he lived in it. Like an angel, he manifested God's presence. Florensky was pursuing truth intellectually. Isidore taught him that it could be found only through self-giving love.

Florensky, however, did not yet know how to embody this truth and express this love. Although the next years brought additional academic successes, he felt increasingly disoriented spiritually. In 1906, he was briefly imprisoned after publicly expressing dismay at the growing political chaos in the country. The next year, he was dismayed when a seminary friend with whom he had had a close emotional relationship, Sergei Troitskii, married Florensky's sister and moved to Tbilisi. Florensky himself continued to have no interest in marriage, a precondition for ordination to the priesthood, yet Bishop Antonii still refused to bless a monastic life for him. Florensky felt further unhinged when early in 1908, his father died—and less than two weeks later, Fr. Isidore, as well.

In the words of his English biographer, Florensky entered a period of "quiet mutiny." Although he now had a lectureship in the history of philosophy at the Academy, he still felt stifled by what he regarded as the church's theological and moral rigidity. He began to live dissolutely, drinking excessively and, by some accounts, even trying out hashish and opium.[12]

Late in 1908, Florensky renewed a correspondence with Vasilii Rozanov, a brilliant but controversial essayist and thinker, who lived in St. Petersburg. At the time of their first contact in 1903, the two men could not have been more different. Rozanov enjoyed being a provocateur. He celebrated sensuality, sexuality, and

12. Pyman, *Florensky*, 69.

family life. He was deeply critical of the Orthodox Church and its claim that believers could or should transcend earthly needs and desires. When Florensky began writing to him again, he knew that Rozanov contradicted everything that Fr. Isidore had taught him. Nevertheless, Florensky now viewed Rozanov as someone to whom he could openly confess his personal doubts and struggles, as he worked out an understanding of Christian faith.

Like Augustine in his *Confessions*, Florensky in his letters to Rozanov reveals both a deep trust in God and a profound awareness of personal sinfulness. On the one hand, Florensky alludes to a profound religious conversion during his seminary years. For the first time in his life, he says, he now feels completely free and at peace. "[Christ] does not judge me. He comforts, he shows that dying, I am capable of resurrection."[13] "In Christ, I see, feel, sense, taste reality.... He gives me a *holy* flesh" and therefore a "firm support" for life in the world.[14] On May 31, 1909, Florensky promises to send Rozanov's wife, a pious Orthodox believer, a biographical account of Fr. Isidore that he has just composed.

On the other hand, Florensky struggles to hold on to his newly realized religious faith. In October of that same year, he writes Rozanov that he has a sense of impending personal crisis. Wishing that he could be a schoolboy again, he dreams of running away to America, becoming a robber, and living in the forest. He despairs that people throughout history have never been able to realize their highest ideals: "Love is impossible. There is no holy flesh (with the exception of the Unique One). Everywhere is loneliness and disunity."[15]

Several weeks later, Florensky again writes of his melancholy. He feels guilty that he cannot help his lonely, widowed mother in Tbilisi. In order to escape his "unbearable thoughts" and "cold condition," he has been getting drunk and visiting prostitutes, even

13. To Rozanov, April 19, 1909, in Rozanov, *Literaturnye izgnanniki*, 21.
14. To Rozanov, April 25, 1909, in Rozanov, *Literaturnye izgnanniki*, 22.
15. To Rozanov, October 17–20, 1909, in Rozanov, *Literaturnye izgnanniki*, 36.

though he feels disgusted with himself afterward.[16] He wonders whether he is fated to suffer a heaviness of spirit forever, because he has been selfishly pursuing his intellectual interests rather than being true to his family legacy of priestly service to the church.

Gradually, the antinomies of his existence resolve themselves. The correspondence with Rozanov makes clear that Florensky had found in Christ the unity that he had sensed intuitively in his childhood encounters with nature—of the infinite and the finite, and of the spiritual and the physical. Christ was the decisive confirmation that the immanent could show forth the transcendent, that flesh could be transfigured by the holy. What the Symbolists had tried to articulate in their poetry and art was now most clearly demonstrated for Florensky in Christianity.

In a particularly poignant letter from this period (August 10, 1909), Florensky refers to Diego Velazquez's famous painting of 1632 of the crucifixion. For Florensky, the painting captures the antinomies of death and life, of darkness and light, and of the "other" world and the primal forces of nature (he alludes again to Böhme's *Urgrund*). The Savior's body, though dead, "glows with an inner, silver light." Florensky goes on to say that he has just seen such a body with his own eyes. After a night apparently spent in a brothel, he walked by a drunken man passed out in a bed with a prostitute. Something suddenly came over Florensky. He felt "beside himself," as though he had fallen into ecstatic prayer. He believed that he was viewing something shameful yet intensely beautiful and holy. As in Velazquez's painting, the man's naked body softly glowed in the morning light.[17]

During these troubled days, Florensky continued to work on what would become his master's thesis and subsequently appear in print as *The Pillar and Ground of the Truth*, in which he treats existential antinomies as the way to knowledge of God. We may again ask whether his philosophical presuppositions shaped the

16. To Rozanov, November 15, 1909, in Rozanov, *Literaturnye izgnanniki*, 37.

17. To Rozanov, August 10, 1909, in Rozanov, *Literaturnye izgnanniki*, 30.

way he remembered and interpreted the scene in the brothel, or whether what he saw in the brothel helped shape the worldview that he set forth in *Pillar and Ground*. In any event, what had changed from his childhood experience of the mysteries of nature was his ability to view the world in the light of Christian faith. God's redemptive light and beauty now appeared to him not only in plants and animals but also in humans, even in the midst of their moral confusion.

A Life Dedicated to the Church

The year 1910 would bring Florensky further clarity. In the spring, he had gone hunting with a friend (Florensky claims that he himself was only pretending). As they slogged through a swamp, rain began to pour; the dreary day, he later wrote, reflected his loneliness and melancholy. He began thinking about the sister of the man (Vasilii Giatsintov) who had become his closest friend after Sergei Troitskii's departure. Florensky suddenly asked himself, "Why not marry her?" At that very moment, he looked down and discovered a four-leaf clover, something for which he had been looking his entire life. A thought from somewhere beyond himself came to him: here was a sign from God that he should marry her.[18] He later wrote Rozanov that they conceived a child on the first night of their marriage.[19]

In 1911, Florensky was ordained to the priesthood, and his first son, Vasilii, was born. Florensky's academic reputation continued to grow. In 1912, he became editor of the Academy's prestigious theological journal and established a close intellectual friendship with the prominent Russian thinker Sergei Bulgakov. That same year, he was appointed to serve as a priest at the church of Mary Magdalene, located at the home for retired sisters of the Red Cross in Sergiev Posad.

18. To Rozanov, September 16, 1910, in Rozanov, *Literaturnye izgnanniki*, 43.
19. To Rozanov, December 16–17, 1910, in Rozanov, *Literaturnye izgnanniki*, 49.

In 1914, Florensky successfully defended the thesis version of *Pillar and Ground* before a prominent group of religious intellectuals, including Bishop Antonii (Florensov), and brought a fuller version of it to publication. The Academy formally appointed Florensky to a professorship in the history of philosophy. In 1915, Florensky bought a house on Dvorianskaia [Court] Street near the Lavra. Later that year, a second son, Kirill, was born.

Florensky became quietly involved in several controversies that provoked intense discussion in church intellectual circles. In one pseudonymous essay, he repeated common anti-Semitic tropes of Jewish "ritual killing." In another case, he defended a group of monks on Mount Athos who had controversially asserted that reciting the name of God evokes the very presence of God.

Here and at other points, Florensky's thinking could take seemingly bizarre turns. Endlessly curious, he sometimes explored and defended positions that strike us today as odd, even indefensible. He took astrology, numerology, and palm reading seriously; romanticized the Middle Ages and called for returning to its "organic unity"; and argued that a person's given name helps determine that person's personality traits. Nevertheless, even when his remarks about these or other matters are disputable, they are provocative and interesting, as when he argues that saying a person's name helps make that person present to us. As for astrology, Florensky argues that its origins were among certain magi who used narcotics; they entered into an ecstatic trance, observed the stars, and experienced a spiritual connection to them. Astrology, he says, only went wrong when it was turned into a "science."[20]

Not only Florensky's thinking but also his personal demeanor could strike people as odd. To be sure, his lectures were riveting. One attendee wrote that the large hall at the Academy was filled to overflowing; people were standing in the aisles and against the walls: "There was a certain magical charm to his speaking. One

20. To Rozanov, December 16–17, 1910, in Rozanov, *Literaturnye izgnanniki*, 52.

could listen to him for hours." Nevertheless, Florensky himself was "unattractive." He "moved stiffly, and his figure was slightly bent over. His voice sounded muffled, and his words came out in spurts."[21]

Later, when Florensky left the Academy and devoted himself to scientific-technical work, he cut an equally odd figure to his communist, atheist colleagues, because he continued to wear a light-colored priestly cassock. Moreover, his personality could be prickly. He once discovered a copy of a book by the pro-Soviet writer Maksim Gorky on a table in his laboratory. Picking it up by a pair of tongs, Florensky carefully placed it on the floor and asked a coworker to remove it, as though it were radioactive or poisonous material.[22]

Florensky's contemporary, the religious philosopher Nicholas Berdyaev, saw a deeply troubled soul beneath Florensky's "great gifts and originality.... His very presence had a strangling, suffocating effect on me. He spoke in a deliberately soft voice, with his eyes on the ground, and never looking straight into your face. He was always hiding something. Indeed, he confessed in an expansive moment that he was battling against the boundless Dionysian element within him."[23]

The 1917 October Revolution immediately put church life and Florensky's own future into jeopardy. In seeking to eradicate the remnants of the old regime, the Bolsheviks attacked the Orthodox Church ruthlessly. Within months, dozens of church leaders had been arrested and executed. Church properties, including the Holy Trinity–St. Sergius Monastery, were nationalized. Although monks continued to live there and to guard the grounds, the

21. T. V. Smirnova, *"... pod pokrov Prepodobnogo": ocherki o nekotorykh izvestnykh sem'iakh zhivshikh v Sergievom Posade v 1920-e gody* [Beneath the protective veil of the Saint: notes about several famous families living in Sergiev Posad in the 1920s] (Sergiev Posad: Sviato–Troitskaia Sergieva Lavra, 2008), 91, 92.

22. Smirnova, *"... pod pokrov Prepodobnogo,"* 98.

23. Nicolas Berdyaev, *Dream and Reality: An Essay in Autobiography* (New York: Macmillan, 1951), 166.

Academy—and Florensky's classes—had to move to a monastery in Moscow.

Florensky now began to think deeply about how Orthodox worship and ritual open people to the "other" world that earlier had so fascinated him in the natural world. A series of lectures for a popular audience—they, too, attracted an enthusiastic crowd—became *Philosophy of the Cult* (further developed in the 1920s but not published until 1977). Here, Florensky focuses no longer on the creation but rather on the church's sacraments. He argues that each sacrament constitutes a hierarchy by which God descends into the world and humans rise toward God.

Preserving Russia's Past

At about the same time, a government Department of Museum Affairs and Preservation of Monuments of Art and Antiquities, headed by Leon Trotsky's wife (Natalia Sedova), established a Commission for the Preservation of Art and Antiquities at the Holy Trinity–St. Sergius Monastery. Florensky, along with several close acquaintances in Sergiev Posad—all were leading experts on church art and history—was appointed to its membership. Initially commissioned to catalog the monastery's vast holdings (including icons; liturgical garments, furniture, and implements; and church bells), the Commission quietly worked to preserve the monastery complex as a whole, believing, as Florensky said, that the Lavra was the very "heart of Russia."

In connection with his work as the Commission's secretary, Florensky wrote several essays about the nature and meaning of church art. Especially groundbreaking would be his interpretation of Orthodox iconography, *Iconostasis* (completed in 1922 but not published until 1969). Similar to his interpretation of his childhood experience of nature, Florensky argues that icons lie on the boundary of two worlds, the earthly and heavenly. A church iconostasis, which separates the altar area (accessible only to the priests) from the nave (where the people gather), hides, yet reveals the kingdom of God. The icons and iconostasis offer the worshipper a glimpse of the world as transfigured by divine glory.

Florensky eventually argued for turning the monastery into a living museum. Its former monks would serve as tour guides, and visitors would experience the monks' rhythms of worship, prayer, and labor. Florensky believed that the unique atmosphere of the Lavra—as created by a synthesis of icons, chanting, incense, and dramatic liturgical action—was an essential part of Russia's historic identity that deserved to be preserved by the state.

Here again we see Florensky's concern to memorialize the past. The new Bolshevik Russia would go astray, if it did not recognize its obligation to the nation's Orthodox heritage. Florensky, like a number of Russian religious thinkers of the time, believed that the country had a special divine commission to set forth to the world Orthodoxy's vision of divine beauty and earthly harmony, in contrast to a West characterized by capitalist exploitation of nature and aggressive competition between individuals.

However, Florensky's proposal was nothing more than wishful thinking, and state officials quickly rejected it. Even while preserving some of the monastery's treasures, such as Andrei Rublev's famous Trinity icon (which in 1928 would be moved to the Tretiakov National Art Gallery in Moscow), the Bolsheviks soon desacralized the Lavra and turned it into an antireligious museum.

The monastery had long housed the relics of its fourteenth-century founder, St. Sergius of Radonezh. Believers could see the shape of a body, wrapped in liturgical robes, beneath the glass cover of a reliquary; many held that his body was incorrupt—that is, that the skin and flesh were still intact. To combat what they took to be religious superstition, government authorities decided in 1919 to unwrap the body, confident that only rags and sawdust, or a puppet, lay within.

While details are murky, it appears that Florensky and another member of the Commission secretly removed and hid the saint's skull, putting a different skull in its place, before the authorities acted.[24] In any event, upon exposing the body, the authorities found neither an incorrupt body nor a puppet but rather a skeleton and some remains of clothing. Hoping to sow doubt among the faithful, the authorities put the decayed body on public display. However, the effect was quite the opposite. The presence of a relatively complete skeleton confirmed believers' conviction that God had miraculously preserved the saint, and they were enraged at the authorities' desecration of his body. In 1920, the authorities forbade further religious pilgrimage to the relics and closed the monastery churches.

The Last Years

From this time on, Florensky began spending most of his time in Moscow. Besides teaching for the Theological Academy, he conducted research at several scientific institutes and gave lectures on the theory of art at the Higher State Art–Technical Studios, whose director (Vladimir Favorskii) was one of Florensky's friends from Sergiev Posad. Florensky traveled back to Sergiev Posad on weekends, where he received a steady stream of guests and devoted himself to his family. A daughter, Ol'ga, had joined his two sons in 1918; his third son, Mikhail, came into the world in 1921; and his last child, Mariia-Tinatin, was born in 1924.

By then, the Commission for preservation of the Lavra had been replaced by a state-operated museum administration; the Theological Academy was no longer able to operate in Moscow; and Florensky's lectures on art had concluded, as the Studios moved toward favoring new artistic expressions consonant with

24. P. V. Florenskii, "Predislovie" [Foreword], in Sviashchennik Pavel Florenskii, *Vse Dumy—o Vas* (St. Petersburg: Satis'/Derzhava, 2004), 10. Another account holds that replacement of the skull took place in 1920, when the relics were no longer available for public veneration and state officials debated whether to bury or destroy them. See Scott Kenworthy, *The Heart of Russia: Trinity–Sergius, Monasticism, and Society after 1825* (New York: Oxford University Press, 2010), 323. The saint's skull was presumably returned to the body when the state allowed the monastery to reopen in 1946.

Figure 1.1. Florensky with Son Mikhail, 1932, Sergiev Posad / Public domain. By courtesy of the Florensky family archive, from *P. A. Florenskij e la cultura della sua epoca* (Marburg: Blaue Horner Verlag, 1995).

socialist-communist ideals.[25] Further constricting Florensky professionally was closure of the Red Cross home in Sergiev Posad, thereby ending his priestly appointment. He and other members of the Commission continued quietly to document the Lavra's treasures, but his professional work shifted almost entirely to scientific work on behalf of the government. Rather than theological treatises, he published scientific papers and soon had particular responsibility for the state's program of nationwide electrification.

In 1927 and 1928, as Stalin consolidated power and instituted the country's first Five-Year Plan, political repression grew. Some state and party officials concluded that Sergiev Posad had become a refuge for Russia's old guard—monks from the closed monastery and prominent intellectuals, many from families of nobility, who had remained sympathetic to the monarchy and the church. A vicious antireligious campaign was unleashed in the local press. Remaining members of the Commission were arrested, and the last of the town's parish churches were closed. Florensky was included in the roundup.

Thanks to connections in high places, Florensky was able after three months to return home and to his scientific work, but the die had been cast. In 1933, he was arrested again, accused of being the chief ideologist of a counterrevolutionary, monarchist group sympathetic to German fascists. He received a ten-year sentence and was exiled to a labor camp in Russia's Far East.

At the end of 1934, Florensky was transferred to the gulag camp on Solovetskii Island in Russia's White Sea, five hundred miles northeast of St. Petersburg. The authorities assigned him to scientific work, this time in a laboratory investigating commercial uses of seaweed. His writing was limited to correspondence with his family. Even here, however, he continued to articulate

25. See Yve-Alain Bois, "School," in *Revoliutsiia! Demonstratsiia! Soviet Art Put to the Test*, ed. Matthew S. Witkovsky and Devine Fore (Chicago: Art Institute of Chicago, 2017), 44–49.

the worldview that underlay his great philosophical writings, now in the form of practical life wisdom and advice for each of his children.

Over the next months, living conditions became increasingly difficult. Although Florensky did not write openly about the deprivations, he seems to have lived on the edge of hunger and mental exhaustion. By 1937, he senses that the end is near.

In June of that year, Florensky's family was informed that he had been sentenced to an additional ten years of imprisonment, "without a right to correspondence," what Soviet citizens later understood as a euphemism for a death sentence. Florensky disappeared from view. Rumors circulated. According to one account, Florensky was executed at Solovki. The prisoners knelt in honor, as guards carried his dead body to the monastery gates.[26] According to other reports, Florensky was transferred from Solovki to one of the most brutal labor camps, Kolyma, in Siberia's far north.[27]

In 1943, Sergei Bulgakov, now in exile in Paris, wrote that he had just received news of Florensky's death at Solovki.[28] But not until 1958, during the Khrushchev "thaw" and program of anti-stalinization, did government authorities finally confirm that Florensky had died of "unknown causes" in February 1943. Florensky's family, which over the years had faithfully preserved his letters and papers, immediately moved to have him memorialized. Thanks to their efforts, the state officially rehabilitated him (1958 and 1959), and Archimandrite Pimen (Khmeleviskii), head of the Holy Trinity–St. Sergius Lavra, celebrated a memorial service (*panikhida*) for him, with family members in attendance, in

26. See Donald Sheehan, "Introduction," in Pavel Florensky, *Iconostasis*, trans. Donald Sheehan and Olga Andrejev (Crestwood, NY: St. Vladimir's Seminary Press, 1996), 23.

27. See Aleksandr I. Solzhenitsyn, *The Gulag Archipelago*, vol. III-IV, trans. Thomas P. Whitney (New York: Harper and Row, 1975), 671.

28. S. N. Bul'gakov, "Sviashchennik o. Pavel Florenskii" [The priest Fr. Pavel Florensky] in Bul'gakov, *Sochineniia v dvukh tomakh: filosofiia khoziaistva/tragediia filosofii* [Essays in two volumes: philosophy of economy and the tragedy of philosophy], vol. 1 (Moscow: Nauka, 1993), 538.

1959. Not until 1990, however, with Gorbachev's policies of glasnost, did Florensky's family finally win access to his secret police files. There they learned the truth: on December 8, 1937, Florensky had been executed and buried in an unmarked grave on the mainland, somewhere north of Leningrad. To this day, no one knows with certainty where his murderers dumped his body.[29]

29. Some Orthodox Church officials believe that he was buried at Levashovo, an execution site twenty miles north of St. Petersburg. For an account of Florensky's last days that draw on archival materials, see P. V. Florenskii, "Sviashchennik, ne sniavshii s sebia sana" [A priest who never renounced his ordination], in Sviashchennik Pavel Florenskii, *Vse Dumy—o Vas* (St. Petersburg: Satis'/Derzhava, 2004), 509–32.

2

CHILDHOOD

"To seek out those places where the otherworldly voice of nature speaks more clearly"

Light, silver clouds dampen the sunlight of a spring sky over the Russian countryside. Two men, deep in thought, walk side by side. Behind them lie ripening fields and greening forests. The man to the left wears a skufia (a priest's tall black stocking cap) and a long white cassock, and he holds a walking stick. The man to the right is in a dark suit and tie; a black cloak hangs loosely over his shoulders. Nothing disturbs the men's reverie. Perhaps here, away from the world's troubles, they are able briefly to contemplate the very mystery of life.

So portrayed artist Mikhail Nesterov two of Russia's greatest religious philosophers, Pavel Florensky and Sergei Bulgakov, on the eve of the 1917 Bolshevik Revolution. The next year, the man in black, Bulgakov, would become an Orthodox priest but in 1922 be exiled to France. Florensky, in white, remained in Russia but soon had to abandon his priestly service and theological writing, in order to devote himself entirely to scientific-technical work on

Figure 2.1. Mikhail Nesterov, "The Philosophers" / Public domain. Wikimedia Commons. Tretiakov Gallery, Moscow.

behalf of the communist government. Each man thought highly of the other, and each had deeply enriched the other's thinking. When Bulgakov learned in 1943 of Florensky's death in the gulag, he wrote a glowing tribute, calling Florensky "the greatest" of their contemporaries.[1]

1. S. N. Bul'gakov, "Sviashchennik o. Pavel Florenskii" [The priest Fr. Pavel Florensky], in Bul'gakov, *Sochineniia v dvukh tomakh: filosofiia khoziaistva/tragediia filosofii* [Essays in two volumes: philosophy of economy and the tragedy of philosophy], vol. 1 (Moscow: Nauka, 1993), 538. Nesterov's "The Philosophers" now hangs in Moscow's Tretiakov Gallery.

The pastoral scene that Nesterov painted was, in fact, what one could see from Florensky's garden in Sergiev Posad, at that time still a sleepy little town in the shadow of the great Holy Trinity–St. Sergius Monastery.[2] Florensky had grown up close to the natural world, and Russia's landscapes would shape his life up to his death. As a child, he had explored the rugged cliffs and deep valleys of Azerbaijan and Georgia. The last years of his life were spent in the gulag, first in a remote corner of southeastern Siberia and then on a lonely island in the White Sea, far to the north of Moscow and St. Petersburg. In the years in between, he had enjoyed, as often as he could, the peace and quiet of Sergiev Posad, where he had studied, taught, and made a family and a home. He wanted his children to grow up there and to revel in the area's natural beauty.

Florensky believed that childhood experiences of the natural world sustain a person through the trials that come all too soon to every adult. Moreover, he was convinced that a child's innocent delight in playing with the little things of nature captures something profound about the very meaning of life. His own childhood remained a key reference point for him, as he became an adult and lived through tumultuous years of revolutionary change and arrest and imprisonment.

Childhood's Joyous Ecstasy

Florensky once wrote that he had so loved childhood that he had never wanted to grow up.[3] To be a child was the height of happiness and perfection. He had freely roamed the natural world and delighted in its wonders. Around him was an Eden, in which he lived in a constant state of "ecstasy": "The joy of existence, the fullness of existence, and my keen curiosity overflowed my entire existence."[4]

2. Prior to the Bolshevik Revolution, the town was known as Sergievskii Posad.

3. Pavel Florenskii to V. V. Rozanov, June 9, 1909, in V. V. Rozanov, *Literaturnye izgnanniki* [Literary exiles], vol. 2 (Moscow: Respublika, 2010), 28.

4. Sviashchennik Pavel Florenskii, *Detiam moim* [To my children] (Moscow: Moskovskii rabochii, 1992), 85. For the reference to "Eden," see p. 73.

After the deaths of his father and the holy elder Isidore in 1908, Florensky spoke of wanting to become a child again: "I often feel like a little boy. I want to play around and be mischievous.... My Dionysian impulses are looking for an outlet."[5] A friend reported how Florensky took delight in playing with the man's little daughter, "pretending to be a bear, teasing her, [and] singing silly children's songs."[6]

Later, Florensky wrote about an open-air puppet theatre that he had attended in Sergiev Posad in the summer of 1922. To get there, he had to walk to the edge of town, descend a slippery slope, and cross a stream into an old, abandoned garden. In one of the few direct references in his writings to the country's social conditions, Florensky describes entering into a child's world, "isolated from all-possible worries, life weariness, and innumerable concerns about existence in such a difficult time. Revolution and the destruction of 1922 [an allusion to the civil war and famine that followed the revolution], impoverishment, and the instability of life in all its dimensions—all this remained on the other side of the [garden] fence."[7]

People of all ages had gathered for the show. They were in a holiday mood, expecting something interesting and unusual, something different from the usual rhythms of their lives. The performance did not disappoint. Florensky writes that it took all of its viewers back into the "hearth" of childhood. The playful puppets opened a "window into the eternally living childhood" that lies somewhere within each of us: "What is deepest and dearest to us—that is our childhood, living in us but thickly curtained off

5. A. V. El'chaninov, "Iz vstrechi s P. A. Florenskim" [From an encounter with P. A. Florensky], *Vestnik* 142, no. 3 (1984): 68.

6. El'chaninov, "Iz vstrechi," 68.

7. Pavel Florenskii, "Predislovie k knige N. I. Simonovich-Efimovoi 'Zapiski petrushechnika'" [Preface to the book by N. I. Simonovich-Efimova, *Punch's Notes*], in Pavel Florenskii, *Istoriia i filosofiia iskusstva* [History and philosophy of art] (Moscow: Akademicheskii proekt, 2017), 169. See Pavel Florensky, "Of the Efimovs' Puppet Theatre," in Pavel Florensky, *Beyond Vision: Essays on the Perception of Art*, ed. Nicoletta Misler, trans. Wendy Salmond (London: Reaktion Books, 2002), 133.

from us. We forget about it and about the primordial closeness to all of being that we had when we still penetrated into the life of nature. We forget that it continues to live in us, and in certain moments it unexpectedly announces itself."[8]

For Florensky, religion, too, returns us to this childhood. Religious holidays, in particular, free us briefly from the demands and trials of everyday life. Without this "emptying out" of ordinary time, life would become boring and wearisome. On holy days, what has been long suppressed in us is able to rise again to the surface: "a sense of rootedness in the world, a way of life that approaches ecstatic joy."[9]

The growing turmoil in Russian society, along with a premonition that his own life would soon be in danger, motivated Florensky to record his childhood experiences in his correspondence with Rozanov, in his "Testament," and in detailed memoirs of his years growing up in the Caucasus. In all of these pieces, Florensky does much more than collect anecdotes. Rather, he demonstrates how his childhood experiences, especially of the natural world, laid the foundations of the philosophical-religious view of God and the world that he would work out more fully as an adult. Although his parents had given him practically no religious training, the natural world had opened him to a sense of transcendence that he would later find realized more completely in Christianity and the church.

Foundations of a Worldview

Florensky believed that one's "first childhood impressions determine the future of one's inner life."[10] As evidence, he cited the fact that his favorite time of the day was at about 7 p.m., the hour at which he had been born.[11] More central to his intellectual development, however, had been conversations with and between his

8. Florenskii, "Predislovie k knige," 171. See Florensky, "Efimovs' Puppet Theatre," 134.
9. Florenskii, "Predislovie k knige," 169. See Florensky, "Efimovs' Puppet Theatre," 132.
10. Florenskii, *Detiam moim*, 31.
11. Florenskii, *Detiam moim*, 30.

parents and relatives, the music and poetry that had surrounded him in the family home, and his personal exploration of the natural world. Each, he came to believe, had left lasting and decisive impressions on him. Now, as an adult, he pondered what it is that all children need to experience in order to lay down solid foundations for the rest of life.

As we noted in sketching out his biography, Florensky emphasized the importance of knowing one's family heritage, something that his own parents had failed to give him. He argued that a family heritage shapes an individual's personality, while relating that person to society as a whole. Every family is a "unified organism" that has been given a particular "idea," "form," "duty, "historical meaning," or "law of development" to fulfill.[12] A family's failure to honor its distinctive commission damages the family as a whole and each of its members in particular.

Florensky came to see priestly service to God as essential to his family's heritage. His grandfather's and, then, father's rejection of this calling—and their turn to "science," instead—had left them professionally unsatisfied and their families unhappy. Florensky pleaded with his own children, "Let there be in each generation at least one priest.... The task of our family is neither practical nor administrative but rather contemplative, reflective, directed to areas related to the spiritual life, culture, education."[13]

Perhaps because of the Bolshevik regime's antireligious policies, all of Florensky's children would eventually enter scientific-technical fields, instead. However, with a grandson (Aleksandr Trubachev), a family member again fulfilled the family's calling. He became not only a priest but also a monk (with the name Andronik), and he devoted much of his life to editing, publishing,

12. As quoted by Igumen Andronik Trubachev, "Predislovie" [Foreword], in Sviashchennik Pavel Florenskii, *Detiam moim* (Moscow: Moskovskii rabochii, 1992), 18–19.

13. Pavel Florenskii, "Zaveshchanie" [Testament], in Sviashchennik Pavel Florenskii, *Vse Dumy—o Vas* [All my thoughts are about you] (St. Petersburg: Satis'/Derzhava, 2004), 26, 27. The entry dates from June 26, 1919.

and commenting on his grandfather's philosophical and theological works.

A second foundation for children is familiarity with great works of art and culture. Florensky remembered how as a little child he had heard his aunt play classical music on the piano. The works of Mozart and Beethoven had particularly captured his imagination: "Only here," he seemed to understand, "is authentic music." Even at this early age, Florensky sensed that such music left him with something more than just a powerful psychological experience. Rather, "it resounded in my head as the music of the spheres, as a formulation of the world's life."[14] Great music brought him into a state of ecstasy. As an adult, he discovered that Bach's music spoke even more directly to what he had experienced as a child.

Florensky had a similar childhood experience with great poetry, especially that of Pushkin and Lermontov. Florensky claims that the sounds and rhythms alone captivated him. Indeed, he argues, children do not have to find a poem's meaning. Their sense of "judgment is ontological," not moral. A poem that is a great human achievement simply impresses itself upon a child as something "good and blessed."[15] Children intuitively recognize what is true, in contrast to adults, who endlessly analyze and evaluate things but come to no firm conclusions.

Florensky claims that in childhood he also felt a special resonance with the spiritual values and aspirations of antiquity, especially as represented by Greek sculpture: "From as long as I can remember (and I have memories from about age two, if not earlier), this attraction to higher human ideals has lived in me, beats in every heartbeat.... I am completely and helplessly indifferent to *evaluating* this striving. But I know that it is *necessary* for me and others, for our education, for science, for the purity of soul, for all of life."[16] It was especially through his Armenian mother, as we

14. Florenskii, *Detiam moim*, 80–81.

15. Florenskii, *Detiam moim*, 84.

16. To Rozanov, April 19, 1909, in Rozanov, *Literaturnye izgnanniki*, 21.

have noted, that Florensky "felt" ancient classical culture in his very "blood."[17]

A Concrete Metaphysics

Florensky devotes even more space in his writings to how children's experience of the natural world grounds them and gives their lives meaning. Here, he draws on a wide range of Western thinkers, including Plato, Aristotle, Spinoza, Goethe, Schelling, and Bergson. The influence of the nineteenth-century Russian religious philosopher Vladimir Solov'ev (1853–1900) is also evident, although Florensky rarely refers to him directly. Florensky wishes to find a way between idealism and materialism, between mysticism and scientific empiricism, and between positivism and an abstract metaphysics. He argues, instead, for a "concrete metaphysics" that unites the noumenal and the phenomenal: "I wanted to see *spirit*, but I wanted to *see* its embodiment."[18]

In his interpretation of the natural world, Florensky sharply contrasts his position with Kant's—a theme that will run through all of his mature writings. For Florensky, Kant represents a rationalistic way of knowing that imposes human categories on the phenomena that it observes. A Kantian metaphysics reduces nature to predictable mechanical processes. Time and space are characterized by consistency and regularity and can therefore be analyzed—broken down into constituent parts. But this way of knowing the world is only from the "outside." It never penetrates into a phenomenon's "inner meaning." Kant places a barrier between the phenomenal and the noumenal.

Florensky can also pose this contrast in terms of a child's way of experiencing the world versus an adult's—as represented by the difference that he saw between himself and his father. Florensky argues that children see the natural world holistically and from

17. To Rozanov, August 10, 1909, in Rozanov, *Literaturnye izgnanniki*, 32.

18. Florenskii, *Detiam moim*, 154; the Russian can also be translated as, "I wanted to see the *soul*, but I wanted to *see* its incarnation."

the inside. Every natural phenomenon seems filled with a mysterious, otherworldly energy. When we grow up, we lose this sense of wonder and delight, without even being aware of what is happening to us. We somehow become "indifferent" to the "serene azure of the spirits of nature."[19] Florensky compares our adult condition to that of Adam and Eve after their fall from paradise.

The mathematical theories of discontinuity that Florensky learned from his mathematics professor, Nikolai Bugaev, seemed to confirm Florensky's childhood intuition that the world's discontinuities, irregularities, and inconsistencies open us to its true character: "Wherever there is deviation from the ordinary—that's where to look for what nature wishes to declare about itself."[20] When Florensky accompanied his father on his expeditions into the wilds, his father, the scientist, was always explaining to him the laws of nature. But Florensky "eagerly asked about the exceptions. It was the exceptions from the laws [of nature], the ruptures in regularity, that stimulated me intellectually."[21] He loved nature's playfulness, those phenomena that defy logical categorization.

In his memoirs, Florensky speaks of his particular fascination with things that lie in a liminal space—such as poisons (on the boundary between life and death), crystals (between rocks and plants), and sparks (between matter and energy). In a letter to Rozanov, Florensky similarly declares, "An attraction to the mysterious has [always] lived within me.... The mysterious concentrated itself in mushrooms, ferns, lichens, mosses, algae—in general, in all those created things that lie close to the boundary of life, to the boundary between the animal and the plant kingdoms."[22] When he studied the layers of rocks in geologic formations, the boundary between past and present disappeared. Holes and openings—such as caves, tunnels, and long passageways—were liminal, transitional

19. Florenskii, *Detiam moim*, 74.
20. Florenskii, *Detiam moim*, 160.
21. Florenskii, *Detiam moim*, 183.
22. To Rozanov, May 10–31, 1909, in Rozanov, *Literaturnye izgnanniki*, 24.

spaces. Plants with elasticity, such as the stems of certain water plants, both manifested and concealed an inner life force. Buds were more interesting to him than fully developed flowers.

Florensky's fascination with nature's mysterious transitions and transformations stimulated his interest in those human interactions with the world that are equally playful, as both revealing and hiding what a thing or a person really is. The young boy Florensky loved magic tricks, chemistry experiments, magnets, shadows, mirrors, costumes, and masquerades. Each seemed briefly to undo "reality"—something suddenly showed itself "to be" different from what it had "seemed" to be.[23] He was equally fascinated by his mother's descriptions of the theatre and by his aunt's accounts of automatons—mechanized human figures that could move or gesture (such as a wax figure of Peter the Great in St. Petersburg's Hermitage Museum).[24]

Later, Florensky tells his children that he had been fascinated by the unique form of each plant, animal, and mineral that he encountered. Each spoke into his inner depths. He would wonder to himself, "'Oh, why am I not that form?' Or, 'Indeed, that form—that's me.'"[25] He even felt sometimes as though he were living within another form. "In my thinking," he continues, "the conviction began to establish itself that what is 'simple' is not so simple … the continuous is not at all continuous, what is identical—not identical but rather differentiated, and what is differentiated—not differentiated but rather identical."[26]

As a child, Florensky had unusually sharp senses and strong reactions to what he perceived. Women's singing voices pleased him,

23. Florenskii, *Detiam moim*, 155.

24. Although museum visitors claimed that the figure sometimes stood up and approached them, it was, in fact, not mechanized. See "Voskovaia skul'ptura Petra I: odin iz samych strannych eksponatov Ermitazha" [The wax sculpture of Peter I: one of the strangest exhibits in the Hermitage], Livejournal, September 9, 2021, https://picturehistory.livejournal.com/6790935.html.

25. Florenskii, *Detiam moim*, 89.

26. Florenskii, *Detiam moim*, 172.

whereas baritones irritated him, as did loud noises. His eyesight was extraordinary. He could recognize objects far in the distance, while simultaneously noticing every little plant, pebble, or bug right in front of him. Red and orange colors seemed threatening to him, whereas he loved sky-blue. He could identify different coins by their feel; each had a distinctive "living energy." Silver, he asserted, was more living than gold or copper.[27] His nose was able to distinguish poisonous from nonpoisonous berries and plants.[28] He was interested in tastes and wanted to know why one thing tastes good to us and another bad.[29] The smells of different spices delighted him, and he made his own perfumes.[30] Moreover, certain smells, he claimed, ruptured the surface of his childhood world and guided him into the "other" world.[31] Especially the smell of water plants seemed to him to penetrate more deeply than other smells into the noumenal world.[32]

Forms and Symbols

Florensky searched in these and other natural phenomena "for the revelation where … the surface of things is thinner and where spiritual unity shines through more clearly."[33] Childhood taught him that the noumenal (the spiritual world) reveals itself through the phenomenal (the material world): "In the depth of the physical lies the mystery."[34]

In the fibrous, elastic surfaces of water plants and certain animals and birds, Florensky sensed a vitality "that could manifest itself, even while restraining itself and vibrating.… Even if they barely touched me, I sensed that something much more powerful

27. To Rozanov, June 25–26, 1912, in Rozanov, *Literaturnye izgnanniki*, 72.
28. To Rozanov, October 17–20, 1909, in Rozanov, *Literaturnye izgnanniki*, 35.
29. To Rozanov, December 16–17, 1910, in Rozanov, *Literaturnye izgnanniki*, 51.
30. Florenskii, *Detiam moim*, 71–73.
31. Florenskii, *Detiam moim*, 76.
32. To Rozanov, May 28, 1910, in Rozanov, *Literaturnye izgnanniki*, 41.
33. Florenskii, *Detiam moim*, 154.
34. Florenskii, *Detiam moim*, 175.

was hidden in them than appeared. Their mystery grabbed me."[35] Similarly, in colors, smells, and tastes, he detected a hidden energy. Echoes, steamboat signals, or a glass lamp tinkling in the wind—each sound had a life source from beyond itself. Shadows and reflections also suggested to him the presence of a mysterious "other" that was nevertheless near to our everyday world.

"Young animals, some birds, tiny lizards with beautiful dark brown eyes, sometimes little green frogs, and, of course, many flowers conversed with me. Minerals, various natural phenomena, and especially many colors, smells, and tastes were penetrated by a deep energy ... [that] directed itself toward me."[36] Florensky was absolutely certain that he and "Nature" were sometimes looking each other in the eye. Nature had become a *litso*—literally, a face—and in Florensky's philosophical vocabulary, that which has a *litso* is transparent to a transcendent power that he, even as a child, somehow knew to be "God."

Florensky would later tell his children that the idea of "the symbol" had helped him to understand the relation of the spiritual and material worlds. In summarizing his worldview, he wrote, "Over my entire life, I have thought, essentially, about one thing—about the relationship of the revelatory to the noumenal, about the uncovering of the noumenal in the phenomena, about the revelatory revelation, about its embodiment. It is the question of the symbol."[37] All of nature is symbolic in the sense that it reveals through itself the divine even as it points beyond itself to the divine.

Florensky related his symbolic thinking to Goethe's understanding of the *Urphänomenon*, the "pure phenomenon" by means of which one senses the infinite that unifies all of reality.[38] Goethe helped Florensky claim a Platonism that does not disparage this

35. Florenskii, *Detiam moim*, 90.
36. Florenskii, *Detiam moim*, 89.
37. Florenskii, *Detiam moim*, 153.
38. Florenskii, *Detiam moim*, 159.

world or view the spiritual as superior to the material. The symbol participates in that to which it points. By means of symbols—"revelations"—the spiritual moves into the empirical world (a movement that Florensky's calls "embodiment" or "incarnation"), and material things guide us into the "other" world (what Florensky calls "the mystery" or "the secret").

Aristotle's understanding of "forms" helps Florensky modify Plato's notion of "ideas." What interests Florensky are not pure "ideas" beyond this world but rather the concrete "forms" of this world, each in its individual uniqueness: "For me [in childhood], the form was reality."[39] Florensky's interest in the natural world is never abstract; he rarely talks of nature in general. Rather, he gives rich descriptions of particular phenomena: specific plants (seaweed, roses, lilies), minerals (gold, silver, copper), animals (frogs, lizards, birds with fibrous skin), colors (red, orange, blue), sounds (tinkling glass, echoes, steamboat signals), and magic-like transformations of reality that humans can effect (costumes, mirrors, puppet theatre).

For Florensky, this close attention to phenomena's "forms" and "symbols" preserves the mystery-secret at their heart—a mystery-secret that we can never entirely comprehend. The forms and symbols tease us; they play with us. Through them, the other world presents itself as something that we "feel, see, smell, taste . . . [even while] always escaping a final analysis, a final determination."[40]

When we enter into this mystery, we perceive how all of reality is interrelated. Here, Florensky is influenced by Solov'ev's notion of "the whole of things" (*vseedinstvo*), which in turn draws on Schelling's idealist philosophy of the unity of spirit and nature.[41]

39. Florenskii, *Detiam moim*, 184.

40. Florenskii, *Detiam moim*, 158.

41. For Schelling's influence on Solov'ev, see Paul Valliere, *Modern Russian Theology: Bukharev, Soloviev, Bulgakov* (Grand Rapids, MI: Eerdmans, 2000), 124. For a good introduction to Schelling's philosophy and its importance for Christian theology, see Walter Kasper, *The Absolute in History: The Philosophy and Theology of History in Schelling's Late Philosophy*, trans. Katherine E. Wolff (New York: Paulist Press, 2018).

Reflecting on his childhood fascination with the multitudinous forms of the natural world, Florensky writes, "Atmospheric displays, colors, smells, tastes, the sky's luminaries, and subterranean phenomena weave themselves together by a multitude of connections; they form a tissue of universal correspondence."[42]

To return to Florensky's way of contrasting two ways of knowing the world: scientific, Kantian, or "adult" thinking breaks forms apart into constituent parts, whereas symbolic and childhood thinking regards the concrete "forms" of this world as wholes that cannot be reduced to anything else.[43] Adult, scientific thinking looks at phenomena from the outside and organizes them into general categories, but symbolic, childhood thinking observes each thing in itself in order to enter into its inner life. In this way, children are able to "overcome the fragmentation of the world." "By perceiving [the world] from *within*," they grasp how all things are interconnected. Moreover, children understand how they themselves are not mere "observers" but rather are integrally connected with what they see.[44] Indeed, asserts Florensky, until one, like a child, appreciates the world's immense variation in its individual forms, one cannot experience its mystical unity.[45]

Florensky's Religion

Florensky had little formal religious training as he was growing up—and little direct encounter with church life. Rather, it was a sense of connection to a family heritage, to classical culture, and to the mystery of the natural world that shaped him "spiritually." Nevertheless, Florensky's father did help him associate this mysterious dimension of life with "God" and Christianity. Florensky reports that his father, despite a personal indifference to religion, sometimes referred to a "Highest Being" or "the Divine." Moreover, in everyday life, his father showed respect to the religious leaders

42. Florenskii, *Detiam moim,* 86.
43. Florenskii, *Detiam moim,* 184.
44. Florenskii, *Detiam moim,* 87.
45. Florenskii, *Detiam moim,* 87.

he encountered. Although he saw a danger of intolerance in any claim to absoluteness, he acknowledged Christianity's greatness and could not imagine a person choosing anything other than Orthodoxy.[46]

In his memoirs, Florensky summarized what his childhood had taught him: religion has to do with "a feeling of reality's limitlessness," "a feeling of the connection between separate individuals," and "the totality of mysterious revelations."[47] Nevertheless, Florensky later came to believe that something had been missing from his childhood. Connection to a family heritage, classical culture, and the mystery of the natural world had brought him only so far; they had not ultimately satisfied his longing for a truth by which he could live. Only as an adult did he understand that he had to take a leap of faith in the God who had revealed himself in Christ.

Florensky would tell his children that his childhood belief in God had actually been a form of self-divinization. A sense of connection to mysterious powers made him feel godlike. He did not yet have an awareness of himself as a sinner. He resisted submitting to God.[48] He believed that his family heritage called him to spiritual pursuits, but he could not yet see what form they would take, and he had chosen, instead, to study mathematics. Classical culture, as profound as it was to him, seemed to point to something even greater that he did not yet know. And as much as the child Florensky longed to experience the primordial energies of the world, he found that "there always remained a thin, transparent layer between us … and my striving for a mystical breakthrough never completely realized itself."[49]

We might add that Florensky's childhood faith lacked an experience of religious community. In his memoirs, he confesses that

46. Florenskii, *Detiam moim*, 121, 122, 128.
47. Florenskii, *Detiam moim*, 119.
48. Florenskii, *Detiam moim*, 145–46.
49. Florenskii, *Detiam moim*, 89.

he was more interested in rocks and plants than in animals or human beings.[50] Participating with fellow believers in divine worship was still far from him; he remained a lonely, individual seeker.

As we noted in our biographical sketch, Florensky, as a seminarian, had an intense religious experience that fundamentally changed his life. In his correspondence with Rozanov, Florensky repeatedly refers to a relationship with the living Christ: "Only *in Him* am I able to find peace."[51] "I will tell the secret of my soul to One alone, because One alone will weep with me."[52] "You can't believe the degree to which the whole structure of my soul holds on to Christ … even when I try to leave Him and break free."[53]

Whatever this breakthrough to faith was about (Florensky gives us no details), it brought resolution to his childhood search for truth in his family heritage, classical culture, and the mystery of the natural world. In the days after his conversion to Christ, he would decide to become a priest and thereby be faithful to his family heritage and commission. He later wrote that on the day of his ordination he experienced an "eternal Pascha [Easter]."[54] His conversion would also help him understand why classical culture mattered. He did not abandon his interest in it; on the contrary, his lectures at the Theological Academy often explored the philosophy and culture of antiquity. However, antiquity now seemed to him to anticipate, and to find its completion in, Christ.[55]

Further, in Christ, Florensky comes to a new understanding of the mystery that inheres in nature. The antinomies of the noumenal and the phenomenal, the spiritual and the material, the infinite and the finite—all of them now come together for him in Christ, the human-divine, who is everything in everyone.[56] "Only

50. Florenskii, *Detiam moim*, 70.
51. To Rozanov, April 6, 1909, in Rozanov, *Literaturnye izgnanniki*, 19.
52. To Rozanov, April 6, 1909, in Rozanov, *Literaturnye izgnanniki*, 18.
53. To Rozanov, May 16, 1909, in Rozanov, *Literaturnye izgnanniki*, 25.
54. To Rozanov, May 11, 1911, in Rozanov, *Literaturnye izgnanniki*, 58.
55. To Rozanov, April 25, 1909, in Rozanov, *Literaturnye izgnanniki*, 22.
56. To Rozanov, May 16, 1909, in Rozanov, *Literaturnye izgnanniki*, 25.

in Christ do I see, sense, feel, [and] taste reality, the 'transsubjective.'"[57] "Christ satisfies the longing in all human religions for the heavenly to enter into our world, and for our world to rise up to heaven."[58]

The mystical interconnections that Florensky had once found in the natural world now become increasingly apparent to him in human relationships. His discovery of a four-leaf clover becomes a sign to him to marry. When his wife Anna conceives their first child, he feels as though an umbilical cord stretches from him into her womb; it is as though he too is pregnant.[59] At his ordination, the bishop lays his hand upon him, and Florensky experiences an immediate, physical unity with all bishops, the apostles, and Christ himself.[60] In the next days, his taste for food and drink changes, because he has become a different person. Family life is now important to him.[61] When he celebrates the Eucharist as a priest, he senses the living presence of the departed souls for whom he prays.[62] Florensky is no longer the loner, wandering in nature, away from others; he knows that he belongs to a communion of saints.

At the end of his childhood memoirs, Florensky, indicating his agreement with the French philosopher Henri Bergson, writes, "All being flows through us and is therefore in our depths ... as a self-intuition." Florensky reiterates that he has had this intuition since childhood, but now he adds that it has to do "not only with the elemental depths of nature and all of its life—the spiritual dimension of plants, cliffs, and animals—but also with human souls and, in particular, the saints."[63]

Florensky continued to love the natural world, but after his

57. To Rozanov, April 25, 1909, in Rozanov, *Literaturnye izgnanniki*, 23.
58. To Rozanov, April 25, 1909, in Rozanov, *Literaturnye izgnanniki*, 23.
59. To Rozanov, December 16–17, 1910, in Rozanov, *Literaturnye izgnanniki*, 49.
60. To Rozanov, May 11, 1911, in Rozanov, *Literaturnye izgnanniki*, 58.
61. To Rozanov, May 11, 1911, in Rozanov, *Literaturnye izgnanniki*, 59.
62. To Rozanov, January 15, 1911, in Rozanov, *Literaturnye izgnanniki*, 56.
63. Florenskii, *Detiam moim*, 217.

conversion to Christ, he increasingly found the church's liturgy and sacraments to reveal the noumenal (the spiritual, the heavenly, the otherworldly). He continued to learn from classical culture, but with the Bolshevik assault on religion, his focus would shift to preserving the church's unique cultural achievements—icons, church buildings, and the special spiritual atmosphere of the monasteries. As for his family—he wanted his children to know their ancestral heritage, but now, even more, he understood how important it was for him just to be physically present to them. He wished to be their father both physically and spiritually; he wanted to hand on to them the sense of the holy that had come to permeate his own life.

To Be like a Child

It is appropriate that Nesterov painted Florensky not by himself in a pastoral setting but rather together with Bulgakov. Friendship—and especially Christian friendship—would be central to Florensky's theological reflections in *Pillar and Ground*. However, as in Nesterov's painting, the natural world remains the essential backdrop to Florensky's faith. Although adult life would soon tear Florensky away from the innocent delights of childhood, he wanted his children to know creation's mystical beauty. He would often take walks with them along the same country path that he had shared with Bulgakov.

Bulgakov later wrote that Nesterov had attempted in "The Philosophers" to capture not only the special friendship of these two men but also a "spiritual vision of the epoch." Nesterov wanted their faces to reflect a sense both of impending "disaster" and of "joyous victory over it."[64] The Soviet years would send Bulgakov into exile, and Florensky to the gulag. The Lavra would be closed, and Sergiev Posad would be renamed Zagorsk, in honor of a revolutionary Bolshevik martyr. The town grew rapidly. Large

64. Bul'gakov, "Pavel Florenskii," 546.

industrial plants were opened, and a military-technical institute was established on the grounds of the nearby Gethsemane Skete, to which Florensky had often walked.

The communist regime regarded the natural world as raw, inert material to be exploited to fulfill ambitious Five-Year Plans. Stalin ordered construction of huge dams and hydroelectric plants. Prisoners of the gulag dug out, mostly by hand, a massive 141 mile-long White Sea–Baltic Canal. Having to abandon seminary teaching and priestly service, Florensky himself participated in the country's industrial transformation by working for its electrification. The view from his garden was changing. Apartment blocks, paved streets, and factory smokestacks were replacing the pristine countryside. What he so vigorously rejected, a scientific, "Kantian" worldview, was triumphing in Soviet society over the mystical, symbolic thinking that he advocated.

With the fall of the Soviet Union in 1991, Zagorsk again became Sergiev Posad. The Lavra, which government authorities had allowed to reopen after World War II, is once again one of the country's largest monasteries. Hundreds of thousands of pilgrims come annually to pray in its churches, venerate the relics of St. Sergius, and draw water from its holy well. But not everything is as before. Busloads of Chinese tourists, most of whom know nothing about Orthodoxy, briefly walk up to the monastery gates and snap photographs. The federal and city governments plan to enhance the town's tourist facilities with upscale hotels, restaurants, and shopping. The relation of the holy and the secular, the spiritual and the material, has again become a question.

Children, however, remain children, and while fewer of them may roam the natural world as freely as Florensky once did, they continue to be fascinated by pebbles and leaves, tadpoles and bunny rabbits. As in earlier generations, many parents still want their children to experience special places in the natural world—the wonders of a geyser or a glacier, or the peace and quiet of a farm, a forest, or a fishing hole. We sense that something essential about humanity is at stake in how we treat animals, plants, and the land. Modernity's massive destruction of the environment has spawned movements to save it and to find a new, harmonious relationship between humans and the natural world. In this regard, Florensky still has something to teach us, also as Christians. The natural world has a revelatory capacity that calls out for our attention and reverence.[65]

Jesus once said to his disciplines, "Unless you turn and become like children, you will never enter the kingdom of God" (Mt. 18:3). He added, "Do not despise one of these little ones; for I tell you that in heaven their angels always behold the face of my Father who is in heaven" (Mt. 18:10). Americans today debate how to combat childhood poverty, but poverty and wealth are not only matters of money and material well-being. How can we ensure that children experience what they need spiritually to sustain them through the trials of adulthood? How can we provide every child time and space to play and take delight in the natural world? And how can the innate curiosity of a child reawaken those of us who have been deadened spiritually in adulthood by constant stimulation and stress, to the mystery that pervades everything that is?

If Florensky is correct, their future and ours depends on encountering the natural world again in all of its wondrous, concrete, and unique forms.

65. In some of his late writings, the German philosopher Martin Heidegger draws on ancient Greek thinking to develop similar themes. See his essays in *Poetry, Language, Thought*, trans. Albert Hofstadter (New York: Harper and Row, 1971).

3

FR. ISIDORE

"He seemed not to walk on earth."

On a warm, late summer afternoon in 2019, I boarded a local train (*elektrichka*) from the center of Moscow for the suburb of Peredelkino, far to the southwest. A Russian friend had told me that a holy man, Fr. Ilii (Nozdrin), would be receiving visitors. I was curious. I had been researching the significance of a group of holy elders who had attracted pilgrims and disciples in the late Soviet era, when believers were no longer being shipped to the gulag but the church had nevertheless been pushed to the margins of society. These elders of the 1960s to 1990s were now deceased, but I wondered whether there were elders today who had preserved their legacy. When I asked, people referred me most often to Ilii.

Ilii was born in 1932 and, in fact, had known several of the prominent holy elders of the late Soviet era. By the time of my visit, Ilii himself was well known throughout Russia. Patriarch Kirill referred to him as his spiritual father, the wise elder to whom he made confession and from whom he sought advice. The friend who sent me to Peredelkino was also one of Ilii's spiritual children; he had counseled her to become a nun in one of the new monastic communities that he had helped found and guide. Other Orthodox friends told me of having visited him for counsel and prayer.

In the 1930s, the communist government founded a writers colony in Peredelkino, previously a nobleman's large estate. Such notable authors as Boris Pasternak received a summer dacha. In 1952, the state gave the Orthodox Church one of the houses of the former estate to use as a patriarchal residence. After the fall of communism, the church erected a huge cathedral next door. The area was forested; the air, fresh and clean.

After some searching, I found a courtyard where people had lined up to visit Ilii. But I had arrived too late. Ilii's personal assistant, a big, burly monk, was gruffly telling people to go home, that Ilii would not receive any more visitors that day. I began to walk away, but something told me to stop and to plead for mercy: "I am a foreigner, and my friends told me that I must meet Fr. Ilii. I am here only today. Please, can't you make an exception?" The monk looked at me quizzically, asked me where I was from, and suddenly declared, "Okay, you're the last one." I joined the end of the line, which by now had moved into a small house. The monk closed the door.

Before me, I saw a long dining room table, with perhaps twenty seats around it. In a far corner of the room, Fr. Ilii was seated on a low chair. People would approach him one by one, ask his blessing, kneel before him, and speak softly into his ear. The rest of us would scooch over a seat, until Ilii had blessed the person again, and the next person went forward. As we waited, kitchen helpers brought out tea and cookies.

Some of the women broke down in tears as they poured out their cares and concerns to Ilii. He would gently comfort them, sometimes taking their hands and praying. On the table in front of him lay dozens of small, inexpensive icons categorized according to the different saints they represented. To his left was a case with tiny glass bottles, each containing an oil. Sometimes, Ilii handed a person a particular saint or oil that was reputed to help with that person's particular ailment or need.

After about forty-five minutes, it was finally my turn. I explained that I was an American Protestant theologian, and I wanted to know more about Russia's holy elders. Ilii listened attentively, made a few general comments, promised to help me, and told me to visit him again.

Holy People

Since that encounter, I have often asked myself, "Was Fr. Ilii 'holy'? What, indeed, does it even mean for a person to be holy?" In my Calvinist Protestant understanding, holiness is a moral category. It has to do with how one lives a good life. In gratitude for God's goodness, believers seek to worship God and to care for their fellow human beings. Western Christians, Catholic and Protestant alike, speak of sanctification, a process of dying to the old self that is infected with selfishness and self-centeredness, and of coming alive as a new self that looks outward and gives of itself to God and others. In this sense, every Christian is called to grow in holiness.

However, equating holiness with moral behavior can be problematic. Holiness easily becomes associated with a "holier than thou" attitude. In reaction against a holiness based on legalism and moralism, Protestants today are more apt to emphasize God's healing power for people who are broken and God's demand for justice for people who are oppressed, than God's call to each follower to be holy. Protestants tend to say that God alone is holy, while we humans fall desperately short and live by God's grace and forgiveness alone.

As I became more familiar with Orthodoxy, my perspective shifted. I learned how believers seek out "spiritual fathers" (and sometimes "mothers"), people whom they trust to encourage their spiritual growth, correct their shortcomings, and counsel them about spiritual questions—and sometimes about everyday practical matters. The role of spiritual fathers in Orthodoxy has made me think about the people in my life who have been mentors and spiritual guides. Their moral example has been important to me, but perhaps even more significant has been their life wisdom.

Were they holy? Even in Orthodoxy, the priest after the consecration of the Eucharistic elements proclaims, "One [alone] is holy, One is Lord, Jesus Christ, to the Glory of God the Father." Nevertheless, there are people who do appear to us to be "bigger than life." They see further, understand the human condition more deeply, than you or I. Just by being in their presence, we seem to stand on firmer ground.

Florensky's Mentors

Florensky had several important mentors as he was growing up. His father was important to him in childhood. During university studies in Moscow, Florensky became close to his mathematics professor, Nikolai Bugaev. As Florensky's intellectual and spiritual interests expanded, Bishop Antonii (Florensov) became his spiritual father, blessing Florensky to take up theological studies, while steering him away from becoming a monk.

After entering seminary in 1904, Florensky met Fr. Isidore (Kozin), who became a second spiritual father to him. Fr. Isidore lived in the Gethsemane Skete, on a hill just outside Sergiev Posad and across a stream and pond from the Chernigovskii Skete, whose subterranean church and famous icon of the Mother of God were favorite pilgrimage destinations. Even after Fr. Isidore's death in 1908, Florensky loved to walk out to Gethsemane, less than two miles from his house near the Lavra, sometimes bringing his children along and having a picnic.[1]

1. See T. V. Smirnova, *"... pod pokrov Prepodobnogo": ocherki o nekotorykh izvestnykh sem'iakh zhivshikh v Sergievom Posade v 1920-e gody* [Beneath the protective veil of the Saint:

By the time Florensky knew him, Fr. Isidore was at least eighty years old and was regarded as one of the skete's holy elders (although he was not the most popular of them). In Isidore's presence, Florensky sensed that spiritual truth and power had entered the material world. Isidore was a steady rock for him in a Russia that was being buffeted by social change and political strife, and as Florensky was still seeking his own way into the future. Isidore meant so much to Florensky that after the elder died Florensky composed a short biography in his honor, entitling it "Salt of the Earth" (after Jesus' words in the Sermon on the Mount). Florensky referred to himself, the author, as the elder's "unworthy spiritual son."

Holy Elders

The phenomenon of holy eldership has a long history in Eastern Christianity (Orthodoxy).[2] The elders of the first centuries were men and women who became known both for extraordinary ascetical accomplishments and for living to an unusually ripe old age. The man associated with the founding of Christian monasticism in the fourth century, Antony the Great, lived most of his life in the Egyptian wilderness, sometimes surviving for weeks on a single loaf of bread. When he died at age 105, it was reputed that his eyesight and hearing had not declined and that his teeth were still healthy.[3] In the fifth century, Simeon Stylites lived for nearly forty years on a small platform atop a high pillar in the Syrian desert; each day, as he prayed, he performed hundreds of deep bows.

Both men had deliberately sought solitude in remote places but

---

notes about several famous families living in Sergiev Posad in the 1920s] (Sergiev Posad: Sviato–Troitskaia Sergieva Lavra, 2008), 99, 101. A photograph of Florensky with his children on these walks is included in Sviashchennik Pavel Florenskii, *Vse Dumy—o Vas* [All my thoughts are about you] (St. Petersburg: Satis'/Derzhava, 2004), 258.

2. See Irina Paert, *Spiritual Elders: Charisma and Tradition in Russian Orthodoxy* (DeKalb: Northern Illinois University Press, 2010).

3. See Athanasius, *The Life of St. Antony and the Letter to Marcellinus*, trans. Robert C. Gregg (Mahwah, NJ: Paulist Press, 1980), 98.

soon drew curious and admiring crowds. Small monastic communities established themselves near St. Antony's cave, and people from all walks of life, even rulers and bishops, came to the two men for counsel and to resolve disputes.[4]

These first elders had extraordinary spiritual gifts. They seemed to be successors to the Old Testament prophets, the New Testament apostles, and Christ himself. Like their biblical forebears, they fought off demons and resisted worldly temptations. Some could look into the future, read a person's mind, or accomplish miraculous healings. However, what mattered most was their wisdom and integrity. Although (and perhaps because) their ascetical deeds, such as extreme fasting and self-deprivation, were beyond the capacity of most believers, people turned to them for sure guidance in how to live the Christian life.

In the next centuries, monastic life became more established and regulated. Monks were organized into communities under an abbot and a rule of life. Elders were no longer popular, charismatic loners, but rather older, experienced monks who provided spiritual direction to newer, younger ones. The disciple was to renounce his own will and to render full obedience to the elder, who himself was to exemplify obedience to the community's rhythms of prayer and mutual service.

The earlier understanding of holy eldership—as a charismatic office—received new impetus with the hesychast movement in Greece in the thirteenth and fourteenth centuries. The hesychasts believed that unceasing prayer under the guidance of a spiritual father could unite a monk with God. In defense of this bold claim, the Greek thinker Gregory Palamas (1296–1359) distinguished God's "energies," which one can receive, from God's "essence," which remains unknowable. Hesychast monasticism established itself firmly in the Russian Empire in the eighteenth century,

4. See Peter Brown. "The Rise and Function of the Holy Man in Late Antiquity," *The Journal of Roman Studies* 61 (1971): 80–101.

under the influence of Paisii Velichkovskii and his spiritual leadership of a large monastery in Moldavia.[5]

Holy Eldership in Russia

In the nineteenth century, holy eldership (in Russian, *starchestvo*) took a turn toward the world, as represented by Seraphim (Moshnin).[6] Born in 1754 in Kursk, a provincial town three hundred miles south of Moscow, Seraphim became a monk at age twenty-two in the monastery in Sarov, a remote, forested area three hundred miles to the east of Moscow. After several years, Seraphim received permission from the abbot to live by himself in a hut in the woods; he returned to the monastery only for the Divine Liturgy on Sundays and holy days, to receive the Eucharist. His ascetical deeds rivalled those of the desert fathers and mothers. He made friends with a bear and fed it. He kneeled on a rock for one thousand days in a row and prayed. He survived on forest vegetation, a few plants that he raised, and the occasional gift of bread that a brother from the monastery brought him. To add to his physical deprivations, he was at one point beaten and robbed, leaving him hunched over and half-crippled. When his assailants were later discovered, he forgave them and insisted that they not be punished.

After sixteen years, Seraphim returned to the monastery to live, but for the next fifteen years he practiced silence and separation and devoted himself to prayer. However, eight years before his death, he suddenly ended his isolation and received visitors. People reported that he radiated extraordinary love, compassion, and wisdom, welcoming them with the Paschal greeting "Christ is risen" and calling them his "joy." He became the spiritual father to

5. See Paert, *Spiritual Elders*, 31–40. For an in-depth study of hesychasm, see John Meyendorff, *St. Gregory Palamas and Orthodox Spirituality,* trans. Adele Fiske (Crestwood, NY: St. Vladimir's Seminary Press, 1974).

6. The classic hagiographical account is Seraphim (Chichagov), *Zhitie prepodobnogo Serafima, Sarovskogo chudotvortsa* (1903) [The life of Saint Seraphim, the Sarov miracle-worker].

the sisters of the Diveevo Monastery, twelve miles from Sarov, and scandalized some of his fellow monks by receiving them and other women privately in his cell. Peasants as well as nobles came to him for prayer and counsel. Seraphim often knew their concerns before they spoke, and his prayers seemed to effect healing and peace.

In 1833, Seraphim was found dead in his cell, kneeling in prayer before an icon of the Mother of God. He was buried against the outer wall of the monastery church. People soon made pilgrimage to his grave. Reports grew of miraculous answers to prayer when people called on him for intercession. Accounts of his life and deeds were composed and widely distributed. By the end of the century, a movement for his canonization, supported by the royal family, had gained impetus. In 1903, the church's Holy Synod declared him a saint, and tens of thousands of believers, including Tsar Nicholas II and his wife, came to Sarov to venerate his relics. Seraphim would become, next to Sergius of Radonezh, the most beloved of Russian saints; one finds their icons today in almost every Orthodox church in Russia.

Seraphim seemed to have a special connection to the spiritual world. His first biographers recorded his several visions of, and conversations with, the Mother of God and other saints. However, one of the most influential accounts of his spiritual power was not discovered and published until 1903, the very year of his canonization. The author, Nikolai Motovilov, who died in 1879, had left behind an account of his conversations with Seraphim from years earlier. Especially famous became Motovilov's account of an encounter with Seraphim one winter day in the forest:

> Then Father Seraphim took me very firmly by the shoulders and said: "My son, we are both at this moment in the Spirit of God. Why don't you look at me?"
>
> "I cannot look, Father," I replied, "because your eyes are flashing like lightning. Your face has become brighter than the sun, and it hurts my eyes to look at you."

"Don't be afraid," he said. "At this very moment you yourself have become as bright as I am. You yourself are now in the fullness of the Spirit of God; otherwise you would not be able to see me as you do."

Then bending his head towards me, he whispered softly in my ear: "Thank the Lord God for His infinite goodness towards us ... But why, my son, do you not look me in the eyes? Just look, and don't be afraid; the Lord is with us."

After these words I glanced at his face, and there came over me an even greater reverent awe. Imagine in the centre of the sun, in the dazzling light of its midday rays, the face of a man talking to you. You see the movement of his lips and the changing expression of his eyes, you hear his voice, you feel someone holding your shoulders; yet you do not see his hands, you do not even see yourself or his body, but only a blinding light spreading far around for several yards and lighting up with its brilliance the snow-blanket which covers the forest glade and the snow-flakes which continue to fall unceasingly ...

"What do you feel?" Father Seraphim asked me.

"An immeasurable well-being," I said.

"But what sort of well-being? How exactly do you feel well?"

"I feel such a calm," I answered, "such peace in my soul that no words can express it."

"This," said Father Seraphim, "is the peace of which the Lord said to His disciples: My peace I give to you; not as the world gives do I give to you [John xiv, 27], the peace which passes all understanding [Philippians iv, 7] ... What else do you feel?"

"Infinite joy in all my heart."

And Father Seraphim continued: "When the Spirit of God comes down to a man and overshadows him with the fullness of His presence, then that man's soul overflows with unspeakable joy, for the Holy Spirit fills with joy whatever He touches ..."[7]

7. G. P. Fedotov, *A Treasury of Russian Spirituality*, (London: Sheed & Ward, 1950), 273–75, as quoted in Timothy Ware, *The Orthodox Church*, new ed. (New York: Penguin, 1993), 119–20.

Historians today doubt the veracity of Motovilov's account.[8] In 1903, however, his description of Seraphim's transfiguration resonated deeply with Russian Orthodox believers' new interest in hesychasm and holy eldership. In *Pillar and Ground*, Florensky himself records Motovilov's story in full.

Holy eldership blossomed elsewhere in Russia as well. Especially well known became the monastery of Optina Pustyn', 160 miles southwest of Moscow. The small monastic community was close to dissolution, until in 1821 one of Paisii Velichkovskii's disciples assumed leadership and succeeded in reviving it. In the following years, a series of remarkable holy elders emerged. Like Seraphim, these men of deep prayer received worldly people seeking spiritual and physical help:

> The senator, the poor peasant, the student—in the eyes of the elder, all seemed equally suffering and in need of spiritual medicine ... Some came to ask whether they should marry their daughter or their son, accept a job, move to another village to find work ... A peasant woman asked advice on how to feed her turkeys ... and received it. To his amazed followers the starets [elder] answered: her whole life is in those turkeys.[9]

Amvrosii (Grenkov) (1812–91) became especially renowned. As one contemporary historian writes, "The era of Amvrosii in Optina signified the emergence of the crowd. People were waiting day and night at the doors of the elder's house, but often had to leave without having an individual meeting with him."[10] Even members of the royal family sought his prayers and blessing.

Some of Russia's leading intellectuals also made pilgrimage to Optina, including the religious thinkers Aleksei Khomiakov and

8. See Valentin Stepashkin, *Serafim Sarovskii,* 2nd ed. (Moscow: Molodaia Gvardiia, 2019), 210–37.

9. S. I. Chetverikov, *Optina Pustyn'* (Paris: YMCA Press, 1926), 76–77, as quoted in Meyendorff, *Palamas and Orthodox Spirituality,* 160.

10. Paert, *Spiritual Elders,* 129.

Vladimir Solov'ev, and the writers Nikolai Gogol, Konstantin Leont'ev, Lev Tolstoy, and Fyodor Dostoyevsky. Tolstoy once joined a group of peasants who walked to the monastery—it took him four days. He seems to have been fascinated by the phenomenon of holy eldership but not particularly impressed by Amvrosii. His daughter later claimed that the visit only deepened his alienation from the Orthodox Church.[11] In contrast, Dostoevsky drew on his visits to Amvrosii to offer a sympathetic portrayal of the holy elder Father Zosima in *The Brothers Karamazov*.

In 1905, Florensky briefly visited Optina Pustyn', although for archival research rather than spiritual counsel.[12] The days of the great elders were already fading. Florensky was nevertheless impressed by the monastery's special spiritual atmosphere, which he would mention in *Pillar and Ground*, and which later motivated him to work to preserve the monastery when the Bolsheviks moved to close it.[13]

Florensky and other religious seekers among the intellectuals of his time were drawn to holy elders in other places, as well—though, again, with mixed reactions. As the religious philosopher Nicolas Berdyaev wryly noted, "Members of the intelligentsia returning to the Orthodox Church made a cult of *starchestvo* and sought spiritual guidance from the *startsy*." Berdyaev once joined friends in visiting the renowned holy elders at Zosimova Pustyn', just north of Sergiev Posad. Florensky "stood behind me in church; on turning round I saw that he was weeping."[14] Berdyaev himself,

11. See Pål Kolsto, *Heretical Orthodoxy: Lev Tolstoi and the Russian Orthodox Church* (New York: Cambridge University Press, 2022), 99, 117–18.

12. See Avril Pyman, *Pavel Florensky: A Quiet Genius* (New York: Continuum, 2010), 57.

13. Pavel Florenskii, *Stolp i utverzhdenie istinny*, 2nd ed. (Moscow: Akademicheskii proekt, 2017), 130–31. See Pavel Florensky, *The Pillar and Ground of the Truth*, trans. Boris Jakim (Princeton, NJ: Princeton University Press, 1997), 92–93.

14. Berdyaev does not give a date but says that Florensky was not yet ordained (1911) and was undergoing "great spiritual difficulties and distress." See Nicolas Berdyaev, *Dream and Reality: An Essay in Autobiography* (New York: Macmillan, 1951), 189. Aleksandr El'chaninov reports that Florensky and others made the visit at the end of January 1910. See A. V. El'chaninov, "Iz vstrechi s P. A. Florenskim" [From an encounter with P. A. Florensky], *Vestnik* 142, no. 3 (1984): 77–78 n. 14.

like Tolstoy earlier in Optina Pustyn', was not impressed. Indeed, the experience "proved highly disappointing and even painful for me. . . . I could not discover anything 'spiritual.'"[15]

Seraphim and Isidore

Florensky strongly associates Isidore with St. Seraphim. While pregnant, Isidore's mother made pilgrimage to Sarov. The elder called her out from the large crowd, bowed to the ground before her, and declared that she would give birth to a son who would become a great ascetic. Then, as a young boy, Isidore remarked one day to his mother about a sweet aroma in the air. She said that Seraphim must have just died, although they would not get that news until a couple of days later.[16]

The Gethsemane Skete, which Isidore joined, also had associations with Seraphim. The skete had been founded in 1843 to renew monastic prayer in the hesychast tradition.[17] One of its founders, Antonii (Medvedev), had briefly been a monk in Sarov and had known Seraphim personally. Other of the first monks had also been inspired by Seraphim's example.[18] Isidore himself greatly venerated Seraphim and seemed to be like him. According to Florensky, "A ray of Saint Seraphim's radiance" always shone in him.[19] When Isidore prayed, his appearance, like Seraphim's, was transformed: "Some kind of light streamed from his eyes, and he himself was radiant with a festal joy."[20] After Isidore's death, the

15. Berdyaev, *Dream and Reality*, 188–89.

16. Pavel Florenskii, "Sol' Zemli," in P. A. Florenskii, *Bogoslovskie trudy, 1902–1909* [Theological works, 1902–1909], ed. N. N. Pavliuchenkov (Moscow: St. Tikhon's University Press, 2018), 476. See Pavel Florensky, "The Salt of the Earth," in Pavel Florensky, *Early Religious Writings, 1902–1909,* trans. Boris Jakim (Grand Rapids, MI: Eerdmans, 2017), 211.

17. See Scott Kenworthy, *The Heart of Russia: Trinity–Sergius, Monasticism, and Society after 1825* (New York: Oxford University Press, 2010), 73–83.

18. See *Gefsimanskii skit i peshchery pri nem* [The Gethsemane skete and its caves] (Sergiev Posad: Sviato–Troitskaia Sergieva Lavra, 1899), https://azbyka.ru/otechnik/Istorija_Tserkvi/gefsimanskij-skit-i-peshhery-pri-nem/#0_1; Florenskii, "Sol' Zemli," 478; and Florensky, "Salt of the Earth," 213.

19. Florenskii, "Sol' Zemli," 476. See Florensky, "Salt of the Earth," 211.

20. Florenskii, "Sol' Zemli," 468. See Florensky, "Salt of the Earth," 204.

most renowned elder at the skete, Varnava, called him a second Seraphim.[21]

In contrast to the Lavra, which had great wealth and attracted thousands of pilgrims, the monks at Gethsemane, as at other sketes, were few in number, lived apart from one another, devoted most of their day to silent prayer, and received few visitors (and no women). For Florensky, the skete was a spiritual refuge. Whenever he walked there, he felt himself entering a holy space apart from the rest of the world. Isidore would welcome him into his small wooden shack, and Florensky's gaze would immediately alight on Isidore's icons, inexpensively produced yet personally precious to the elder. Nearby, on the wall hung photographs of people who had been spiritually connected to Isidore: although "of no earthly value, [they were nonetheless] … symbols of the heavenly world."[22]

The tiny garden behind the shack and up against the enclosing wall of the skete reproduced events of salvation history as recorded by Scripture and the Church Fathers. Isidore regarded the garden's willow trees as symbolizing the oaks of Mamre, where Abraham received the Holy Trinity in the three angelic visitors. A bench constructed out of rocks represented the cliffs of the Thebaid in Egypt, where Antony the Great and other hermits had lived. A wooden cross nailed between tree branches resembling stag horns reminded Isidore of the second-century martyr St. Eustace, who converted to Christianity when he had a vision of a cross while he was out hunting.[23] On a large rock in the garden, Isidore frequently knelt in prayer, like Seraphim of Sarov.[24]

Although constantly focused on God, Isidore nevertheless cared about this world. Florensky particularly emphasizes Isidore's extraordinary hospitality, comparing it to Abraham's. Isidore always insisted on preparing tea for his guests, and he would not

21. Florenskii, "Sol' Zemli," 465, 487. See Florensky, "Salt of the Earth," 201, 221.

22. Florenskii, "Sol' Zemli," 429. See Florensky, "Salt of the Earth," 166.

23. Florenskii, "Sol' Zemli," 430–31. See Florensky, "Salt of the Earth," 167.

24. Florenskii, "Sol' Zemli," 453. See Florensky, "Salt of the Earth," 189.

let anyone leave without a gift, even if just a few old candies, a *prosphora*, or a turnip from his garden. Whatever anyone gave to him, he soon gave to others, especially to the poor and needy. He shared his meager meals and gave away any new clothes or shoes that the monastery provided him.[25] As Florensky recalls his many visits to Isidore, he interrupts his narrative and exclaims, "Dear reader! You perhaps won't believe that, as I write these lines, tears of gratitude and consolation fill my eyes.... These slices of melon, morsels of dry bread, or pieces of apple were not simply food; no, they always represented slices and pieces of love and tenderness."[26]

Isidore graciously received all who came to him and had an encouraging word for each. He had a special place in his heart for Jews and liked to tell of how his love for them had moved several to embrace Christianity. He prayed for the unity of the Orthodox and Catholic Churches: "We are all children of one Mother [the Mother of God]; we don't want to see her suffer."[27] He sometimes cared for unsavory characters who took advantage of him, but he never gave up on them, always hoping that they would reform themselves.[28] He took pity on birds and animals, even befriending and feeding the mice in his cell.[29]

Equally remarkable was Isidore's capacity for forgiveness. People, especially other monastics and even those guilty of sordid sins, liked to come to him for confession. Only when he saw that someone had come to him in an unrepentant spirit would be become severe and turn the person away. Generally, however, he refused to condemn others, even covering up their sins by accusing himself, instead.[30] Rather than prescribing penances, he assured them of God's boundless mercy.[31] Florensky declares, "The spiri-

25. Florenskii, "Sol' Zemli," 439–40. See Florensky, "Salt of the Earth," 174–76.
26. Florenskii, "Sol' Zemli," 436–37. See Florensky, "Salt of the Earth," 173.
27. Florenskii, "Sol' Zemli," 448. See Florensky, "Salt of the Earth," 185.
28. Florenskii, "Sol' Zemli," 441–42. See Florensky, "Salt of the Earth," 178–79.
29. Florenskii, "Sol' Zemli," 443. See Florensky, "Salt of the Earth," 179.
30. Florenskii, "Sol' Zemli," 444–46. See Florensky, "Salt of the Earth," 181–83.
31. Florenskii, "Sol' Zemli," 459. See Florensky, "Salt of the Earth," 195.

tual simplicity of the Elder softened even the oldest sores on the soul."[32] In Isidore's presence, people who had held on to particular sins for twenty years suddenly felt free to confess them.

Although Isidore deeply cared for others, he often presented himself as an odd simpleton—one of Orthodoxy's holy fools—who did not entirely fit in this world. He would pick up weeds that others had pulled, replant them in his garden, and try to revive them.[33] What he called his "furniture," he had constructed from knotty tree branches. His "marmalade" was a disgusting mixture of "cherries, grapes, strawberries, raisins, kvass, and turnips," which he reserved for himself and his "special guests."[34] He sometimes prepared a salad that combined whatever odd leftovers he had at hand. If his guests politely declined, he would grin lovingly and say, "At least, try it."

Florensky regarded Isidore's simplemindedness as a form of irony. Isidore wanted people not to take themselves and their attachments to the luxuries of this world too seriously: "He pushed each person from the heights of human self-contentment and lay him flat on the ground; he stamped into the dirt any self-conceit."[35] Even so, he managed not to offend others, even when he poked fun at them.

Isidore treated traditional Orthodox rules and authorities in the same way. During the first week of Lent, as Orthodox believers begin strictly to abstain from meat, fish, and dairy products, monks eat little to nothing. One Lent, however, Isidore asked his bishop to forgive him for drinking milk. In astonishment, the bishop asked, "How did that happen?" Isidore replied, "I had some milk left over. It would have been a shame to throw it out, so I drank it."[36]

32. Florenskii, "Sol' Zemli," 457. See Florensky, "Salt of the Earth," 193.
33. Florenskii, "Sol' Zemli," 443. See Florensky, "Salt of the Earth," 180.
34. Florenskii, "Sol' Zemli," 434. See Florensky, "Salt of the Earth," 171.
35. Florenskii, "Sol' Zemli," 435, See Florensky, "Salt of the Earth," 172.
36. Florenskii, "Sol' Zemli," 455. See Florensky, "Salt of the Earth," 191.

Another time, Metropolitan Sergii (Stragorodskii), a great theologian (and later head of the Russian Orthodox Church), took a personal retreat at the skete. Although the other monks tried to keep Isidore away, Isidore still managed to find Sergii: "Father," he exclaimed, "what I want to say to you is this: the newspapers are reporting about famine in India; people in India are starving, while we have so much. Send some money (i.e., from the Lavra) there."[37] Isidore was similarly foolhardy—or courageous?—in promoting his goal of uniting the churches. He sent letters of appeal to Alexander III, Gladstone, and Bismark. Only the tsar responded—with a reprimand.[38]

Although Isidore had little book learning, he deeply knew and respected Orthodox doctrine. He especially emphasized the dogmatic centrality of the Mother of God, the church, and the suffering Christ, whose death won human salvation.[39] But Isidore was more a man of deep prayer than of doctrinal scholarship. He composed a meditation on Christ's five wounds on the cross, continually prayed it by himself, and taught it to others. Those who recited it said that it saved them from sinful thoughts and unhealthy desires.[40]

Like Seraphim of Sarov, Isidore had a special spiritual connection to God. Filled with the Holy Spirit, he "seemed not to walk on earth."[41] When he gave a blessing to his visitors, it was not an empty ritualistic gesture but rather a powerful communication of God's grace.[42] His words affected people as though they had touched an electrical current.[43] Moreover, because his heart was pure, Isidore was able to see miraculous occurrences and divine energies in the natural world.[44] He often had dreams of the Mother

37. Florenskii, "Sol' Zemli," 450. See Florensky, "Salt of the Earth," 186.
38. Florenskii, "Sol' Zemli," 449. See Florensky, "Salt of the Earth," 185.
39. Florenskii, "Sol' Zemli," 464. See Florensky, "Salt of the Earth," 201.
40. Florenskii, "Sol' Zemli," 469–70. See Florensky, "Salt of the Earth," 204–5.
41. Florenskii, "Sol' Zemli," 427. See Florensky, "Salt of the Earth," 164.
42. Florenskii, "Sol' Zemli," 432. See Florensky, "Salt of the Earth," 169.
43. Florenskii, "Sol' Zemli," 435. See Florensky, "Salt of the Earth," 172.
44. Florenskii, "Sol' Zemli," 473. See Florensky, "Salt of the Earth," 209.

of God, Seraphim of Sarov, and other saints.[45] Like Seraphim, he had spiritual gifts of reading a person's heart and mind and of effecting miraculous healing through prayer. But, as with Seraphim, these gifts were secondary to the extraordinary love, compassion, and joy with which the Holy Spirit had endowed him.[46]

In trying to explain Isidore's character, Florensky poses a series of "antinomies"—a term so central to *Pillar and Ground*, where Florensky thinks about how one comes to know divine truth. Isidore is both humble and self-assertive. He fasts faithfully, yet sometimes breaks the rules. He is gentle, yet strict, with others. He lives continually in "the other world" but reads the newspaper. He turns away from the material world, yet loves every created thing, even mice and weeds—and sinful human beings. What appears contradictory to scientific rationality (*rassudok*) is nevertheless complementary and in unity for "purified" reason (*razum*), which alone can discern spiritual realities.[47]

Florensky is especially impressed by Isidore's sense of freedom. Because Isidore was above "this world," he was spiritually free within it. He looked at others through the window of eternity.[48] He humbled himself before others but never allowed them to manipulate him, no matter how much worldly power or influence they had. Florensky writes, "It will be apparent to you, reader, that Abba feared no one, yielded to no one, never forgot his human dignity before anyone, and always felt sovereign and free. He submitted to God alone."[49] Isidore insisted that the Sabbath was made for man, not man for the Sabbath. He felt free to violate the letter of the law for the sake of the spirit of the law.[50]

Moreover, Isidore helped others attain spiritual freedom. When people came into Isidore's simple cell, they suddenly breathed

45. Florenskii, "Sol' Zemli," 472. See Florensky, "Salt of the Earth," 208.
46. Florenskii, "Sol' Zemli," 470–71. See Florensky, "Salt of the Earth," 206.
47. Florenskii, "Sol' Zemli," 487. See Florensky, "Salt of the Earth," 221.
48. Florenskii, "Sol' Zemli," 435. See Florensky, "Salt of the Earth," 172.
49. Florenskii, "Sol' Zemli," 448. See Florensky, "Salt of the Earth," 184.
50. Florenskii, "Sol' Zemli," 454. See Florensky, "Salt of the Earth," 190.

freely.[51] In making confession of sin before him, they sensed that they no longer stood before a mere human witness; rather, "Eternity itself" was looking at them. "In a word," says Florensky, "they knew with a certainty that they had come into the kingdom of freedom."[52]

As Florensky writes about Isidore's last days, he notes the many hardships that the elder endured over his lifetime. Isidore was probably the illegitimate son of the landowner for whom Isidore's parents were serfs. Isidore had wanted to be a monk on Mount Athos but had abandoned the idea, because he had too little money to support himself there. Other monks at Gethsemane, especially older ones, resented Isidore for his spiritual freedom: "They didn't like his independence and frankness.... His disregard for the prescribed fasting earned him disdain, as did his food and drink.... Some even ... called him 'a freak.'"[53] His relationship with Antonii, head of the skete, was strained.[54] Even as Isidore grew old, weak, and ill, Antonii sent no one to help. By the time the local bishop, one of Isidore's spiritual sons, visited him on his deathbed, a thin layer of dirt had settled on Isidore's face, and the bishop had to remove several fleas.[55] Florensky asserts that Isidore nevertheless remained a true Christian in every circumstance: Christianity was for him "no mere decorative element but rather the very tissue of life."[56]

Aleksei Mechev

At Isidore's funeral, the bishop called him the last representative of the monasticism that originated with the great hermits in ancient Thebaid; or, perhaps, he was the first blossom of a great

51. Florenskii, "Sol' Zemli," 460. See Florensky, "Salt of the Earth," 196.
52. Florenskii, "Sol' Zemli," 458. See Florensky, "Salt of the Earth," 194.
53. Florenskii, "Sol' Zemli," 474–75. See Florensky, "Salt of the Earth," 209–10.
54. Apparently, a different Antonii from the one who helped found the skete.
55. Florenskii, "Sol' Zemli," 475. See Florensky, "Salt of the Earth," 210.
56. Florenskii, "Sol' Zemli," 475. See Florensky, "Salt of the Earth," 211.

monasticism that was about to be renewed in Russia.[57] But signs of renewal proved not to be immediately evident. After the October Revolution, the Bolsheviks began closing monasteries, and the last of the holy elders had to flee into the deep forests and distant mountains. Nevertheless, holy eldership did not disappear. Besides those monastic elders to whom believers in the underground continued to come, there were remarkable parish priests around whom spiritual families gathered.[58]

Perhaps the first great manifestation of holy eldership in a parish, rather than a monastic, setting was John of Kronstadt.[59] Born in 1829 in Russia's far north, John was ordained a priest in 1855 and began serving the Orthodox cathedral in Kronstadt, a large naval base on an island across the bay from St. Petersburg. John had boundless energy, maintained a strict ascetic regime (even refusing to have sexual relations with his wife), served the liturgy as often as possible, and encouraged frequent confession and communion, in contrast to the common practice of receiving once a year.

John also had a deep social conscience. He visited the city's worst slums, brought medicine and food to people in need, and eventually organized settlement houses, in which homeless people could find shelter and learn trades. Like the great monastic elders, he gave away money as soon as he received it—sometimes huge sums that he divided up for the many poor who looked to him daily for assistance.

John seemed to live entirely for God and for others, with disregard for his own health and well-being. He constantly traveled between Kronstadt and St. Petersburg; he slept only four or five hours a night. Nevertheless, like Seraphim of Sarov, he radiated joy and love and manifested spiritual gifts of prescience and healing.

57. Florenskii, "Sol' Zemli," 485. See Florensky, "Salt of the Earth," 219.

58. See V. I. Vasilevskaia, *Women of the Catacombs: Memoirs of the Church in Stalin's Russia*, ed. Wallace L. Daniel (Ithaca, NY: Cornell University Press, 2021).

59. See Nadieszda Kizenko, *A Prodigal Saint: Father John of Kronstadt and the Russian People* (University Park: Pennsylvania State University Press, 2000).

By the 1890s, he was attracting huge crowds—sometimes in the tens of thousands—both in Kronstadt and in other parts of the empire to which he traveled.

One of the persons whom John deeply touched was Aleksei Mechev, the priest of the Moscow parish of St. Nicholas in Klennikakh, a commercial district near Red Square. The parish was in bad shape when Fr. Aleksei arrived in 1893. The tiny building was in disrepair, and few people attended services. Aleksei immediately went to work. He instituted a daily cycle of morning and evening prayer and a daily celebration of the Divine Liturgy. For the first eight years, no one came, but Fr. Aleksei did not lose heart. He visited prisons and working people's dining halls, organized a church school for neighborhood children (they met in his own apartment), and raised funds to renovate the church building. Slowly, a group of spiritual children gathered around him. According to one account,

> Those who came [into the parish] unexpectedly felt as though they had landed in an earthly paradise, where everything radiated simple, honest, holy joy. The priest was a living expression of this joy. One look from him removed any deadly sin from a person's heart and broke down any barriers separating people. He strove to give his parishioners what those longing for spiritual life had sought and received in monasteries. He called forth love for divine worship … and set people on the path to active love for others.[60]

In 1902, Fr. Aleksei's wife died after a lengthy illness. Aleksei became deeply despondent and lost interest in his work. A friend invited him to meet John of Kronstadt, who happened to be in Moscow at the time. Aleksei assumed that John would share in his sorrow. But John replied that, on the contrary, he had come to share his joy with Aleksei: "Leave your cell, and go out to others. …

60. "Moskovskii starets Aleksei Mechev" [The Moscow holy elder Aleksei Mechev], *Al'fa and Omega* 23, no. 1 (2000), http://aliom.orthodoxy.ru/arch/023/023-mechev.htm.

You think that there is no greater sorrow on earth than your own.... But now you will be with the people. Enter into others' sorrow, take it upon yourself. Then you will see that your grief is insignificant in comparison with theirs, and you will feel better."[61] A few days later, John invited Aleksei to celebrate the liturgy with him in one of Moscow's churches.

After Fr. Aleksei's death in 1923, Florensky wrote a moving tribute to him. Florensky noted that the meeting with Fr. John became a turning point in Aleksei's ministry. He now gave himself entirely to others. He took their burdens upon himself and, in exchange, shared his love and joy with them.[62] For the next two decades, he led his parish through three Russian revolutions and a world war. He became a skilled doctor of the soul, who was able to read people's hearts before they spoke, diagnose their spiritual condition, and offer healing.

Now, the church overflowed with worshippers. From early morning until late in the night, people crowded on to the staircases and into the courtyard of his apartment building. On days that he received visitors, people would arrive the night before and sleep by the courtyard gate, hoping to get a few minutes with him the next day. Florensky reports that not only simple believers but also "professors, doctors, teachers, writers, people in technical fields, artists, and other people in the arts world"—and not only Orthodox but also Lutherans, Muslims, Jews, and even unbelievers—were drawn to him. He opened the spiritual world to each person according to that person's ability to receive it.

A unique community developed, consisting of "all social strata, conditions, ages, professions, levels of intelligence, [and] nationalities. Each person ... labored and sacrificed for the good of

61. "Moskovskii starets."

62. Pavel Florenskii, "Otets Aleksei Mechev," in Sviashchennik Pavel Florenskii, *Sochineniia v chetyrekh tomakh* [Collected essays in four volumes], vol. 2 (Moscow: Mysl', 1996), 624.

the Community. There were no legal ties, no institutional arrangements, not even any rules; nor was there any formal membership in the Community. Nevertheless, it was a tightly integrated whole."[63] Its members brought a Christian spirit into their different areas of secular work and used their skills to relieve the suffering of any who appealed to Fr. Aleksei for aid. Some called it a "monastery in the world."[64]

Florensky notes Fr. Aleksei's close ties to Optina Pustyn'. Aleksei personally knew several of the monastery's last holy elders. One of them, Feodosii (Pomortsev), visited the St. Nicholas parish and praised Aleksei for doing by himself alone what in Optina required several elders. Of the famous Amvrosii, Aleksei exclaimed, "We are of one spirit." Because Amvrosii and Aleksei trusted each other so fully, they did not hesitate to send their spiritual children to each other. Another of Optina's holy elders, Nektarii (Tikhonov), said to a visitor, "Why do you come to us? You have Fr. Aleksei."[65]

For Fr. Aleksei, Christianity was a matter of experience, not of doctrine—a principle that Florensky embraces at the beginning of *Pillar and Ground*. In Aleksei, Florensky saw someone who was able to draw others into an encounter with the living God, because they encountered in him, as in the monastic elders, one who was divinely transfigured and therefore holy.[66]

Holy Elders as Mediators

As we have seen, Florensky in childhood had a profound sense of the "inner mystery" of every created thing. If one knows how to look, the natural world reflects the glory of God. An "other world" reveals itself in and through "this world." Some scholars have

63. Florenskii, "Aleksei Mechev," 625.
64. Florenskii, "Aleksei Mechev," 626.
65. Florenskii, "Aleksei Mechev," 626.
66. Florenskii, "Aleksei Mechev," 621.

asserted that Florensky, despite his denials, does not escape panentheism, the philosophical position that God is "in" all things, even though God is categorically different from them. But what Florensky wanted to assert was not so much a natural theology but rather a principle of mediation—that the things of this world lie on a boundary with the heavenly world. If we have eyes to see, each world will lead us to the other.

In Fr. Isidore, Florensky, perhaps for the first time in his life, found a person who lived on that boundary. Florensky's fascination shifted from minerals and water plants, mushrooms and shadows, to a frail, odd human being who nevertheless seemed transparent to the divine. For Florensky, Isidore was not simply an exemplary moral figure; rather, his very being glowed and resonated with divine glory. Isidore brought together the "other world" and "this world." Even his corpse radiated a beauty that overcomes death: "In him lay a 'fleshly, spiritual beauty' ... a Sabbath-rest beauty."[67] Florensky tells his readers, "If Fr. Isidore does not seem to you an Angel from heaven rather than a man on earth, forgive me. The fault lies not with the venerable Elder but rather with the inability of the author of this account."[68]

Protestants have typically objected to the notion that there could be mediators between God and humanity other than Jesus Christ. But the great German church historian Adolf Harnack argued that it was the seemingly limitless "love and service" of the first Christians that drew others into their fold: "The gospel thus became a social message. The word—which took hold of a man's innermost being, removed him from the world, and joined him to God—was also the word of solidarity and brotherhood."[69] To be

67. Florenskii, "Sol' Zemli," 485. See Florensky, "Salt of the Earth," 219. Florensky attributes the words in quotation marks to St. Gregory of Nyssa.

68. Florenskii, "Sol' Zemli," 428. See Florensky, "Salt of the Earth," 165.

69. Adolf von Harnack, *Die Mission und Ausbreitung des Christentums in den ersten drei Jahrhunderten* (Leipzig: J. C. Hinrichs, 1902), 108. See Adolf von Harnack, *The Mission and Expansion of Christianity in the First Three Centuries* (New York: G. P. Putnam's Sons, 1908), 149.

sure, Harnack emphasizes the holy community, not the solitary holy man or woman. But, as we have seen, Isidore and especially Aleksei Mechev did not live for themselves. Rather, they shaped interpersonal relations that mediated Christ's love in the way of the first Christians.[70]

In *Pillar and Ground*, Florensky will reflect more explicitly and theologically on the phenomenon of asceticism and holy eldership. There, he will argue that the extraordinary love of the ascetics and elders is rooted in the inner love of the Trinitarian persons: Father, Son, and Holy Spirit. Because the ascetics and elders bear the Holy Spirit, they have a "true love" for the creation.[71] They are able to see its original beauty.[72] Similarly, they see each person as a unique being loved by God and as capable of responding to God's love.[73] The ascetics and elders do not take the place of Christ; rather, they represent him as the unique mediator. Christ himself is a holy elder—indeed, he is "the tender Elder," as Florensky calls him.[74]

After my meeting with Fr. Ilii, I asked a prominent Moscow priest—he himself has several hundred spiritual children, some of whom regard him as a holy elder—whether Russia still has holy elders. He replied thoughtfully, "Well, some people say, Fr. Ilii. But I think that if holy eldership exists today, it is on a much lower level than the elders I knew in the late Soviet period." Then, he added, "But we do have the Bible and the elders' words. Perhaps that is enough."

70. For a contemporary Orthodox understanding of mediation, see Edith Humphrey, *Mediation and the Immediate God: Scriptures, the Church, and Knowing God* (Crestwood, NY: St. Vladimir's Seminary Press, 2023). The Anglican (later Catholic) John Henry Newman made a similar point: nothing can replace "personal influence" in drawing others to Christian faith. See Newman's 1832 sermon "Personal Influence: The Means of Propagating the Truth," in John Henry Newman, *Fifteen Sermons Preached before the University of Oxford* (London: Longmans, Green, and Co., 1900), 75–98.

71. Florenskii, *Stolp i utverzhdenie*, 300. See Florensky, *Pillar and Ground*, 215.

72. Florenskii, *Stolp i utverzhdenie*, 295, 300. See Florensky, *Pillar and Ground*, 212, 215–16.

73. Florenskii, *Stolp i utverzhdenie*, 296. See Florensky, *Pillar and Ground*, 212.

74. Florenskii, *Stolp i utverzhdenie*, 17. See Florensky, *Pillar and Ground*, 12.

Notwithstanding Ilii's promise to help me, we never had another opportunity to meet. But I will always remember his kindness and attentiveness to me at the end of what must have been a very long day for him. And I will remember those who came to him because they believed that he was holy. They so longed for him to help.

4

SEARCHING FOR THE PILLAR AND GROUND OF THE TRUTH

"The Truth overcomes everything else."

Florensky understood his life to be a search not simply for truth but rather for the Truth. As we have seen, he had inklings of this Truth already in childhood, especially in his experience of the beauty and wonder of the natural world, but he did not yet know how to speak of it. Instead, as he grew up, he was trained by his father and in school in a rationalistic, scientific way of thinking that aimed only at truth, not the Truth. Later, Florensky would speak of the contradiction that he experienced between the ideal and the empirical, the infinite and the finite, and the concrete and the abstract.

Faith in the Christian God eventually gave Florensky a way beyond these contradictions. But his way to Christianity was fraught with difficulty. He had not been brought up in the church, and he had had no religious training. A first turning point came at a moment of deep, personal despair, when those two strange dream-visions shook him. Florensky now became convinced that he could not search for the Truth apart from God.

Another turning point came after Florensky went to Moscow. Elated by the Truth to which Bishop Antonii (Florensov) introduced him, the Christian Truth that the Orthodox Church guards, Florensky dreamt of becoming a monk. Antonii, however, refused to bless his intentions and, instead, directed him to enroll in theological studies.

At the Academy, Florensky achieved great academic successes but had new moments of spiritual crisis. Of great help to him in resolving them was Fr. Isidore, the "holy elder." Florensky moved from an abstract understanding of Christ as the Truth to a living encounter with someone who embodied that Truth.

Florensky perhaps hoped to embody that Truth for himself by becoming a monk, but Antonii continued to tell him that his path lay elsewhere. In the meantime, Florensky drew together what he had learned about the Truth into what would become his best-known work, *The Pillar and Ground of the Truth*. Here, Florensky declares that humans will not rest until they find the Truth. The Truth "overcomes everything else."[1]

Sometime during these turbulent years, Florensky had profoundly experienced Christ personally. This living Truth had mysteriously appeared to him in the midst of his despair about life's meaning. In response, Florensky eventually married and was ordained to the priesthood. In family life and in the church's liturgy and prayers, he found new sources for plumbing the depths of the Truth that had taken hold of him.

1. Pavel Florenskii, *Stolp i utverzhdenie istinny*, 2nd ed. (Moscow: Akademicheskii proekt, 2017), 49. See Pavel Florensky, *The Pillar and Ground of the Truth*, trans. Boris Jakim (Princeton, NJ: Princeton University Press, 1997), 33. Florensky notes that he is alluding to 3 Esdras 3:10–12.

Mediation

Pillar and Ground explores an idea that Florensky will develop in detail in later writings: the symbol as a mediating principle. For Florensky, what otherwise appears to human rationality to be sheer antinomies—as we noted earlier, the ideal and the empirical, the infinite and the finite, and the concrete and the abstract—expresses the capacity of created things to point to and to participate in spiritual realities. Florensky was endlessly fascinated by this process of mediation—by what seems to bring together heaven and earth, or, we could say, by what seems to become transparent to divine glory.

In *Pillar and Ground*, Florensky gives this mediating principle the name Sophia (Wisdom). He can even describe Sophia as (almost) a fourth hypostasis next to the three of the Trinity. But it is clear that Sophia, for him, can be understood as encompassing, or standing next to, other broad mediating principles. On the very last page of his treatise, he writes,

> Asking ourselves what the Pillar and Ground of the Truth is, we mentally run through the whole series of answers given here. The Pillar of the Truth is the Church; it is certitude; it is the spiritual law of identity; it is ascesis; it is the Trihypostatic Unity; it is the Light of Tabor; it is the Holy Spirit; it is chastity or spiritual integrity; it is Sophia; it is the Most Pure Virgin; it is friendship; it is, once more, the Church.[2]

This answer is all the more interesting in light of the opening words of *Pillar and Ground*: "Living religious experience [is] the sole legitimate way to gain knowledge of . . . the spiritual treasures

2. Florensky, *Pillar and Ground*, 348. See Florenskii, *Stolp i utverzhdenie*, 482. Here, and throughout the rest of the chapter, I am citing Jakim's English translation, which so beautifully captures Florensky's lyrical prose. In the notes, I list the page numbers in the translation, followed by the corresponding page numbers in the Russian text.

of the Church."[3] Florensky's own "living religious experience" began in his childhood as he encountered the natural world—and although he does not include nature here as a feature of Sophia, the ninth letter of his treatise is devoted to "Creation" and precedes the chapters (letters) on "Sophia" and "Friendship."

Florensky's encounter with Fr. Isidore, his intense friendships, his intellectual struggle for the Truth, and his immersion in the church's liturgical life—each, along with the natural world, becomes for him a place where heaven and earth meet, where one is drawn out from sinful solipsism into a vision of God's glory in and through the things and people of this earth. Moreover, each way of encountering God informs the others.

A Theodicy

Florensky calls *Pillar and Ground* his "theodicy," an effort to justify the ways of God to Russia's intelligentsia at the beginning of the twentieth century (the book carries the subtitle "The Experience of an Orthodox Theodicy in Twelve Letters"). Various ideologies and philosophies had attracted the country's leading thinkers: German idealism, revolutionary Marxism, Nietzschean nihilism, theosophy, and Tolstoyan pacifism. Florensky himself had dabbled in each. Eventually, however, he turned to Russia's ancient Orthodoxy for orientation, as did such fellow intellectuals as Sergei Bulgakov and Nicolas Berdyaev, both of whom foreswore Marxism for Christianity.

Florensky addresses *Pillar and Ground* to the intelligentsia's seekers of truth. He calls his book a treatise for catechumens—that is, for those thinkers who have turned toward the Orthodox Church in pursuit of truth-Truth but have not yet entered into church life. Florensky wants to persuade them that the church, as the apostle Paul declares in 1 Timothy 3:15, is indeed the pillar and

3. Florensky, *Pillar and Ground*, 5. See Florenskii, *Stolp i utverzhdenie*, 9.

ground of the Truth. One knows the Truth as one prays, receives the sacraments, and practices ascesis.

In this search for truth-Truth, *Pillar and Ground* has parallels with Schleiermacher's *Speeches to Religion's Cultured Despisers*. Both Florensky and Schleiermacher seek to make a case for Christianity to the secular thinkers of their day. Because they are not composing a dogmatic, theological work for people already inside the church, they do not focus on Christ and his atoning work. Rather, they try to find a nontheological language that the intelligentsia will understand. Both choose a dialogical genre: Schleiermacher writes "speeches," while Florensky composes letters.

Florensky and Schleiermacher are also similar in their arguing for the priority of religion as experience, rather than as doctrine or ritual. Both want to demonstrate to their readers that they, the readers, have religious sensibilities, whether they know it or not. Both wish to cultivate in their audience a sense of wonder at being, which, if one learns to see rightly, unites the infinite and the finite. In this regard, both Florensky and Schleiermacher regard Plato's thinking as helping to articulate Christian teaching.

The differences between Florensky and Schleiermacher are equally important. Florensky's audience does not consist of "cultured despisers" of religion. He assumes that his readers are already interested in learning more about the church. Schleiermacher appeals to Romanticism and its aesthetical categories, whereas Florensky, while interacting with a variety of Western philosophies (including Romanticism), ultimately frames them in terms of Orthodox ascetical practice.

Throughout his lifetime, Florensky was a prolific correspondent. He regarded the letter as a high literary genre. But the letters of *Pillar and Ground* are not recognizably letters. While several allude to friends from his past, most seem addressed to no one in particular, and none reads like personal correspondence.

Perhaps "letters" freed Florensky from composing a formal treatise as an extended, logical, linear argument. In any case, his style is meditative and associational. One thought seems to trigger another. Florensky moves easily from word studies (drawing from numerous languages, including Hebrew, Greek, Latin, Sanskrit, German, French, and Russian) to the philosophy of logic, to observations about particular Orthodox icons or holy days. His language can be intimate and personal, descriptive of his own state of mind at the time he writes, while at other times, it is intellectually demanding, even obscure. As in his other writings, he interacts with a wide variety of prominent Western thinkers; explicates Scripture and Orthodox hymnody; and incorporates insights from contemporary mathematics.

This eclecticism perhaps reflects his intense aversion to philosophical systematization. Florensky regarded "systems" as inevitably failing to respect the uniqueness of the beings or things that they categorize. Nevertheless, Florensky's mind is synthetic, always finding interconnections and interrelationships between the truths that different areas of knowledge uncover. Florensky is insistent that truth-Truth is one. Reality in its multiplicity has, at the same time, an inherent unity, because reality is grounded in the God who, as the Orthodox liturgy declares, is "Father, Son, and Holy Spirit, the Trinity one in essence and undivided."

The Printed Book as Symbol/Icon

Even the "packaging" of *Pillar and Ground* for publication reflects Florensky's broad intellectual interests and synthetic spirit. Florensky carefully chose colors, illustrations, and type size. The physical book, not only its ideas, should be "a fabric made from many interwoven strands."[4] It should serve, like a symbol or an icon, to reveal the "other" world to which its words on the page point.

4. Richard F. Gustafson, "Introduction," in Pavel Florensky, *The Pillar and Ground of the Truth*, trans. Boris Jakim (Princeton, NJ: Princeton University Press, 1997), xvi.

Florensky says that the sky-blue (azure) color of the book's hardcover corresponds to the background of the Novgorod icon of the Wisdom of God (Sophia), an icon whose meaning Florensky will explicate in the treatise's chapter on Sophia.[5] The book's frontispiece reproduces a seventeenth-century Dutch emblem that depicts two cupids standing side by side on a pedestal in front of the sea; on the shore to the left stands a church, while to the right, rocky cliffs jut up. The Latin motto reads, "The Goal of Love: Two Are One," a theme that Florensky will explore in depth in his chapter on "Friendship."

Illustrative plates at the head of each chapter derive from an eighteenth-century Russian collection of Western European emblems, each of which includes a Latin motto (along with its Russian translation).[6] While the reader might easily regard these emblems as mere (and rather curious) decorative features, each, in fact, captures (even if enigmatically) something of that chapter's theme. Consider the emblem of the treatise's first letter, "Two Worlds": a slender pyramidal column, one side of which is white and turned to the sun, while the other is black and turned toward dark clouds. The motto reads, "Sic semper. – Always such." Here, visually, Florensky suggests the importance of antinomies for expressing divine truth.

Florensky dedicates the book to the Virgin, whom he will equate with Sophia in his chapter by that name. The title page includes words of St. Gregory of Nyssa, "Knowledge becomes love," a theme that Florensky develops throughout the treatise. At the end of the treatise, Florensky declares (in capital letters), "LET US BOW DOWN BEFORE THE FATHER, AND HIS SON, AND THE HOLY SPIRIT, THE HOLY TRINITY ONE IN

5. See Pavel Florensky, "The Turquoise Environment of Sophia and the Symbolism of Sky-Blue and Dark-Blue" and "Clarification of Certain Symbols and Drawings," in Florensky, *Pillar and Ground*, 390–406, 589. See Florenskii, *Stolp i utverzhdenie*, 546–70, 812.

6. See Anthony Hippisley, "Introduction," in *Emvlemy i simvoly (1788): The First Russian Emblem Book* (New York: Brill, 1989), xi–xlvii.

Sic semper.—Всегда такова.

II.—ПИСЬМО ПЕРВОЕ: ДВА МІРА.

Мой кроткій, мой ясный!

Холодомъ, грустью и одиночествомъ дохнула на меня наша сводчатая комната, когда я въ первый разъ послѣ поѣздки открылъ дверь въ нее.

Теперь,—увы!—, я вошелъ въ нее уже одинъ, безъ тебя.

Это не было только первое впечатлѣніе. Вотъ, я примылся и прибрался. По прежнему выстроились на полкахъ ряды матеріализованныхъ мыслей. По прежнему постлана твоя постель, и твой стулъ стоитъ на своемъ мѣстѣ неизмѣнно (пусть будетъ хоть иллюзія, что ты—со мною!). На днѣ глинянаго горшечка по прежнему горитъ елей, бросая снопъ свѣта вверхъ, на Нерукотворенный Ликъ Спасителевъ. По прежнему поздними вечерами шумитъ въ деревахъ за окномъ вѣтеръ. По прежнему ободрительно стучатъ колотушки ночного сторожа, кричатъ грудными голосами паровозы. По прежнему перекликаются подъ утро горластые пѣтелы. По прежнему около четырехъ часовъ утра благовѣстятъ на колокольнѣ къ заутрени. Дни и ночи сливаются для меня. Я, какъ будто, не знаю, гдѣ я и чтò со мною. Безмірное и безвременное водворилось подъ сводами, между узкихъ стѣнъ нашей комнаты. А за стѣнами приходятъ люди, говорятъ, разсказываютъ новости, читаютъ газеты, потомъ уходятъ, снова при-

Figure 4.1. Emblem from *Pillar and Ground*, Letter #1 / Public domain. Wikimedia Commons. Pavel Florenskii, *Stolp i utverzhdenie istinny* (1914).

ESSENCE, WITH THE SERAPHIM CRYING OUT, 'HOLY, HOLY, HOLY, IS THE LORD!'"—words from the Orthodox liturgy. Throughout the book, he sets off certain sections in small type to indicate that they provide extended but secondary commentary. He carefully chooses when or when not to capitalize key words, such as "friend," "truth," or "the other."

Influenced by the Neo-Platonism of the Symbolists, whom he had gotten to know in Moscow through his friend Andrei Bely, Florensky regarded symbols not as mere signs or signifiers but rather as worldly realities that participate in the higher reality to which they point. When Florensky later immersed himself in Orthodoxy, he found it to be a further stimulus to thinking symbolically.

Indeed, key to understanding *Pillar and Ground*—and, indeed, all of Florensky's corpus—is Florensky's concept of the symbol. Symbols mediate between humans and God, between this world and the "other" world. The symbol reveals the depth of being, its grounding in God's being. The symbol is synthetic. The person or thing that becomes a symbol retains a unique individuality, even while bringing together the observer (we who contemplate the symbol) and the One (God) who makes it possible for us to step outside of ourselves in order to know and to love what is other.

A commitment to symbolic thinking may clarify Florensky's decision to frame *Pillar and Ground* as a series of letters. Florensky understands the one to whom he writes, often addressed as a "friend," to serve as a symbol, a mediator, between several spheres of reality: Florensky's inner self, people who have been special friends to him in the past, the present reader of the treatise, the Christ whose icon is before him as he writes, and God himself, the source of all friendship and mediation.[7]

7. Gustafson, "Introduction," xvii.

Friends as Symbols/Icons

The letter-chapters of *Pillar and Ground* follow events in Florensky's life as a seminarian in the Theological Academy, although at points the chronology is not entirely clear. In any event, the accuracy of the history is less important than the symbolic character of the different addressees, each of whom was important to Florensky at a particular point in his life. These "friends" are somehow still present to him, though now absent. They are past, historical realities and, at the same time, an eternal presence.

Pillar and Ground opens with a "Word to the Reader." Florensky then addresses the first letter, "Two Worlds," to "my humble one, my radiant one."[8] Florensky continues by describing his melancholy and loneliness. He has just returned from a trip. Now, sitting alone in his cell in the monastery, he feels the painful absence of the friend who used to be there, right next to him. The allusion is clearly to Sergei Troitskii, a fellow seminarian and his best friend at that time. Florensky accompanied him to Tbilisi (Florensky uses the earlier name "Tiflis"), when Troitskii graduated from the seminary in 1907. Letters Two, "Doubt," and Three, "Triunity," have no addressee but continue the line of thinking of Letter One.

In Letter Four, "The Light of the Truth," an addressee appears again. Florensky writes to his "winged Friend" and "Protector," perhaps still alluding to Troitskii but now, seemingly, more symbolically than personally. Florensky, lamenting, as earlier, his loneliness, confesses that he is writing more for himself than for his friend, but "perhaps you will hear me to some extent in these letters, and then a stream of quiet reconciliation, purity, and faith will pour into me."[9]

Regardless of when these words were first written, they came to be especially poignant by the time of *Pillar and Ground's*

8. Florensky, *Pillar and Ground*, 10. See Florenskii, *Stolp i utverzhdenie*, 15.
9. Florensky, *Pillar and Ground*, 53. See Florenskii, *Stolp i utverzhdenie*, 76.

publication in 1914. Florensky, with his history of emotionally intense male friendships, felt rejected and hurt when Troitskii married Florensky's sister in 1909. A year later, in November, Troitskii was brutally stabbed to death by one of his students at the school where he was teaching in Tbilisi, a tragedy that only intensified Florensky's emotional distress about the broken relationship.

Letter Five, "The Comforter," begins like Letter Four with enigmatic allusions to Florensky's "far yet eternally near Friend," the "Brother" who once "shared one soul with me." Florensky recalls "our long walks in the forest" in the autumn, how we "listened to the mysterious evening rustlings" as "an ineffably exultant mystery grew in our souls."[10] Now, however, as Florensky had written in the previous letter, the friend is gone, and Florensky is again by himself. Death seems near. Nevertheless, "I will attempt to write something—in your memory. Let the pages of this letter be the dried flowers of that autumn."[11] Letters Six, "Contradiction," and Seven, "Sin," have no addressee.

In Letter Eight, "Gehenna," a new addressee appears: "My *starets*! I cannot tell you with what apprehension I approach the writing of this letter.... Perhaps your hands alone will receive it," despite, says Florensky, the poverty of his words.[12] Florensky is referring to Fr. Isidore, the elder (*starets*), in whom Florensky had found a symbol, a living icon, of the risen Christ. Fr. Isidore lived in the two worlds, the spiritual and the empirical, that Florensky was seeking to hold together as the Truth. Fr. Isidore had become holy in his humanity, because his humanity had become transparent to God's glory.

Here, again, Florensky's chronology is murky. Florensky tells Fr. Isidore about a nightmare of darkness and personal annihilation, seemingly a reference to his dreadful dream-vision of being buried alive; according to his memoirs, he was seventeen at

10. Florensky, *Pillar and Ground*, 80. See Florenskii, *Stolp i utverzhdenie*, 115.

11. Florensky, *Pillar and Ground*, 81. See Florenskii, *Stolp i utverzhdenie*, 116.

12. Florensky, *Pillar and Ground*, 151. See Florenskii, *Stolp i utverzhdenie*, 210.

the time (the summer of 1899). But here, in *Pillar and Ground*, Florensky says that the event took place "almost four years ago."[13] Since Florensky did not enter the Moscow Theological Academy until slightly more than four years after the nightmare—and, as we now know, did not write this letter-chapter until 1907—the timing is difficult to square.[14] The event, though historical, has become an archetype for Gehenna, separation from God.

Letter Nine, "The Creation," opens with an allusion to yet another time of spiritual crisis: "The last connecting thread with the earth has been broken. The gravestone presses on my breast.... Everything is dim." Florensky's father had died in January of 1908; ten days later Fr. Isidore passed away. Florensky describes walking through a cemetery. He reads on a cross, "The ashes of a holy soul rest beneath this holy abode."[15] He continues beyond the cemetery into ripening fields of rye and toward the setting sun. While he does not address (the soul of) Fr. Isidore directly, Florensky does think about the character of the spiritual person, the ascetic, who is defined not by "fasts and other bodily exercises" but rather by "a personality restored in its integrity."[16]

Letter Ten, "Sophia," continues Florensky's autobiographical meditations: "It was just then that I began to live on my own." In August 1908, having completed his seminary education with distinction, he moved out of the monastery into "a small lonely house" across from the Lavra.[17] It was a season in which quiet desperation continued to afflict him. In the evenings, the world "would grow dark, and rain would begin to fall," bringing "desolation and fear" upon him.[18] But remembering Fr. Isidore, who "gave me ... the

13. Florensky, *Pillar and Ground*, 152. See Florenskii, *Stolp i utverzhdenie*, 211.

14. Igumen Andronik Trubachev, "Prilozhenie: iz istorii sozdaniia knigi '*Stolp i utverzhdenie istinny: opyt pravoslavnoi teoditsei v dvenadtsakh pis'makh*'" [Appendix: The History of the Composition of *The Pillar and Ground of the Truth: The Experience of an Orthodox Theodicy in Twelve Letters*], in Pavel Florenskii, *Stolp i utverzhdenie istinny*, 2nd ed. (Moscow: Akademicheskii proekt, 2017), 831.

15. Florensky, *Pillar and Ground*, 190. See Florenskii, *Stolp i utverzhdenie*, 264.

16. Florensky, *Pillar and Ground*, 192. See Florenskii, *Stolp i utverzhdenie*, 267.

17. Florensky, *Pillar and Ground*, 231. See Florenskii, *Stolp i utverzhdenie*, 322.

18. Florensky, *Pillar and Ground*, 231–32. See Florenskii, *Stolp i utverzhdenie*, 322.

purest perception of a spiritual person I have had in my entire life," Florensky would again be inspired to understand and pursue "the beauty of the spiritual life."[19]

Soon Florensky adds, "Dear one, forgive me for these crude and hateful pincers and scalpels with which it is necessary to prepare the most delicate fibers of the soul."[20] We, the readers, wonder who exactly this friend, this "dear one," is. "Dear" (the Russian word *milyi* can also suggest innocence and childlikeness—one who is sweet and loveable) seems too intimate a way to address either Fr. Isidore or God, about both of whom Florensky has just been thinking. Has Sergei Troitskii come back into his mind?

Alternatively, could Florensky now be speaking to his new, intimate friend in Sergiev Posad, Vasilii Giatsintov (whose sister he would later marry)—or to the reader in general? Again, the personal and the symbolic merge. By the end of the chapter, Florensky has declared that "friendship, as the mysterious birth of *Thou*, is the environment in which the revelation of the Truth begins."[21]

Letter Eleven, "Friendship," is addressed to a "Distant Friend and Brother!"[22] Florensky seems to be alluding again to Troitskii, but now as one who can be present only spiritually, because he is deceased. Florensky declares, "Again I am with you. Every day I remember something about you.... From day to day, my life slides toward 'the other shore,' so that I could look at you at least from there." Florensky recalls when "you and I were walking to the Paraclete Skete.... You and I took communion together. That was the seed to everything that I now have." Only now, after Fr. Isidore's "departure, do I begin to understand the secret meaning of his repeated, persistent words: 'A brother helped by a brother is as strong as a fortress' (Prov. 18:19). That is what I wish to elucidate to some extent in the present letter."[23]

19. Florensky, *Pillar and Ground*, 233. See Florenskii, *Stolp i utverzhdenie*, 323.
20. Florensky, *Pillar and Ground*, 236. See Florenskii, *Stolp i utverzhdenie*, 327.
21. Florensky, *Pillar and Ground*, 283. See Florenskii, *Stolp i utverzhdenie*, 396.
22. Florensky, *Pillar and Ground*, 284. See Florenskii, *Stolp i utverzhdenie*, 397.
23. Florensky, *Pillar and Ground*, 285. See Florenskii, *Stolp i utverzhdenie*, 398.

The twelfth and final letter, "Jealousy," continues the discussion of friendship. Florensky does not identify an addressee. Nor does his "Afterword," which offers a brief summary of the treatise as a whole. We have seemingly returned to the general reader, whom Florensky has addressed at the very beginning of *Pillar and Ground*.

By means of this symbolist style of writing, Florensky makes clear that he is not simply setting forth information or abstract ideas. He wants to draw the reader into a different way of seeing the world. He offers a vision of a higher reality penetrating and illuminating our everyday world. In this respect, *Pillar and Ground* resembles Augustine's *Confessions* (which, in fact, Florensky cites at the end of Letter Four, "The Light of the Truth"). Like Augustine, Florensky combines autobiography and theological meditation and turns them into prayer. Significantly, the last words of Letter Four come from the Orthodox vespers service: "Glory to Thee, Who hast shown us the light," which is chanted just before the ancient hymn, "O Gladsome Light."[24] Florensky, it appears, is inviting his readers into prayer, whether they are consciously aware of what he is doing or not.

Time as Symbol/Icon

Florensky's careful design of *Pillar and Ground* includes attention to the passage of the seasons—the seasons of his own state of mind, as well as of the natural world around him. Whether or not the intimate descriptions of Florensky's internal state at the beginning of Letters One, Four, Five, Eight, Nine, Ten, and Eleven strictly follow a chronology of events in Florensky's life, they clearly have symbolic meaning. Through them, Florensky finds the Truth beyond himself. Indeed, the flow of time (his life, the seasons) becomes revelatory of eternity. What happens in history is not accidental; rather, it flows from and returns to the life of God.

24. Florensky, *Pillar and Ground*, 79. See Florenskii, *Stolp i utverzhdenie*, 114.

In Letter One, Florensky reports, "I rose today in the early morning and seemed to sense something new. Indeed, in a single night the back of summer had broken. Golden leaves whirled over the ground.... Flocks of birds were set in motion." The sudden change of seasons from summer to autumn stirs Florensky to lament the passage of time. "So many, so many have I lost these last years." Nevertheless, the soul "has a foretaste of resurrection" in these fluttering, dying leaves.[25]

In Letter Four, where Florensky turns directly to his "winged Friend," the setting is "a silent, late autumn night. Snow lies deep beneath the window."[26] As earlier, Florensky languishes by himself in his cell in the monastery. But as he thinks of his friend, he senses something springlike already in the air.

In Letter Five, Florensky recalls again that glorious beginning of autumn to which he referred in Letter One. He and his friend (Sergei Troitskii) are walking "at sunset through the cornfield," reveling in "the flaming west." But time has moved on. The "dying August" of Letter One, which passed into the late autumn of Letter Four, has now become winter. The "evening light in the window seems blue and majestic like Death."[27] Florensky nevertheless feels "an unearthly joy."[28]

Letter Eight, to his *starets*, gives no indication of a season of the year, but Fr. Isidore did not die until February 1908, so perhaps the letter is set in the winter days just before. Letter Nine belongs to high summer. Florensky sharply feels the loss of Fr. Isidore. Outside, the winter rye is ripe and ready for harvest. As Florensky smells its "yeasty aroma," he recollects "something familiar, familiar from distant eternity, eternally dear, and beckoning."[29]

Letter Ten seems to take us forward to the next autumn. Cold rain is falling. Gusts of wind shake the iron roof of Florensky's

25. Florensky, *Pillar and Ground*, 11. See Florenskii, *Stolp i utverzhdenie*, 16.
26. Florensky, *Pillar and Ground*, 53. See Florenskii, *Stolp i utverzhdenie*, 76.
27. Florensky, *Pillar and Ground*, 80. See Florenskii, *Stolp i utverzhdenie*, 116.
28. Florensky, *Pillar and Ground*, 81. See Florenskii, *Stolp i utverzhdenie*, 116.
29. Florensky, *Pillar and Ground*, 191. See Florenskii, *Stolp i utverzhdenie*, 265.

little, unfurnished house, into which he moved after graduating from the Academy. But, then, the memory of his "deceased *starets*" awakens him out of his melancholy: "I suddenly wanted to comprehend the beauty of spiritual life."[30]

Letter Eleven opens with a description of a snowstorm, "covering the window with a fine snowy ash and beating against the window glass." Whereas the previous winter had brought melancholy on him, Florensky now declares, "Let the window be covered by the snow. It's good when that happens. The lamp inside burns more brightly; the incense is more fragrant; the flame of the fragrant candle is more even."[31]

In sum, *Pillar and Ground's* twelve chapter-letters seem to cover events sequentially in Florensky's life from the summer of 1907 to the winter of 1910–11—that is, from the trip to Tbilisi with Sergei Troitskii to the winter after Troitskii's death. But if we follow the sequence of seasons that Florensky describes, they come to only a year and a half—from the beginning of fall in one year to winter in the next. Just as the "friend" is definite yet indefinite, so too time is measured not so much by human calculation but rather by divine mystery. In each season of the year (and of his life), feelings of melancholy have haunted Florensky, and he recalls happier days. But these memories also awaken in him new hopes, new horizons. As we shall see, death and life, time and eternity, loss and hope—Florensky always found truth-Truth at these boundaries, in these seemingly irreconcilable oppositions that defy rationalistic resolution.

Interestingly, the emblem at the beginning of the afterword bears the motto "Propter constatium. For constancy." A smooth, rounded pillar has replaced the tall, slender pyramid of Letter One, which was divided into light and dark. The "two worlds" are now in harmony, rather than in opposition. The sun shines

30. Florensky, *Pillar and Ground*, 233. See Florenskii, *Stolp i utverzhdenie*, 323.
31. Florensky, *Pillar and Ground*, 285. See Florenskii, *Stolp i utverzhdenie*, 398.

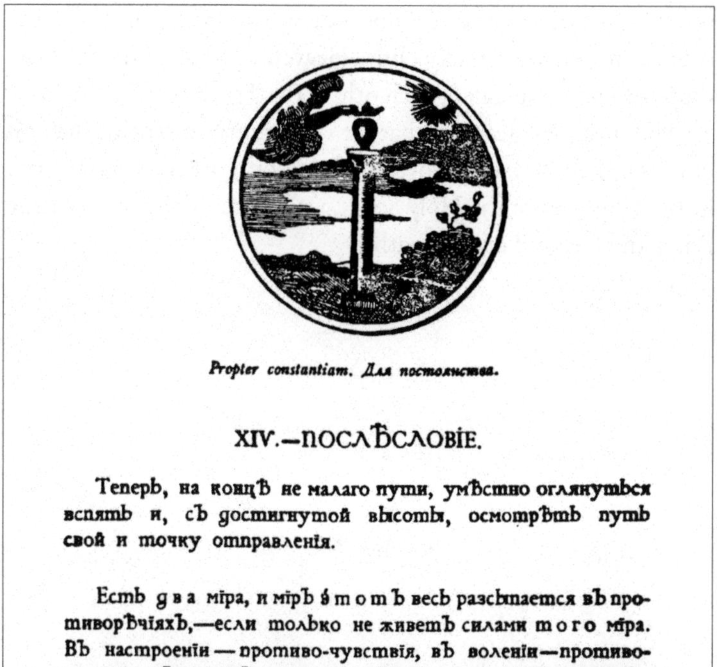

Propter constantiam. Для постоянства.

XIV.—ПОСЛѢСЛОВІЕ.

Теперь, на концѣ не малаго пути, умѣстно оглянуться вспять и, съ достигнутой высоты, осмотрѣть путь свой и точку отправленія.

Есть д в а міра, и міръ э т о т ъ весь разсыпается въ противорѣчіяхъ,—если только не живетъ силами т о г о міра. Въ настроеніи — противо-чувствія, въ воленіи—противо-желанія, въ думахъ—противо-мысліи. Антиноміи раскалываютъ все наше существо, всю тварную жизнь. Всюду и всегда противорѣчія! И напротивъ, въ вѣрѣ, препобѣждающей антиноміи сознанія и пробивающейся сквозь ихъ все-удушливый слой, обрѣтается каменное утвержденіе, отъ котораго можно работать на преодолѣніе антиномій дѣйствительности. Но какъ подойти къ тому Камню Вѣры?

Противорѣчія чувства толкаютъ къ волѣ, но и тутъ —выкрики нестройныхъ голосовъ; тогда мы обращаемся къ разсудку. Однако и онъ—не цѣленъ, и онъ разсыпается въ антиноміяхъ. Ихъ — безъ числа много; ихъ—столько же, сколько можетъ быть актовъ разсудка. Но, тѣмъ не менѣе, какъ уже было сказано ранѣе, антиноміи, въ существѣ своемъ, приводятся къ дилеммѣ: «к о н е ч н о с т ь и л и б е з к о н е ч н о с т ь». Эта противо-борственность к о н е ч н о с т и и б е з к о н е ч н о с т и въ грѣховномъ ра-

Figure 4.2. Emblem from *Pillar and Ground,* Afterword / Public domain. Wikimedia Commons. Pavel Florenskii, *Stolp i utverzhdenie istinny* (1914).

brightly, while clouds gently float through the sky. On the ground below, vegetation grows on one side of the pillar; on the other is bare ground with rocky cliffs. Heaven and earth are at peace. Oppositions complement each other. The Truth is one.

Florensky has learned that we cannot attain truth-Truth on our own. But he has discovered that God guides us, as we seek it. By the power of the Holy Spirit, we do eventually arrive at the Pillar and Ground of the Truth.

5

THE PILLAR AND GROUND OF THE TRUTH

An Interpretive Guide

"The Pillar of the Truth is the Church."

The Pillar and Ground of the Truth established Florensky's reputation as a brilliant thinker. But the treatise is sometimes hard to penetrate. Its sentences are long and complicated; Florensky's train of thought, difficult to follow. The following guide proceeds chapter by chapter, setting forth Florensky's major ideas, briefly interpreting them, and placing them in historical context. I occasionally comment on how, I believe, Florensky compares to other theologians and religious philosophers who have addressed questions similar to his own.

My summary is intended not to replace but rather to supplement Florensky's text—indeed, to encourage readers who may be encountering Florensky's thought for the first time to read *Pillar and Ground* for themselves, notwithstanding the time and effort that it demands. I avoid exhaustive footnoting of Florensky's text and do not interact with secondary literature that I have consulted.

The headings in my text, below, correspond to Florensky's chapter titles.

Word to the Reader

Florensky begins his work by offering a personal word to his readers. He says that he is writing to catechumens—that is, to those who are curious about the Orthodox Church and are seeking a truth that, they hope, it has. They will be able, he continues, to find this truth only by entering into the church's life. Only the experience of the church's spiritual treasures will open them to the truth. Florensky thus makes clear from the outset that one discovers the truth not through logical, rational analysis but rather through experiencing the fullness of divine life that one finds in the church alone.

According to Florensky, Christian churches differ in how they seek to draw people into truth. Catholicism defines canons—rules, laws—that believers should follow in order to know God and obey his will; Protestantism asks believers to use their reason to determine the truth. Orthodoxy, in contrast, points believers to beauty. In the Orthodox Church, one experiences a beauty that goes beyond church canons and personal rationality. This beauty is spiritual, not simply aesthetical. While it characterizes the entire life of the church, it especially manifests itself in certain people: the church's holy elders and ascetics (*podvizhniki* or "spiritual warriors"—that is, those who accomplish great deeds).

In sum, to know the truth, one must encounter these special, saintly people. They embody the truth. They mediate between God and the world. They are in the world and, nevertheless, beyond the world.

Letter One: Two Worlds

Having addressed his readers, Florensky now speaks of his personal condition. He laments how, over recent years, he has lost one close friend after another. Desperately lonely, he has fallen into melancholy. He grieves, as did Mary after the death of her brother Lazarus, and, like Mary, he turns now to Christ, the One who is the true life, the center around which all history revolves. Christ is the tender "Holy Elder."

In seeking Christ, Florensky understands himself to be seeking truth—not a disputable, wavering human truth but rather a truth that has "a pillar and ground," as the apostle Paul says of the church (1 Tim. 3:15). How does one acquire this pillar and ground? Florensky thinks of the relics of St. Sergius of Radonezh. When Florensky began his theological studies in 1904, he and the other seminarians regularly joined the monks at the Holy Trinity–St. Sergius Monastery in venerating St. Sergius's relics. The prayers to St. Sergius included the words of Matthew 11:27–30: "All things are delivered unto me of my Father: and no man knoweth the Son, but the Father; neither knoweth any man the Father, save the Son, and he to whomsoever the Son will reveal him. Come unto me, all ye that labour and are heavy laden, and I will give you rest. Take my yoke upon you, and learn of me; for I am meek and lowly in heart: and ye shall find rest unto your souls. For my yoke is easy, and my burden is light."[1]

Florensky appeals to a preceding verse: "Jesus answered and said, I thank thee, O Father, Lord of heaven and earth, because thou hast hid these things from the wise and prudent, and hast revealed them unto babes." The truth is not attainable through human rationality and scientific analysis. Rather, it must be revealed by God himself. When we enter into the life of the church,

1. Here, I use the King James Version, as does Jakim's English translation. Florensky is quoting from the Slavonic translation of the Bible, which was at that time (and today in the Russian Orthodox Church is still) used liturgically.

we encounter the God who in his Son Jesus Christ promises to take our burdens upon himself. He is the Truth that humans seek.

Letter Two: Doubt

Florensky reflects further on the search for truth. Human efforts to arrive at truth take two forms. The first approach is what Florensky calls the intuitive. We sense that a thing is identical to itself: A=A. We cannot say why this is; it simply seems obvious to us. Intuitive truth is concrete, practical, and unphilosophical.

The second approach is the discursive. We know the truth of something only in relation to other things. We can explain and understand why a thing is what it is; we find reasons or causes that account for it. We make judgments. Discursive truth characterizes science.

To understand Florensky's distinction better, we might think of how we know ourselves and of what we take to be true about ourselves. Intuitively, I know that I am who I am. It seems obvious to me that I have a unique identity. I affirm myself as myself. Discursively, however, I know that I am who I am because of the influence of people and events on my life. I was born to particular parents. I inherited certain genes from them. I was raised with distinctive intellectual and moral values. Moreover, not only my parents but also my social location has shaped me, such factors as race, gender, and nationality—and each of these factors has been shaped historically. Each cause, we quickly see, has a chain of causes behind it.

For Florensky, neither approach to truth is ultimately satisfactory. On the one hand, the intuitive approach cannot explain why something is true. We simply assert that something is what it is. On the other, the discursive approach results in an endless chain of reasons and causes for why something is what it is. Again, if I take the example of how I know the truth of who I am: the intuitive approach does not allow me to say why I am what I am, and the discursive approach gives me no ultimate reason or cause for why

I am what I am. Both approaches result in skepticism, the gnawing uncertainty that I could ever know the truth about myself or anything else.

Florensky nevertheless believes that this skepticism must ultimately become skeptical about itself. If skepticism questions the truth of everything, it must also question its own assertion that truth is unknowable. Moreover, says Florensky, the very fact that we search for truth suggests that it must really exist, and that it must bring together the intuitive and the discursive. Truth, he therefore concludes, is "intuitive-discursive." It is an intuition that differentiates itself, and a discourse that integrates everything into a unity. Truth is an absolute Truth that is higher than either the law of identity (the intuitive approach) or the rules of substantiation (the discursive approach). This Truth nevertheless grounds them both. It has the character of the coincidence of antinomies: it is both a "knowing that is real" and a "reality that is known."

Because Truth cannot be attained by either our intuitive or discursive efforts, it must be given to us. Here, Florensky returns to his call for the searchers of truth to enter into the life of the church—for him, the Orthodox Church. Truth is not something that we achieve intellectually; rather, it is life in its fullness in God. Truth is revealed to us as a "self-demonstrating Subject"—that is, as the God who comes to us in Jesus Christ.

Letter Three: Triunity

Florensky continues his reflections on truth. Having noted in the previous chapter that Truth expresses itself as antinomies, he now turns to the church's language for God, which also expresses itself in antinomies. In the fourth century, the Church Fathers, especially Athanasius, drew on Greek terminology to speak of God's oneness and God's threeness. The term *ousia*, commonly translated as "substance" or "essence," was used to refer to God's oneness; the term *hypostasis*, commonly translated as "person," to God's threeness. Florensky notes, however, that the terms are interchangeable. They do not offer a rational, logical explanation of God's triunity; rather, they point to the unique mystery of God's being.

The church's ancient heresies made more sense to human reason but reduced God to something less than God. One heresy was tritheism, for which Father, Son, and Holy Spirit are three different subjects. They may cooperate, but they are not truly one. At the other extreme was the heresy of modalism (Sabellianism): God is one, and Father, Son, and Holy Spirit simply designate three different modes of activity by which God works in the world, such as creating (Father), redeeming (Son), and sustaining (Holy Spirit). In contrast, only the church's paradoxical language of antinomies rightly expresses the truth about God.

Florensky notes that Christians have struggled over the centuries to understand the relationship between faith and reason. He believes that they took a great step forward when they were able to assert neither "I know" nor "I believe," but rather "I know, because I believe." This kind of knowing faith is not, however, Tolstoy's "reasonable faith" that reduces Christianity to morality. Florensky sees an infinite gulf between reason and faith, insofar as reason is fallen. Human rationality has to deny itself and submit to the Truth.[2]

Therein lies a problem, however. We long for this Truth but have not the strength to attain it by our own efforts. Although we are free to choose it, we are trapped within ourselves and within our human categories of thinking. It is one thing to recite the church's language of antinomies (as expressed in church dogma, as in the Nicene-Constantinopolitan Creed); it is another thing to have a living experience of the Truth. Here Florensky alludes to a matter that he will develop later in his treatise: because human rationality breaks the world apart, it is unable to grasp the world's

2. In asserting a gulf between reason and faith, Florensky sounds much like Kierkegaard (whom he does not mention by name). Unlike Kierkegaard, however, Florensky elsewhere affirms the possibility of a redeemed reason that is able to contemplate divine mysteries.

essential unity. Only by experiencing the Truth that is one can we also experience that which binds us to one another and, indeed, to the whole creation.

All that we can do, then, in our fallen condition is to cry out to God: "O Lord, Lord, if you exist, help my unreasoning soul. Come, you yourself. Lead me, you yourself, to you! Whether I want it or not, save me. According to your desire and knowledge, let me see you. By your power and sufferings, take hold of me!"[3] For Florensky, the very longing of the soul for God is the beginning of faith, "the realization of what we hope for and the assurance of what we cannot see" (a reference to Hebrews 11:1).[4]

Letter Four: The Light of Truth

In taking another step forward in explicating the character of truth, Florensky argues that one knows the truth about an object only as one loves that object. True knowledge is more than an intellectual act; it brings about a union between the knowing subject and the known object. Moreover, when an object is loved, it is no longer merely an "object" to the lover. It now has an integrity, a "face," of its own. It becomes a "Thou." Here, Florensky seems to be thinking primarily of relations between human subjects, although in a later chapter he will develop the thought that even things are not mere things, if we truly know and love them. They too have a "face," as we saw in his reflections about his childhood encounters with plants, animals, and minerals.

Foundational to Florensky's understanding of knowing and loving is the character of the inner life of the Trinity. Father, Son, and Holy Spirit know and love one another as three persons, yet as one essence. Love is not simply something that they do; it is what they are. God is Truth, and therefore God is Love.

3. Pavel Florenskii, *Stolp i utverzhdenie istinny*, 2nd ed. (Moscow: Akademicheskii proekt, 2017), 72. See Pavel Florensky, *The Pillar and Ground of the Truth*, trans. Boris Jakim (Princeton, NJ: Princeton University Press, 1997), 50.

4. Florenskii, *Stolp i utverzhdenie*, 74. See Florensky, *Pillar and Ground*, 51.

Human knowing has a Trinitarian shape of truth, love, and beauty. The person who knows another person attains to truth. The person who is known experiences the love of the first. And, says Florensky, a person who contemplates the love between the "I" (the knowing one) and the "Thou" (the loved one) becomes a third, a "He," who sees the beauty of the relationship between the "I" and the "Thou." Moreover, this "He" can enter into the love of the "I" and the "Thou," himself becoming an "I" and a "Thou," and thereby adding a link to an ever-widening circular chain of truth, love, and beauty, which reflects the character of Father, Son, and Holy Spirit, as they relate to one another.

Florensky understands knowing-loving to be a kenotic act. To know-love another I must go out from myself. I must abandon what Florensky calls the empirical self, the self that is self-enclosed and that therefore identifies itself with itself (the principle of A=A). When I truly know-love another, I find myself in one who is not myself (A≠A). I become a new self, the self that God created me to be: "Each 'I', as it sees the image of God in the other, sees itself as the image of God, as though looking in a mirror."[5]

In becoming this new self—the self that has overcome the rational, empirical self—I enter not only into the life of the other but also into the life of God. I am lifted out of time into eternity. However, I am able to go out from myself to love the other only by the power of God, as he pours out his love through me to the other, and as that love returns to me from the other. Communion with the other is simultaneously communion with God, and vice versa, although Florensky clarifies that our experience of both is incomplete in this life and therefore happens by faith.

Florensky contrasts this kind of love with other human concepts of love. A typical Western notion of love, he says (referring to Leibniz and Spinoza), is psychological. Love is, then, a feeling, a taking of delight in something that exists outside of me. This

5. Florenskii, *Stolp i utverzhdenie,* 98. See Florensky, *Pillar and Ground,* 68.

kind of love, however, cannot be differentiated from lust, which objectifies what it loves. A second notion reduces love to morality (Tolstoy), a love that seeks the earthly well-being of another. Still other kinds of love may be based on a shared human identity, such as race or nationality. None of these loves, however, brings about a unity that Florensky calls ontological—a unity of being. Human loves are based on principles of "similarity," whereas Christian love draws people into the same kind of oneness with God and with others that characterizes the triune life of God.

Here, Florensky explicates the ancient church's Trinitarian disputes and the difference that the church eventually drew between *homoousia* ("one in essence," as stated in the Nicene-Constantinopolitan Creed) and *homoiousia* ("similar in essence," which the Arian "heretics" used to describe the relationship between Father and Son). "Similarity" is the principle by which we organize different "things" (objects) into categories. We group them together on the basis of their external characteristics. In contrast, when we truly know-love another, the other reveals its inner life to us. It becomes, as we have said, a "face," a "Thou," with whom we become one.

Florensky believes that Orthodoxy, in contrast to Western philosophies and theologies, has best preserved this distinctive Christian understanding of love, as in the symbolic language of the Divine Liturgy. Just before receiving the Eucharist, the congregation chants, "Let us love one another, that with one mind we may confess Father, Son, and Holy Spirit, the Trinity one in essence and undivided." Here, we see that mutual love, not just "similarity" of thought, is a precondition for oneness of being. Conversely, says Florensky, oneness of thought about God is a precondition for love of one another. This unity of thought and love, and of God and humanity, characterizes the (Orthodox) church, the body of Christ. The life of the church opens us to the life of the Trinity. In the church, we confess the Son, through him we know the Father, and through the Holy Spirit we contemplate the beauty of God's essence.

Florensky's emphasis on the church echoes the opening "Word to the Reader" of *Pillar and Ground*: those who seek the truth find it by entering into the life of the church. Moreover, as in that opening, Florensky again emphasizes that the church's holy people—its saints and ascetics—have already experienced the truth-love-beauty that the rest of us are still seeking. Because these holy ones of long ago composed the liturgical forms and prayers in which we may participate today, we too may enter into life of God. And there are holy ones still among us in whom we encounter God's presence.

In this regard, Florensky reflects on the light of God, which has such a prominent place in Orthodox hesychasm. As we have noted, St. Gregory Palamas taught that, although God's essence remains unknowable, a believer, through prayer and ascetical exercise, may receive God's energies, the same light that filled Christ at his transfiguration on Mount Tabor and that shone on Sergius of Radonezh, as he contemplated the mystery of the Trinity. Although Florensky does not mention it here, he believes that he himself glimpsed this light in the holy elder Fr. Isidore.

Florensky associates light with revelation and beauty. Whenever something discloses its inner life in God to us, it shows forth light, and for humans, light is "intuitively" beautiful. In this sense, nothing is more beautiful than the transfigured Christ. But in contemplating the light of Christ, the ascetic, too, shines with light, even if to a lesser degree. Florensky notes that Moses shone with light after he came out of the tent of meeting. What was, however, still the exception under the Old Testament becomes the rule under the New. The halo that the iconographer places around a saint represents the light that the saint bears and shows forth. The ascetic's purity of heart is not simply a matter of moral purity; his or her very being is beautiful with light.

This light is the Holy Spirit. The person who receives the

Spirit's illumination experiences peace, joy, and the warmth of God's presence. Florensky again lifts up the example of Seraphim of Sarov and quotes Motovilov's account of the transfiguration of the saint, who is filled with light brighter than the sun.

At the conclusion of this fourth letter, Florensky recalls that the Neo-Platonists spoke of an inner light that illuminated their minds, and he asks whether this light is the same as that which the saints receive. He concludes that even if it is, the Neo-Platonists were unable to resolve their skepticism about attaining to truth, because they lacked the doctrine of the Trinity. Their experience of an inner light never became a self-evident intuition for them that transcended rationality and logic. Augustine, however, did make the connection. With the help of Neo-Platonic thinking, he discovered a light above his mind that he associated with the God who is Trinity.

Letter Five: The Comforter

Florensky now meditates on the Holy Spirit, who, as he has said in the previous letter, illuminates us and guides us into the truth. Florensky argues that the Spirit is still revealing itself to the church. At present, we get only glimpses of the Spirit. Those moments when, in the Spirit, we rise above time to eternity are rare. We do not really know the Spirit yet as a "person," a *hypostasis*, a "face." For this reason, the church, even while emphasizing the Spirit's importance, has had difficulty speaking clearly about it.

Might we, then, asks Florensky, understand more about the Spirit by examining the church's references to it in worship? In particular, might the church's celebration of Pentecost (in Orthodoxy, also known as the Day of the Holy Trinity), when God poured out his Spirit upon the apostles in Jerusalem, give us insight into the character of the Spirit? Even here, however, references to the Spirit are muted, says Florensky. To be sure, the long prayer to the Trinity (in the kneeling prayers after the Divine Liturgy on Pentecost) has three parts. But while the first is addressed to the Father, and the second, to the Son, the third is more clearly addressed to the Son again than to the Spirit.

Similarly, the church's dogmatic teaching about the Spirit typically transfers attributes of the Son to the Spirit. The church's ascetical literature offers not much more help. Language about the Spirit frequently elides into a description of the "spiritual" character of particular individuals, whose purification from sin is assigned as much to the Son as to the Spirit. The same imbalance is evident in the church's Scriptures. The Old Testament speaks primarily of the Father; the New Testament, of the Son. Neither develops a full understanding of the Holy Spirit. Where Scripture does refer to the "spiritual," it again focuses on the spiritual gifts that believers may attain.

To be sure, there have been particular individuals or groups that over the course of history have claimed to know the Spirit, but they have usually been outside the church and have been guilty of heresy. Florensky is thinking of Tolstoy, as well as of the Russian advocates of a "new religious consciousness," to whom Florensky himself had been attracted before going to seminary.[6]

Only within the church have there been genuine manifestations of the Spirit. The Spirit revealed itself to the great ascetics of the early church in Palestine, who became the "almost superhuman centers of the Church."[7] With Seraphim of Sarov and the holy elders of Optina Pustyn'—and especially in the holy elder Amvrosii—the church received even more of the Spirit. Where the Spirit is present, not only does it give individuals joy and comfort, but it also endows the church as a whole with an objective power (manifested especially through the church's sacraments) that heals soul and body, and that endows the church's holy people with the capacity to perform miracles and to peer into the future.

6. Specifically, the circle gathered around Dimitrii Merezhkovskii. See Avril Pyman, *Pavel Florensky: A Quiet Genius* (New York: Continuum, 2010), 34–35.

7. Florenskii, *Stolp i utverzhdenie,* 126. See Florensky, *Pillar and Ground*, 88.

Florensky believes that these manifestations of the Spirit will gradually increase over the course of history, until the kingdom of God itself establishes itself on earth. Florensky notes the church's equation of the Spirit and the kingdom, as in some ancient versions of the Gospel of Luke, which substitute "Thy Spirit come" for "Thy kingdom come" in the Lord's Prayer. Life in the Spirit is life in the kingdom. When the day comes that the kingdom manifests itself fully, all people will know the Spirit as a person who reveals the Father as king, the Son as the One whom the Father anoints, and itself as the oil that the Father uses to anoint the Son. If earlier, Florensky characterized the three persons of the Trinity in terms of mutual kenosis, now he emphasizes that they affirm and glorify one another.

For Florensky, the Son, the Logos, is the principle of order, and an ordered universe is open to rational, scientific investigation. The Spirit, in contrast, endows humans with freedom, creativity, and a sensitivity to beauty. Only through the Spirit can humans know the heavenly character of the creation. The Spirit enables us to break out of our self-enclosure, to reach out to what is other, and to discover our essential unity with what is other—a unity that is the "one in essence" of the Trinity itself.

Florensky concludes the letter with a citation of an extended prayer of St. Simeon the New Theologian, in which Simeon asks the Spirit to reveal itself.

Letter Six: Contradictions

The Spirit leads us into truth. Because, however, the Spirit is still revealing itself, we do not yet fully know the truth either about God or about ourselves. We have truths, but not the Truth. Florensky believes that we can nevertheless find a truth that will disclose to us the Truth, a truth that will serve as a symbol of the Truth. We arrive at this truth not through logical deduction but rather through experiencing ourselves as free "persons." Here, as earlier, Florensky uses the term *lichnost'* (personality), central to the vocabulary of all of Russia's early twentieth-century religious philosophers. A "person" is a creative agent.

Because earthly existence is in constant flux, none of our rational judgments about what is true are final or exhaustive. We continually encounter new dimensions of existence that supplement and even contradict our prior judgments. The truth that we seek as the Truth will have to stand above and gather together all of these diverse and even conflicting judgments. Truth, therefore, will inevitably have the character of antinomy—of thesis and antithesis. We will be able to receive this kind of truth only by faith; it will not make rational sense to us. Indeed, this truth demands that we renounce our capacity for rational judgment (*rassudok*)—which, as we saw in Letter Four, just keeps us trapped within ourselves, unable to know what is outside of us.[8]

Florensky believes that the church's inherited dogma, especially that of the Incarnation and the Trinity, takes the principle of antinomic truth to its limit. Christ is fully human and fully divine. God is three in one and one in three. Through antinomies, dogma rightly expresses truth that points to the Truth. For Catholics, using mere rationality, these antinomies seem irresolvable; their church therefore needs an authority, the pope, to guarantee the truth of dogma. For Orthodox believers, by contrast, dogma in its antinomic character calls forth our freedom to believe.

Florensky notes the genius of the Greek mind in holding oppositions together. The pre-Socratic philosopher Heraclitus saw both the essential harmony of all reality and the tragic brokenness of the world with its enmities and wars. Plato intensified these antinomies, as he contrasted perfected, true "ideas" with human

8. Florensky uses two terms for reason: *rassudok* and *razum*. See Florensky, *Pillar and Ground,* 7 n. 7, where Jakim offers helpful definitions. Generally, *rassudok* refers to reason in its fallen, sinful condition; it is an analytical rationality that imposes itself on reality. *Razum* refers to reason as redeemed by God and therefore as able to perceive reality in its essential unity within itself and with God. Florensky often condemns "scientific," Enlightenment, "Kantian" rationality. Nevertheless, he also believes that God makes "science" and rational observation of the creation possible. Further complicating matters is that Florensky is not always consistent in his use of the terms.

blindness to truth. The Jews, too, recognized the antinomic character of truth. The book of Job is built on antinomies; Job experiences something wondrous about God and God's ways within the moral disorder of the world. Christian dogma draws on both Greek and Jewish antinomic thinking; the medieval thinker Nicholas de Cusa speaks of the "coincidence of opposites" (*coincidentia oppositorum*) in God.

What is one in heaven appears on earth in the form of antinomies; therefore, the Truth seems mysterious to us and beyond rational understanding. Humans in their sinfulness reject this mystery. As a consequence, dogma falls apart into competing heresies, each of which elevates one dimension of the Truth—one side of the antinomy—while rejecting its opposite. Rather than entering by way of antinomies into the mystery of God, the heretic tries to make truth rational. "Science" (built on rational judgment, *rassudok*) replaces "revelation" (given to a purified conscience and mind, *razum*).

For Florensky, Orthodoxy puts the broken pieces back together. In this sense, it is catholic—that is, truly inclusive. It points to Christ, in whom all these oppositions have already been reconciled. Moreover, Christ promises us the Holy Spirit, who begins to bring about this reconciliation in each of us. Florensky again mentions the ascetics, who to a higher degree than the rest of us live in the Spirit and who experience (and offer) Christ's healing of the splintered, fragmented human condition.

Truth, dogma, religious experience—each is constituted by antinomies that, as Florensky never tires of emphasizing, demand the self-sacrifice of the rational mind. Although there is no evidence that Florensky and the Swiss Protestant theologian Karl Barth (1886–1968) knew of each other, they share this interest in antinomic truth. Both, at almost the same historical moment, declare that antinomic truth finds especially intense expression in the apostle Paul's letters. Using imagery similar to Barth's in his first (1919) and second (1922) commentaries on Romans, Florensky writes, "The most fitting example [of antinomic truth] is the most dialectical and most fiery of [Paul's] Letters—to the Romans—this antinomy-charged bomb that explodes the rational mind (*rassudok*)."[9]

Letter Seven: Sin

Florensky continues his harsh criticism of *rassudok*, the judging, rational mind that is closed in on itself. "Sin," he asserts, "is the unwillingness to exit the condition of self-identification," "from the identification of 'I=I', or, more exactly, 'I'" (see, again, the fourth letter).[10] When we assert ourselves as self-sufficient, having no necessary relationship to God or to others—when we seek a unity based on ourselves, rather than on the Trinity—we lose our integrity (chasteness, wholeness, unity) and, instead, become divided, fragmented, and alienated from ourselves. The "person" (*lichnost'*) becomes a mere "mask" (*lichina*) behind which he hides his sinfulness and brokenness. Florensky extends his critique of *rassudok* to social-political arrangements. In his view, the extreme specialization of work and material consumption that characterizes modern societies reflects humanity's fallen, fragmented condition.

The sinful, fragmented person loses creative freedom. Our life becomes nothing more than mechanical processes that control and define us. We are like Legion, the man possessed by many demons, whom Jesus encounters among the graves. We become depraved; our acts are shameless. Our heart is hardened. We can no longer see reality; everything around us becomes dark with the darkness that is hell.

Florensky's line of thought now shifts from defining sin to explicating its effects. He proposes to explore, first, what more precisely constitutes the chasteness (integrity, unity, wholeness) that

9. Florenskii, *Stolp i utverzhdenie*, 169. See Florensky, *Pillar and Ground*, 121.
10. Florenskii, *Stolp i utverzhdenie*, 182. See Florensky, *Pillar and Ground*, 132.

sin takes from us and, second, how we are to understand the ontological status of the one who is chaste—that is, the character of the chaste person's enduring existence before God.

The answer to the first—what constitutes chasteness—Florensky finds in "blessedness," which he defines as release from the endless striving to assert oneself and to impose oneself on the world. After extensively discussing the German philosopher Schelling's explication of the Greek word *makarios* (blessed), Florensky equates blessedness with the Buddhist Nirvana and the Christian "eternal Sabbath." The spirit of blessed, ultimate peace is especially evident, says Florensky, in the writings of the Church Fathers of the second century (such as the Second Letter of Clement) and in the church's prayers and hymns for the dead. Blessedness is the condition of the ascetic, who rises above time and touches eternity. The ascetic is able to move out from himself and to see all of reality as a symbol, an opening to, the divine.

Here, we again see how Florensky's personal experience of the church's liturgy and the church's elders (especially, at this time, Fr. Isidore) underlies his philosophical language. Both sources of holiness have drawn him beyond his sinful self-enclosure. He has been granted a vision of a different kind of existence; he has a growing awareness of the presence of God. Florensky wants his "catechumens" to have this experience too. His philosophical meditations are more than an intellectual exercise in Christian apologetics; he hopes that he will succeed in drawing other "seekers" into the life of the church with its holy things and holy people.

The answer to Florensky's second question—about the ontological status of the chaste person—lies in "eternal memory." Memory, for Florensky, is more than passive recollection, which eventually fades into oblivion. Rather, memory is active and creative. Florensky calls it the deepest kind of thinking. Memory makes the past present and turns the present into an anticipation of the future. Memory lifts us above time. It forms images that are transparent to eternity (what Florensky again calls "symbols"). Our ultimate blessedness is to remember God and to be remembered by God. As the thief on the cross said to Jesus, "Remember me, when Thou comest into Thy kingdom" (words that Orthodox believers recite in prayer just before receiving the Eucharist).

All of human life is a striving to be remembered eternally. A person makes or finds things that he hopes will pass on something of his existence to others. A pagan culture commemorates ancestors in order to secure their continuing existence. Only Christianity, however, fulfills the longing for "memory eternal," the very words that the church lifts up to God in its prayers for the dead.[11] Florensky further notes the central place of memorializing in the Orthodox Divine Liturgy. As the priest prepares the Eucharistic elements, he cuts out small pieces from the special bread called *prosphora*, and with each piece, he asks God to remember a particular person who has passed away. Later in the liturgy, the priest recites aloud the names of these people in his prayers. In some mysterious way, says Florensky, the church is calling them back into existence before God.

Here, again, Florensky's philosophical reflections (which, he notes, are indebted to how Plato, Kant, and Bergson think about memory) are inseparable from his personal experience. We know from his autobiographical writings how much the church's prayers for the dead moved him, whenever he served as a priest.

Letter Eight: Gehenna

As Florensky meditates further on the nature of sin, he develops ideas about the self and its salvation, and he identifies antinomies that characterize God's existence, humanity's, and the relationship between God and humanity. Florensky's reflections span the entire range of Christian salvation history, from creation

11. For a moving description of the Orthodox funeral service, see the opening lines of Boris Pasternak's *Dr. Zhivago*.

to a last judgment, but focus on the destiny of the individual soul, which has been created for life in God, resists it, and nevertheless with God's assistance may attain it.

Florensky argues that God loves humans but does not force humans to love him in return. Indeed, a God who forced us to love him would not be a God who loved us. In his love for humanity, God restrains his power and gives us the freedom to love or to reject him. Nevertheless, when humans reject God, they lose their freedom and, thus, the very feature that makes them truly human. Sin is a loss of self, a diminution of existence. Antinomies arise: the God who loves humanity must also judge it because of its sinfulness; humans are free before God, yet enslaved by sin. Florensky again emphasizes that human rationality cannot resolve these contradictions, only God can. Indeed, the believer experiences a foretaste of their resolution in the church's sacraments.

The resolution of humans' relationship to God, says Florensky, is not moral or legal in character (he is perhaps referring to and rejecting Protestant notions of a forensic atonement). Rather, something ontological is at stake. Sin and salvation have to do with humans' very being—which either falls into nonbeing in separation from God or finds its life in God. Humans are to use their freedom to seek God and thereby to be their true selves.

Two pairs of terms frame Florensky's discussion of the self as perched between salvation and sin, heaven and hell. First, a human is both "person" (*lichnost'*) and "character." The "person" is free, creative will; one's character is the result of how one lives out this freedom and creativity. Florensky's second pair of terms picks up a traditional Christian theological distinction (especially important in Catholicism): a human is made both in the "image" and in the "likeness" of God (see Gen. 1:26). Both pairs of terms—person and character, image and likeness—help Florensky explicate the dynamics between an "ideal self" and an "empirical self." Sin brings these different dimensions of the self into opposition; salvation consists in their integration.

As a "person," I should shape my "character" to love and know God and others. My "person" should create a likeness of God in myself that corresponds to the image of God. In contrast, the sinner seeks to be "like God." However, in asserting for myself the independence and self-sufficiency that I associate with God, I remove myself from God and others. In asserting my subjectivity, I am no longer an objective reality either to them or to myself. The sinful self is turned in on itself. It is stuck in the here and now. It seeks to identify itself and to satisfy itself with what is empirical and therefore finite. The sinner thereby becomes a slave to himself, with insatiable desires that eat away at his very being (Florensky notes Jesus' images of an eternal worm and fire that characterize hell). Sin is then no longer simply a particular, misguided act; it becomes the very essence of a person.

Picking up themes from previous letters, Florensky says that the sinful self is incapable of creativity. It is unable to transcend itself or to love what is not itself. As a result, the sinner experiences an agonizing, debilitating skepticism. One longs for truth, yet sees no way to attain it. One is filled with doubt and, therefore, with despair.

Here, Florensky offers an analysis of the human condition that still rings true today. Modern, pluralistic societies teach people to respect diverse points of view. We encounter many truths, each of which apparently demands respect. However, the question of truth then seems to be reduced to a matter of subjective judgment. What is true for me may not be true for you. We easily lose confidence that there is any ultimate, objective truth. We can no longer say why one should believe one thing rather than another about God or about the meaning of human existence.

Florensky asserts that, with God's help, we can begin to separate ourselves from this skepticism, which results from sin. In particular, the church's sacrament of penance releases us to a new lightness of being. Having received forgiveness, we do not simply model our life according to Christ's example or his moral norms. Rather, we discover Christ's transformative power in our life. In communion with Christ, we are able to see the image of God—that is, our deified nature—in ourselves. We awaken to the truth of our existence—namely, that we are united to God, and that we have a place within God's Trinitarian life.

In this respect, Florensky picks up a central theme of Orthodox theology: *theosis* (deification, sanctification). In the words of the fourth-century Church Father Athanasius, "God became man, so that man might become God." This assertion does not mean that the human is absorbed into God; each of us remains a distinct "person." But we can become transparent to God. We can experience and show forth, in the terminology of St. Gregory of Palamas, God's "energies."

Through Christ, one's creative will (one's "person") is able to examine and reshape one's "empirical life." By breaking out of self-enclosure—by reaching out to others, loving them, and discovering the image of God within them—we intensify and even "grow" the image of God in ourselves and, simultaneously, transform our empirical "character" into the likeness of God. "Holiness," says Florensky, "is the provisional self-perception of one's freedom" to transform oneself.[12] As we become aware of our life in God, we experience joy and blessedness. While philosophy can point us to this task, each person uniquely realizes it. Each of us has a distinctive personality that will show forth God in a distinctive way.

Florensky argues that our words have an especially important role in this process of self-transformation. Words are more than arbitrary signs that humans use to communicate meaning; our words convey our very life to others. Words are "symbols" of, windows into, the self; they are an invitation to others to enter into our unique being. In other writings, Florensky explores how

12. Florenskii, *Stolp i utverzhdenie*, 222. See Florensky, *Pillar and Ground*, 160.

a person's name captures something of the essence of that person. Here, however, he focuses on the power of church teaching to show forth God and God's beauty to ourselves and to others.

The antinomy of sin and salvation that characterizes humans' earthly existence also comes to expression in the question of an existence after death. Florensky reviews three Christian positions. According to Protestants, he asserts, a hell of eternal torment awaits some, because sin has become the very essence of their souls. Catholicism, by contrast, argues that because sin remains external to the soul, the possibility remains that a person, even after death, may eventually be cleansed and saved. True to his own method, Florensky argues that only the antinomy between these two positions preserves the truth: in one sense, we are condemned; in another, we are saved. The sinful self must somehow be separated from the deified self, if we are to find true blessedness.

Florensky's meditations in this letter are framed by his personal encounter with "hell." At the beginning of the letter, he reports a nightmare in which he felt darkness come over him, bringing him to the edge of annihilation. He awoke in a cold sweat. The letter ends with his reflections on another time of deep personal trial and tribulation. He felt lost and enslaved. He was unable to pray. So tortured inwardly that he wanted to die, he was nevertheless delivered, when a "Friend," an "Angel," made the Sign of the Cross over him and chanted a prayer to the Mother of God.

At the vigil service that Florensky attended afterward, the hymns to the Virgin further cleared his mind. He says that he suddenly understood that sin and temptation are necessary elements of the human search for truth. Only by battling them do we discover our freedom. In order to come to the Truth, we must destroy the evil in us that resists God. Here, Florensky's personal experience again seems integral to his theology, even though to confirm his position, he turns not to the Church Fathers but rather to German idealism, with its assertion that the fall was necessary for man's maturity into a free being.

The view of humanity that Florensky advances in this letter was and is controversial. Traditional Christian (and Orthodox) teaching has denied that sin is in any way "necessary." Moreover, the church has rejected the notion that one dimension of human existence (the image of God) remains untouched by sin (although theologians have disputed the degree to which the image becomes impaired). Nevertheless, even if seemingly "unorthodox" in this regard, Florensky draws deeply, as we have seen, from Christian theology as expressed in Orthodox worship. He is certain that only in the church and in our experience of the cult do we remember who we truly are before God: beings who see the glory of God in all things, bear that glory in ourselves, and reflect it into the world.

Letter Nine: The Creation

Florensky now reflects on the character of those believers who properly relate to the creation. As with his other letters, he begins with a lyrical description of his personal state of mind as he writes. He is in a cemetery, grieving the loss of someone who was dear to him. As the sun sets, the surrounding fields turn a golden color, and for a moment, he is able to see the world's beauty again. Nevertheless, he knows that the day is quickly drawing to a close. He wonders how to get out of his self-absorption, so that he can retain this vision of God's glory in creation, in the midst of a fallen world.

Florensky argues that God created the world to be distinct and independent from him. God allows the world to be other than himself, and therefore to develop according to its own laws and according to the free choices of its human actors. Nevertheless, because the creation has its foundation in God's triune being, it is essentially characterized by unity within its multiplicity: the creation is one within itself and with God. We again encounter Florensky's antinomy of the ideal and the empirical. The creation is from the outset "deified" but must still realize its deification in time, a task that has become complicated by sin. Like the father of the prodigal, God patiently waits for the world to return to him.

Florensky further argues that only this Christian conception of creation makes science possible. God has provided for a created order that humans can investigate. They are able to discover the interrelationships that hold the creation together within itself and with God. Science is not possible where polytheism prevails; for it, the world has no essential unity. Science is also not truly possible under a pantheistic worldview; for it, the world does not have an integrity of its own apart from God. The pantheist's observation of the world remains superficial, unable to penetrate into the distinctiveness (today, we might say, "otherness") of each of its entities. One sees only the "phenomenal," not the thing itself. As a result, the pantheist fears that demonic, chaotic forces actually lie beneath the apparent unity of the world. For Florensky, in contrast to either the polytheist or the pantheist, the triune God establishes a unity of creation that respects the creation's distinction from God and that honors differentiation within the creation.

Florensky compares the unity of the cosmos to the unity of the human body. The very word for "body" in the Russian language, *telo*, is related to the word for "whole," *tseloe* (Florensky sees a similar relation in ancient Greek: *soma*, "body," and *sos*, "healthy"). For Florensky, this wholeness is none other than what the Church Fathers meant by the Greek term *homoousia*. The body, like the cosmos, has an inner form, an integrity, a unity within itself, even while it is related and united to what is not itself.

Sin violates this wholeness, relatedness, and unity, but a proper kind of asceticism is able to restore them. Florensky distinguishes three types of asceticism (he also calls them three types of "mysticism"): that of the head (represented by Eastern yoga and Western theosophy), that of the chest (or heart) (represented by Orthodoxy), and that of the abdomen (represented by the ancient pagan cults and, to some extent, by Catholicism). Only the mysticism of the chest reaches into the life of the Trinity and preserves the "person" and his creative freedom. The mysticism of the head, if not fed by the heart, tries to master and manipulate the creation. It falls into the sin of pride. The mysticism of the abdomen falls into lust and impurity—the sin of sloth. By avoiding both pride and lust, the mysticism of the heart is able to penetrate into the secrets of heaven and earth; it is able to see in this world that "other world" to which Florensky refers in his first letter.

In recovering the integrity of his own bodily existence, the ascetic achieves purity of heart, and his body becomes a beautiful image of God. His body and soul are united to God, and both body and soul shine God's light into the rest of creation: "Through the rootedness of the spiritual person in the heavens, grace illumines everything around the ascetic and pours itself into the inner life of the whole creation."[13] "Even nonspiritual people receive from the ascetic the power to relate better to the creation."[14] The ascetic transforms not only himself but also everything and everyone around him; he activates the creation's capacity to become transparent to God's energies. This transfigured world is an anticipation of the new heaven and earth that God will bring about at the end of time.

Florensky's experience of Fr. Isidore's holiness surely shapes these reflections on asceticism. The ascetic is a charismatic, a "Spirit-bearer." The ascetic longs for the renewal of the world, feels responsible for it, pities it, and remembers that it has become helpless because of human sin and impurity. The ascetic so loves the creation that he is able to look past its empirical, fallen condition to its inner, original, ideal beauty. Florensky refers to the many stories of ascetics who lived at peace with wild animals and even tiny worms. St. John of the Ladder overcame sexual lust and was able to see women, even whores, in their created beauty. St. Seraphim of Sarov became the chaste spiritual father of a female monastery.

13. Florenskii, *Stolp i utverzhdenie*, 275. See Florensky, *Pillar and Ground*, 198.
14. Florenskii, *Stolp i utverzhdenie*, 278. See Florensky, *Pillar and Ground*, 199–200.

As elsewhere in his treatise, Florensky contrasts self-transcendence with self-absorption. Here, he refers specifically to the contrast between the holy man and the typical Russian intellectual. Members of the intelligentsia do not understand asceticism, because they do not understand deification or the idea of a holy body. Closed in upon themselves—stuck in the law of self-identity—they wish to absorb all of reality into themselves. Their love for the world is abstract, ideational. They do not know how to relate to it in its concrete reality: "Wherever he looks, the intellectual wants to see only what is artificial, only formulas and concepts—and only his own—but not life."[15] As elsewhere, Florensky associates this posture with Enlightenment thinking, especially as articulated by Kant. Rather than seeking the inner essence of things, the intellectual imposes abstract schemes of categorization and organization upon them. Florensky refers to the Enlightenment preference for what is artificial and human-created over what is natural and God-given, whether in relation to gardens, languages, morality, government, or religion.

The contrast between the ascetic and the intellectual extends to how each experiences the antinomies of God and world, spirit and flesh, and the self and the other. The ascetic sees the beauty of both the thesis and the antithesis, whereas the intellectual is frustrated because he cannot logically reconcile them. Rejecting fasting, he does not know how to receive food as God's gift. Finding no meaning in virginity, he fails to understand that marriage is not simply a human institution but also a divine ordinance. Unable to contemplate deification of the body, he is ashamed of his flesh.

As we have seen in his earlier letters, Florensky believes that the liturgy, like the holy person, draws us into a vision of a transfigured world. This ninth letter includes references to church hymnody that associate the image of God with the beauty of the transfigured human body. The wisdom of the liturgy inspires Florensky

15. Florenskii, *Stolp i utverzhdenie*, 299. See Florensky, *Pillar and Ground*, 215.

to call for a new kind of theology, different from the dry scholasticism characteristic of his time:

> At present, we still do not have a liturgical theology, that is, a systemization of the theological ideas contained in our liturgy. But the Church's living self-consciousness is precisely there, for the liturgy is the flower of Church life and also its root and seed. What richness of ideas and new concepts in the domain of dogmatics, what abundance of profound psychological observations and moral guidance, could be gathered here even by a not terribly diligent investigator! Yes, liturgical theology awaits its creator.[16]

Later in the twentieth century, prominent Orthodox theologians, such as Fr. Alexander Schmemann, would take up Florensky's proposal.[17] Some Catholics and Protestants, too, have come again to understand that patterns and forms of worship shape belief. Remembering the early church's formula *lex orandi, lex credendi* (the rule of prayer is the rule of faith—and vice versa), they have called for liturgical renewal in their churches. They would agree with what Florensky never tires of saying: that one knows the faith only by entering into the life of the church and, one might add, of its worship in particular.

Letter Ten: Sophia

Having discussed the ascetic, who is able to relate properly to the creation, Florensky now turns to the creation itself. What is its status in relation to God? How is it different from God, yet united to him? Florensky finds a key in the Orthodox veneration of Sophia, the Wisdom of God. This personification of wisdom (in Greek, *sophia*) appears in the Old Testament (Prov. 8:22–31), and

16. The quotation is from Jakim's translation: Florensky, *Pillar and Ground,* 217–18. For the Russian, see Florenskii, *Stolp i utverzhdenie,* 302–3.

17. Fr. Alexander Schmemann (1921–1983) was a leading Orthodox theologian in the United States and played a key role in the formation of the Orthodox Church in America (OCA). He develops a liturgical theology in such books as *Introduction to Liturgical Theology* (1966).

the early church associated it with Christ, the preexistent *Logos* (John 1:1–4).

Florensky's reflections on Sophia, the Wisdom of God, have been controversial since their formulation. At the advice of the rector of the Moscow Theological Academy, Florensky did not include this letter (or the next two) as part of his master's thesis. Florensky's thinking is speculative and provocative—and not entirely easy to follow. He picks up ideas from German idealism and the Russian philosopher Vladimir Solov'ev (1853–1900); in turn, Florensky's close friend Sergei Bulgakov would develop a more sophisticated Sophiology that eventually resulted in charges of heresy against him.

Whatever his debt to other philosophers, Florensky remains true to his commitment to draw on religious experience, especially on our experience of the church's holy people and of the church's prayer and worship. The wisdom of the ascetic lies in perceiving the unity of the whole creation with the God who is Trinity. This wisdom, asserts Florensky, is nothing other than the Sophia whom the church honors in its hymnody and iconography.

The letter opens with Florensky's description of another bout of melancholy on a dark, rainy night. Florensky feels desperately alone. But then he remembers Fr. Isidore, and suddenly the spiritual world becomes more real to him than his material surroundings. Returning to the themes of Letter Nine, Florensky says that because holy people such as Fr. Isidore are filled with the Holy Spirit, they are beautiful both in themselves and in relation to others. In seeing and loving the creation in its original, ideal state, they themselves are transfigured into their original, ideal state.

As in his earlier letters, Florensky affirms that in an act of love and self-limitation, God gives the creation an independent existence. God does not compel the world to love him in return for his love for it. Rather, he allows it to determine its own development. Nevertheless, God's love for the world does stimulate a movement of love within the world toward him. Indeed, the inner meaning of each thing that exists in the creation (Florensky says "monad," borrowing a term from Leibniz)—its *logos*—is to love and know God and therefore to realize its essential unity with him. It does so by loving and knowing other monads.

Picking up a theme of the second letter, Florensky describes how in receiving love (ultimately, from God), a monad is moved to love another (ultimately, God). One empties oneself, gives oneself to another, and in so doing realizes oneself, moving from a state of potentiality to actuality. One is no longer enclosed within one's subjectivity but rather becomes objective both to oneself and to others. We retain our individuality (*hypostasis*), even as we realize our essential unity ("of one substance") with others (and God). In this receiving and giving of love—what Florensky calls a "steady-state exchange of energy"—the creation ultimately enters into the inner life of the Trinity and attains eternal life.[18] The creation in its ideal state, says Florensky, is something like a fourth hypostasis (person) of the Trinity. It is "Sophia." However, Florensky quickly adds that he is speaking "symbolically." Sophia is a window into the inner life of God, and God's energies shine through her into the world.

As Florensky recognizes, he is positing antinomies that the rational mind will not be able to resolve. How can the creation be separate from God, yet essentially united to him? How can the world have an inner unity, yet preserve the integrity of each individual thing? How can one realize oneself by losing oneself? Is the world's "steady state" a description of what is or of what should be? Florensky will only tell us that he is speaking about a Truth that presents itself to religious experience. In the presence of the holy man or by participating in the liturgy, one has the experience of the creation becoming Sophia and therefore of becoming transparent to God.

18. Florenskii, *Stolp i utverzhdenie*, 327. See Florensky, *Pillar and Ground*, 236.

Florensky is sketching out incomplete ideas; he has not worked them out systematically. However, his earlier distinction between the ideal (or ideational) and the empirical suggests his line of thinking. Before creating, God has an idea of creation. From eternity, he conceives of the types and forms of what he will create. Sophia represents the world as God thinks it. Sophia is "the God-established unity of the ideal determinations of the creation."[19] In this sense, creation is preexistent in the mind of God.

Through God's creative act, this ideal, ideational world, Sophia, is realized as an empirical reality—that is, as the world that humans experience in time and space. Sinful human beings see the world only from the outside. They impose themselves upon it, regard it as a mere extension of themselves, and reduce it to an object to manipulate for their own selfish purposes. In contrast, when humans (such as the ascetic) properly love the empirical creation and penetrate into its inner meaning, it becomes a "revelation," disclosing its ideal, ideational dimension to them—its unity within itself and with God. Humans then realize the world's potential to show forth God and, therefore, to be beautiful and to evoke humans' wonder and gratitude. The ideal shines through the empirical.

Florensky differentiates his position from Gnosticism. For the Gnostics, he says, the ideal world preexists in time, whereas for Florensky "preexistence" means the world as a spiritual entity above time. Because Gnosticism disparages the material, empirical world, it leads humans into moral decadence. For Florensky, the empirical is not evil but rather has the capacity to open us to the ideal, if we are pure of heart (as is the ascetic).

Florensky adds that his position is also different from that of the pantheist. For the Orthodox believer, the ideal and the empirical remain distinct. The believer does not say that all things are divine; rather, the believer affirms that the world remains distinct from God, even when it becomes transparent to God.

19. Florenskii, *Stolp i utverzhdenie*, 347. See Florensky, *Pillar and Ground*, 249.

Florensky associates Sophia with other biblical, liturgical, and philosophical images of an original perfection that is to be realized in, yet beyond, history: the heavenly Jerusalem, the church (the body of Christ, the fullness of the Holy Spirit), the kingdom of God, the "ideal person," and a person's guardian angel. Each image opens us to the world's spiritual dimension. Each functions as a mediating principle between God and the world, the infinite and the finite. Each is the place where heaven and earth meet.

At times, Florensky suggests a hierarchy of mediating principles. The highest is the Savior, the second person of the Trinity, the Logos. Next follows Sophia, after which comes the Mother of God. However, because they are so closely interrelated, the church has often transferred the attributes of one to another, such that we are not able to distinguish one wholly from the other. Accordingly, Florensky can say that Wisdom, like the Logos, imprints its name on every created thing. Here, Florensky is alluding to his understanding of names as symbols, not simply signs. A name mysteriously shapes a thing's inner being

Florensky proceeds to explore Sophia from different points of view, both heavenly and earthly. For the Father, Sophia is ideal essence; for the Son, the inner meaning and truth of creation; and for the Holy Spirit, beauty. From a human perspective, Sophia has an antinomic character: she is the preexisting church, yet also the empirical church of those holy people who purify their hearts. We exercise purity of heart, virginity, and chasteness in order to see her, yet only she by her grace can enable us to see her.

For Florensky, the church's veneration of the Mother of God offers additional insight into the character of Sophia. The Mother of God is more than a saint, more than even the highest of the saints. Church hymnody and iconography give her a place almost equal to that of the Son of God. She is set above the rest of creation, She connects heaven and earth; she is the heart both of the church and of Christ himself. Dionysius the Areopagite calls her the light both around and within him. For Ambrose of Milan, she is not only chaste in herself but also the giver and protector of chasteness in others. The great ascetics such as Seraphim of Sarov dedicated themselves entirely to her. Indeed, Seraphim's one and only icon (which he was holding as he died) was that of the Mother of God of Tenderness (unusual among Orthodox icons, because it presents the Virgin by herself, without the infant Jesus in her arms).

The church's major, historic icons of Sophia, the Wisdom of God—from Novgorod, Iaroslavl', and Kiev—also set forth her character. Taken by themselves, these icons seem to many scholars to be nothing more than personifications of wisdom. However, Florensky again emphasizes that the church has understood Sophia as something far more. She is intimately related to the Logos, the Trinity, the Mother of God, the church, and even humanity as a whole. Over time, says Florensky, believers have discovered three major aspects of Sophia. For the Greek Church (Byzantium), Sophia was the object of dogmatic speculation. For the Russian Church, Sophia has historically been associated with chasteness and beauty. Contemporary Russian religious thought (especially Solov'ev) has added the third dimension: Sophia is the church as "the most true, pure, and complete humanity" and, indeed, as the mystical union of all creation in God. Sophia is "God's memory, into whose holy interior belongs everything that is—and outside of which is Death and Meaninglessness."[20]

This transfigured world opens itself to us when we go out from ourselves and find ourselves in the other. Florensky therefore concludes that the way to Sophia is through friendship, the love of one person for another.

20. Florenskii, *Stolp i utverzhdenie*, 395. See Florensky, *Pillar and Ground*, 282.

Letter Eleven: Friendship

In this letter, Florensky further develops the theme of love, which, indeed, runs throughout *Pillar and Ground*: Christian love draws a person out from self-enclosure; we discover ourselves in others and see them (and ourselves) as they and we exist before God. However, Florensky states that he is now going beyond what he has written in the fourth letter. He is thinking about love among Christians and, especially, about the "brotherly love" that unites one Christian to another.

Appropriately, the letter opens with another lyrical passage. Florensky is by himself in his cell, looking out the window at a snowstorm. He recalls another such day when he and "his friend" walked together from Sergiev Posad to the Paraclete Skete and received the Eucharist. Fr. Isidore had often told him that two brothers strengthen each other (in reference to Proverbs 18:19). The love between two friends enables them to grasp the Truth that is the "pillar and ground"—namely, their essential oneness with each other and, indeed, with the whole creation in its unity with the triune God.

Florensky proceeds to set forth a biblical understanding of love, as explicated in church tradition. He notes that the Greek language has four words for love: *eros* (a passionate, desiring love), *philia* (an intimate, tender love), *storge* (a calm, peaceful, abiding love), and *agape* (a rational, moral, respectful love). Florensky is especially interested in agape and philia and their interrelationship. From different angles, they seem synonymous, complementary, or even antinomic.

Both philia and agape, biblically understood, involve self-sacrificial love. One person takes on the burden of the other. One breaks out of self-enclosure and enters into the reality of the other. However, philia and agape also play different, though complementary, roles in the Christian community. On the one hand, the community is held together by each member's agape for the community as a whole. Florensky calls this agapic love "brotherhood." It reaches its zenith in the Christian agape meal as completed by the Eucharist. On the other hand, the unity of the community depends on relations of philia between individual members of the community. This philial love is "friendship." It finds its most complete expression in the ancient Orthodox "sacrament" of *adelphopoesis* ("brother-creating"), in which two people of the same sex make a covenant with each other before the rest of the church and seal this covenant by receiving the Eucharist together.[21]

This complementariness can also be expressed as an antinomy. In order to live together with "brothers" in the Christian community, one needs the experience of "friendship," whereby one overcomes self-enclosure. Nevertheless, it is equally true that to have a "friend," one needs the experience of agapic "brotherhood," so that philial love does not become closed in upon itself. One form of love is not logically prior to the other; their antinomic character points us to a higher truth.

Other antinomies characterize the Christian community. The Gospel is accessible to all, yet rightly understood only with the help of the "tradition of the elders," as handed down from one generation to another. Christians constitute a community of equals, yet this community is hierarchical, as evident in the different circles of disciples around Christ, with some (such as the apostles) closer to and others farther from him. Christianity gives absolute value to the "person" (*lichnost'*), yet only as the individual is in communion with others, who also are of absolute value.

This antinomy of self and other is, for Florensky, basic not only to human relationships in general but also to the Christian life in particular. He notes that Christ sends out his disciples in pairs. In their philial love for each other, they become a "third." No longer

21. For the history of *adelphopoeisis*, see Patrick Viscuso, "Failed Attempt to Rewrite History: Review of *Same-Sex Unions in Premodern Europe*," *New Oxford Review* (December 1994).

are they only disciples and friends; now they are also Spirit-bearers. They glimpse the kingdom of God and embody the church, the body of Christ, who is of one essence with the Father.

Florensky contrasts Christian friendship with a "pagan" understanding of the family as the most basic social unit. Scholarly commentators have noted that Florensky's emphasis on same-sex friendship, rather than male-female marriage, is perhaps unique within the Christian tradition. In this regard, Florensky may be influenced by his own experience, as we have noted, of several intense male friendships before his marriage (which did not take place until after he had completed *Pillar and Ground*). There is no evidence that any of these relationships were consummated sexually or that Florensky saw "brother-creating" as a context for sexual relations.[22] Rather, Florensky calls for a "chasteness" (wholeness) that God grants us; this chasteness is a "charism."

This chaste love enables friends to be unconditionally faithful, trusting, and forgiving. They continually humble themselves before each other. They guard each other from sin; for this reason, adds Florensky, a monk should not live alone. Parish life, too, requires that people be physically present to one another and assist one another. Florensky acknowledges that this way of "life together" is difficult; he refuses to romanticize it, calling it nothing less than an "ascetical deed"—and in this sense, he says, all Christians lead a "monastic" life. They bear one another's burdens, including one another's sins. Florensky quotes extensively from the diary of a man whose friend has fallen into an awful sin. The man does not scold or reject his friend, but neither is he able to help him recover.

22. Whether Florensky's thought provides a basis for positively evaluating same-sex marriage and same-sex sexual relations today is another question. A negative answer is given by Viscuso (see note 21) and by Paul Ladouceur and Fr. Richard Rene, "Father Pavel Florensky, *Philia*, and Same-Sex Love," *Public Orthodoxy* (February 26, 2021), https://publicorthodoxy.org/2021/02/26/florensky-philia-same-sex-love/. For the opposite point of view, see John Boswell, *Same-Sex Unions in Premodern Europe* (New York: Villard Books, 1994), 272 n. 44; and Giacomo Sanfillipo, "Conjugal Friendship," *Public Orthodoxy* (May 2, 2017), https://publicorthodoxy.org/2017/05/02/conjugal-friendship/.

He simply stands by his friend and follows him wherever he goes. He makes space for his friend and forgives him (though he does not say so openly, lest that encourage the friend or others to sin).

As difficult as friendship may be, it releases great spiritual power in Christians. One does not lose oneself, but rather discovers oneself in the other and before God. "Friendship," says Florensky, is "contemplation of oneself through the Friend in God."[23] Friendship creates an unbreakable bond between two people. One's friend is the being closest to one's heart. Florensky extols friendship as necessary for human existence—indeed, as the very pinnacle of human existence. Conversely, absence of friendship is the source of all disasters and heresies, and to lose a friend is to experience a kind of death.

Here, Florensky again picks up his theme of the essential unity of humanity, creation, and God. Friends become one will, one spirit, and one voice. They mutually enrich each other. Their friendship is characterized by consonance and harmony, and they are able to see each other in their original, ideal wholeness. The unity that friendship achieves is ontological, not simply psychological.

As he brings the letter to a close, Florensky returns to the Orthodox ceremony of "brother-creating," which, he believes, gives expression to the special status of friendship within Christianity. Just as marriage is for a particular man and a particular woman, yet takes place before the gathered community, so too the church's "brother-creating" ceremony establishes that the special friendship of two "brothers" is not a private matter but rather of significance to the whole church community. Their friendship is for the sake of strengthening the church, and the church's rituals affirm and strengthen the special relationship that the two friends have with each other.

Relationships in their particularity depend on what Florensky calls "jealousy" (or "zealousness"). Love is never simply general.

23. Florenskii, *Stolp i utverzhdenie*, 440. See Florensky, *Pillar and Ground*, 314.

Its object can never be humanity in general or an abstract human cause. Rather, it is necessarily directed toward particular things and particular individuals or groups of people. Florensky believes that jealousy protects love from being reduced to a social program (communism) or a moral principle (Tolstoyism). Only in its particularity can love open us to the unity that pervades all of reality.

Letter Twelve: Jealousy

Florensky notes that jealousy is commonly regarded as a moral defect. As Spinoza defines it, you now hate the person whom you once loved and envy the one who has taken your place. Florensky offers an alternative understanding. Jealousy, he says, is a necessary dimension of love, when we rightly understand what love is. The problem with Spinoza is that he fails to differentiate between love and desire (lust). If I love in such a way that I seek to absorb the other person into myself (desire as lust), I will feel hatred and envy if another comes between us. In contrast, if I love the other as a "person" (*lichnost'*), as a "Thou," I am jealous of that person in the sense of wanting that person to remain, and grow as, a "person."

This kind of jealousy does everything possible to overcome the law of identity that leaves me enclosed within myself. I reach out to the other and am zealous for the other to reach out to me. Jealousy seeks to overcome any barrier between us. I want our relationship to endure and for nothing to get in the way of it. This kind of jealousy is characterized by strength, power, and determination. It earnestly seeks to do good. It is a virtue, not a vice. It is the holiest thing of the heart.

Florensky notes that Scripture attributes jealousy to God himself; he is zealous for his people Israel. Divine jealousy is no mere anthropomorphism. It is an ontological, not a psychological or moral, category. It affirms the essential oneness of reality.

Florensky again notes the antinomic character of this kind of love. It limits itself to one other person, yet this limitation opens the lovers to a universal unity with others and God. Love has no limits, yet it freely selects one person out of many, as in marriage or in friendship. For calculating, instrumental reason, these antinomies appear to be irresolvable contradictions. Florensky, however, once again affirms that human experience—and, specifically, our experience of God's love and of human friendship—proves the antinomic character of truth.

Afterword

In a short afterword, Florensky again emphasizes that our lives in this world are filled with antinomies. Even our reasoning is divided. It moves between the finite and the infinite, what is static and what is dynamic, and what is continuous and what is noncontinuous. On the one hand, reason means thinking, and thinking requires the law of identity. A thing is identical to itself. A=A. On the other hand, reason means explaining, and explaining relates a thing to something else. I understand A only as it is conditioned by B, and so on, to infinity. Reasoning requires both thinking and explaining, yet they contradict each other. How then is reasoning possible? How is truth possible?

Our reasoning can find the truth, answers Florensky, only as it is grounded in the Truth of the Trinity, "one in essence and undivided." Under the conditions of this world, however, truth-Truth necessarily appears to us as antinomic: the ideal, absolute character of the creation versus its empirical character; the human as the image of God versus the human as the likeness of God; and the mystical church versus the historical church. Each believer is called to ascetical deeds of love and friendship that overcome these antinomies, but our efforts always fall short.

By our efforts alone, we are unable to align the empirical with the ideal, the image with the likeness, or the mystical with the historical. If we nevertheless so attain to the truth-Truth, it is because God himself guides us. He gives us the pillar and ground of the

Truth. This pillar and this ground are the church, asceticism, the Trinity, the light of Tabor, Sophia, the Virgin, and friendship. I have called them mediating principles that bring together God and the world, the infinite and the finite, and the ideal and the empirical. Through them, the world becomes transparent to God's energies, the finite becomes an icon of the infinite, and the empirical realizes the ideal. The other world shines into and through this world and transfigures it.

Florensky hopes that this vision of divine, transfiguring beauty will win his readers over to the church. No matter how philosophical his language, Florensky is writing from the heart. What he himself has experienced in holy elders, such as Fr. Isidore, and in the church's worship and prayers, he now offers to others.

6

THE CULT

"The goal of the cult is to sanctify humans and, more broadly—the whole creation."

Fr. Ephrem did not like me. A professor in an Orthodox seminary in Russia had asked me to teach his class at the beginning of the semester. Fr. Ephrem was one of the students. I was to speak about the riches that I as a Protestant had found in Orthodoxy, as well as about the reasons that I remained Protestant. It turned out, however, that I would be covering for the professor while he was out of town. The class members—monks and priests—were restless. The problem was not just with my limited, though coherent, Russian. Rather, what disturbed them was that I, a Protestant, was teaching them.

Fr. Ephrem was among those who kept interrupting me. Didn't I see that Orthodoxy was superior to Protestantism? Didn't I know that Protestantism was a heresy? If I appreciated Orthodoxy so much, why hadn't I converted? I found myself getting irritated. Soon I had that sinking feeling you get when you know that you are losing control of the classroom. Finally, I impatiently raised my voice and asked the students to allow me to finish my lecture. Fr. Ephrem fell silent but grinned and gloated. The professor would not ask me to teach the class again.

The seminary librarian later assured me that Fr. Ephrem was not a bad person—a bit zealous perhaps, but not one to hold resentments. Nevertheless, the encounter had left me wary, if not hurt. The first semester ended, then the second, and Fr. Ephrem and I had not crossed paths again. My sabbatical in Russia was soon ending. A couple of days after Pascha, I resolved to seek him out to make peace—not to ask him to make amends, but rather just to let him know that I was genuinely interested in him and his ministry.

It was true—Fr. Ephrem did not hold grudges. When I contacted him, he immediately invited me to visit his parish. He suggested the next Tuesday, a day on which Russian Orthodox believers traditionally visit cemeteries and ask the priest to bless the graves of their deceased relatives. He told me how to take the bus to the small village where he served. From the bus stop, I could try hitchhiking the last three miles to the church.

It was a beautiful, warm spring day. I found the right bus, disembarked at the right stop, and started down the right road. But my efforts at flagging down a ride were in vain; I ended up walking the whole way. By the time I arrived at the church, I was hot and sweaty, and the memorial liturgy was almost over. I nodded to Fr. Ephrem and joined the parishioners as they walked across the road to the cemetery.

People went over to their relatives' gravesites, which they had tidied up beforehand, and waited patiently. For nearly two hours, Fr. Ephrem went from one grave to another, conducting a short *panikhida* (memorial service) at each. As the deacon swung his censer, clouds of incense rose into the air. "Lord, have mercy. Lord, have mercy," intoned Fr. Ephrem again and again. People crossed themselves. Some had tears. Heaven and earth, the living and the dead, blessing and remembrance had come together. For a moment, I had entered another world. But I wondered whether I as a Protestant really belonged there.

The Cult and Culture

Soon after the 1917 October Revolution, the Bolsheviks closed the Theological Academy in Sergiev Posad. Classes, including Florensky's, moved to Moscow. In May and June of 1918, Florensky took on an additional series of lectures—on "the philosophy of the cult"—to which the public could subscribe for a small fee.[1] The auditorium, which seated up to 150 people, was packed for each of the ten sessions (two sessions a week over five weeks). The audience included members of the intelligentsia who were "religious seekers," a cultural elite that had dabbled in theosophy and occultism but was suspicious of the Orthodox Church.

Florensky did not use the lectures to explicate traditional Orthodox dogma, at that time still deeply shaped by scholastic thinking and categories, about prayer or the sacraments. Rather, as in *Pillar and Ground*, he argued for beginning from religious experience. *Pillar and Ground* had drawn especially from the human search for ultimate truth and had emphasized that kenotic love is central to this search. The truth that is God reveals itself as I empty myself and find myself in the other. *Philosophy of the Cult* takes a different approach. Picking up his call in *Pillar and Ground* for a "liturgical theology," Florensky now explicates Orthodox worship. However, *Philosophy of the Cult* is not just for church insiders. Florensky—uniquely among the religious philosophers of his time—used Orthodox liturgical texts and practice to set forth the meaning of every human life.[2]

1. Florensky lectured from notes. He later (1922) added to the text and dictated it to his secretary. See Igumen Andronik Trubachev, "Istoriia sozdaniia tsikla 'Filosofiia kul'ta …'" [History of the composition of *Philosophy of the Cult*], in Pavel A. Florenskii, *Filosofiia kul'ta* (Moscow: Akademicheskii proekt, 2018), 19.

2. Trubachev, "Istoriia sozdaniia tsikla," 23.

Florensky regarded his lectures as part of a larger project. If *Pillar and Ground* had been his theodicy, *Philosophy of the Cult* was to be part of an "anthropodicy," never completed, that would explore what it means to be human before God.[3] Florensky argues that the structure of the cult corresponds to the structure of human beings. By means of the cult, humans are able to approach God, and God is able to come near to them, without destroying them. The cult employs symbols (both as words and as rituals) that mediate between the divine and the human. Florensky wants to persuade the religious seekers in his audience that Orthodox worship offers a more genuine encounter with ultimate mystery than that which they try to conjure up through spiritualist techniques.

The cult helps us grasp our true humanity in relation not only to God but also to one another. Florensky tirelessly asserts that human culture arises from the cult. He believes, therefore, that Russians will truly know who they are as Russians only as they experience the cult, for it sanctifies the objects and activities of their everyday lives. A generation earlier Vladimir Solov'ev had called for a philosophy of culture.[4] Now Florensky contributes to this enterprise by examining the cult.

Returning to Eden

As we have seen, Florensky looked back at his childhood as a time in which he was in a state of continual mystical wonder. The natural world seemed transparent to divine energy; in created things, he sensed a mystery that resonated with that of his own existence. Everything earthly had symbolic character; the creation pointed beyond itself to another reality, a world of ultimate beauty

3. Florensky's lectures, "At the Watersheds of Thought: The Elements of a Concrete Metaphysics" (part of which has been translated by Boris Jakim into English as *At the Crossroads of Science and Mysticism* [Kettering, OH: Semantron Press, 2014]); "Analysis of Space and Time"; and several of his works on art, such as *Iconostasis*, would have been included in this larger work. See Trubachev, "Istoriia sozdaniia," 6.

4. See Paul Valliere, "The Theology of Culture in Late Imperial Russia," in *Sacred Stories: Religion and Spirituality in Modern Russia*, ed. Mark D. Steinberg and Heather J. Coleman (Bloomington: Indiana University Press, 2007), 377–95.

and harmony. Florensky was convinced that every child experiences this kind of wonder. In contrast, adulthood is shaped by scientific observation and technological manipulation. The world now appears to be nothing more than lifeless material. We lose our capacity for awe and wonder.

Florensky is not entirely clear why this change takes place. He sometimes suggests that humanity has experienced an ontological "fall" from Eden. More often, he argues that modern, "rationalistic" thinking, as represented by the Renaissance, Protestantism, and Kant, has infected humanity. Or it may be that Florensky simply sees Kantianism as the contemporary philosophical expression of the world's fallen condition. In any event, Florensky longed as an adult to return to the enchanted world of his childhood.

In *Philosophy of the Cult*, Florensky proposes a primordial state of affairs, an ontological foundation to created reality, in which various antinomies—idea and reality, meaning and object, time and eternity, humanity and the natural world—complement rather than contradict each other. Reality is meaningful, and ideas are real. We know ourselves as we know what is not ourselves. God comes downward toward humans, and humans move upward toward God.[5] The transcendent and the immanent are not opposites; rather, each is in necessary relation to the other.

With the rise of Western civilization, this original unity falls apart into irreconcilable antinomies: "(Human) activity turned away from Reality and Meaning—to realities and meanings.... Realities became empty, and meanings, false. Things became nothing more than utilitarian (useful), [and] understanding—merely a matter of persuasion.... Everything [now] resembled Truth, while no longer participating in Truth, no longer being Truth or in the Truth. In short—everything became secularized."[6]

The loss of our primordial unity with the world is paralleled by

5. Pavel A. Florenskii, *Filosofiia kul'ta* (Moscow: Akademicheskii proekt, 2018), 54–56.
6. Florenskii, *Filosofiia kul'ta*, 57. See also Florensky, *At the Crossroads*, 138.

a fragmentation of the self: "The human personality falls apart and decomposes into specializations, particularities, and partialities, of which not even one is necessary. Everything becomes accidental and conditional. . . . The soul dissolves into an accumulation of seductive temptations, that is, into a condition of being blown about by arbitrary winds from outside of oneself."[7] Humans' promethean energy no longer "plays" delightfully with the multitudinous forms of the natural world but rather sows chaos both in the world and in the self.[8] Elsewhere, as in *Pillar and Ground*, Florensky describes the fallen self as turned in on itself—"locked up."

Florensky argues that Christ reenchants the world and restores the organic unity of self and world that Florensky had experienced in childhood. We know that, for Florensky, these were not simply abstract ideas; he had experienced a personal conversion to Christ during his seminary years. What we do not know is whether Orthodox worship played a decisive role in this event. Certainly, from the time that he entered the Moscow Theological Academy in 1904, he would have attended worship services almost every day. He would have received the Eucharist, although we do not know how often—many believers at that time communed only once or twice a year.[9] Nor do we know just how disciplined he was about keeping the church's fasts or hours of prayer in his cell. As we have noted, much about life in the Academy disgusted him, and he went through a period of "quiet mutiny" in 1908. Moreover, his letters to Rozanov make no reference to the Orthodox liturgy or sacraments until after Florensky's ordination to the priesthood in 1911.

Only in the *Philosophy of the Cult* lectures of 1918 do we learn

7. Florenskii, *Filosofiia kul'ta*, 57.

8. Florenskii, *Filosofiia kul'ta*, 133.

9. The "Rules and Regulations" of the St. Petersburg Theological Academy refer to the Eucharist only in relation to the Great Lent. A student's frequency of communion apparently depended on the counsel of his spiritual father. The situation at the Moscow Academy was likely similar. See "Instruktsiia S.–Peterburgskoi Dukhovnoi Akademii" (1894), reprinted from the Archives of Americans of Russian Descent in Minnesota.

just how much Orthodox worship had come to mean to him. Florensky now argues that the cult returns humans and their world to their original condition: "In the cult, the creation does not find norms external to itself, but rather its own proper, inner ... foundations as purified from everything accidental."[10] "Humans leave their subjective self-enclosure and [find their] support in absolute objective reality."[11] They are no longer defined by a Dionysian or promethean "dark desiring" but rather by their being a divinely "illuminated image."[12]

Florensky here uses terminology that he developed earlier in *Pillar and Ground*. Through the cult, a person recovers a *litso* (face), thereby enabling that person to turn toward God. In so doing, a person, moreover, becomes a *lik*—that is, a face that is transparent to the divine—and knows the world as "the embodiment of the heavenly world in ... concrete symbols."[13] We then experience reality in its original, God-willed "concrete idealism."[14]

To and from Golgotha

As it flows from and to Christ and his crucifixion, the cult reunites heaven and earth. Christ in his self-sacrifice overcomes the destructive dichotomies of human existence. There, at Golgotha, Christ brings together the human and the divine, time and eternity, the ideal and the real, meaning and life, and "Dionysian" freedom to play with the world and "Apollonian" attention to its concrete forms.[15] The antinomies of human existence that Florensky could not resolve through scientific rationality now point him to a truth beyond it—a truth embodied in a divine life that becomes human flesh and that, in dying a human death, becomes wholly open to God.

10. Florenskii, *Filosofiia kul'ta*, 136.
11. Florenskii, *Filosofiia kul'ta*, 398.
12. Florenskii, *Filosofiia kul'ta*, 136.
13. Florenskii, *Filosofiia kul'ta*, 109.
14. Florenskii, *Filosofiia kul'ta*, 279, 109.
15. Florenskii, *Filosofiia kul'ta*, 133–36.

In an allusion to Plato's allegory of the cave, Florensky argues that humans "remember" reality's primordial unity. The loss of that unity, because of sin, makes them so angry that they seek to regain it by their own "titanic," unconstrained efforts (Prometheus, Faust). Drawing on ideas that Ludwig Feuerbach and other German idealist philosophers had advanced, Florensky argues that humans ultimately satisfy their resentment toward God only by killing God. But the death of God also means the end of human rebellion. Paradoxically, the crucifixion effects reconciliation between humans and the God who dies, yet lives.[16]

At Golgotha, heaven and earth meet. Even a physical cross in a church or home defines a space in which humans are able to encounter God and the other world (the noumenal, the transcendent). A Christian cross is more than mere wood. It is a living, divine substance—a "Thou." It is "the light of the Lord's face, the revelation of his glory."[17] The cross, therefore, first calls forth from a believer not sentimental love but rather awed veneration. There, we stand in fear and trembling before a power that is capable of destroying us, mortal and sinful as we are, but that nevertheless promises to lift us up and fill us with wonder before the living God.

The cross reveals not only who God is but also who we are and what our world truly is. Florensky notes that the saints are often depicted as praying with lifted and outstretched hands, as though in the shape of the cross. Basil the Great declared that the whole world was created in the image of the cross. Moreover, prayer and worship are acts of self-sacrifice that correspond to Christ's crucifixion. In mediating between heaven and earth, the cross stirs us to "remember" (in a Platonic sense) that God's glory fills us and, indeed, all of reality around us. From the cross, God's energies flow into the world.

The cross demonstrates what the cult in general is about: demarcating a space in which the two worlds meet. The cult "brings

16. Florenskii, *Filosofiia kul'ta*, 143.
17. Florenskii, *Filosofiia kul'ta*, 31.

us into contact with other worlds. Our sense of the presence of ... mysterious substances, forces, and powers around and before us cannot be anything but fearful."[18] Or, as Florensky would write a few years later, "The liturgy is a representation of an event that, though it occurred at a particular moment of time, is primordially and eternally present.... We begin to see another reality, whose light shines to us from beyond our empirical world."[19]

Because this other, divine reality is so glorious, humans are unable to take it in all at once. Just as the unique forms of the natural world mediate the child's encounter with creation's inner mystery, the liturgy with its symbols and rituals mediates God's self-revelation at the cross to fallen humanity. Citing John of Kronstadt, the great pastor and holy man of the late nineteenth century, Florensky says, "If the light of the Holy Mysteries shone forth, not concealed by the sight of bread and wine ... no created eyes would be able to bear their brightness."[20]

For Florensky, alluding to the writings of Pseudo-Dionysius, this mediation of the holy through the cult takes place by means of an intricate network of hierarchies.[21] Through mediating agents, God permeates every corner of reality with his holiness and prepares us to appropriate it:

> The task of the cult may be fulfilled only by a hierarchical organization of life, in order that all of life be sanctified. But this

18. Florenskii, *Filosofiia kul'ta*, 41.
19. Florensky, *At the Crossroads*, 11.
20. Florenskii, *Filosofiia kul'ta*, 41.
21. See Florenskii, *Filosofiia kul'ta*, 147, where Florensky cites Dionysius's words that the Eucharist is the "sacrament of sacraments." Although Florensky's sacramentology does not exactly parallel Dionysius's, Florensky shares his interest (characteristic, more broadly, of Neo-Platonism) in hierarchical categories and symbolic thinking. What scholar René Roques says of Dionysius's worldview is equally true of Florensky's: "The totality of this two-fold universe, the angelic and the human, constitutes a sacred order ... regulated by the law of hierarchical mediations, both in the sense of the 'descent' of divine illumination and the 'ascent' of divinization." See René Roques, "Preface," in *Pseudo-Dionysius: The Complete Works*, trans. Colm Luidheid (New York: Paulist Press, 1987), 5. For Dionysius's view of the Eucharist, see "The Ecclesiastical Hierarchy," in *Complete Works*, 209.

> sanctification involves steps, layers, levels, degrees of the transfiguration of the earthly by the heavenly. The earthly should rise entirely into the heavenly, but in a differentiated way—on different levels. Not everything rises at once to Tabor [the mountaintop on which Jesus was transfigured]. In correspondence to the earthly that moves heavenwards, the heavenly should lower itself toward the earthly, for the sake of the latter's salvation.[22]

The movement, as we see, is two-way. In one direction, the cult slowly leads us above this world toward the holy. In the other, the cult gradually brings the holy into the world: "Ritual is necessary as a path of elevation to the holy.... [But] by means of the ritual we also return from the holy back into life."[23] Each step downward accommodates more of God's glory to our frail human condition. Conversely, the same step strengthens us to move upward and closer to Christ.[24]

At each level, the cult separates out and "isolates"—makes "holy"—a thing, action, space, or word; Florensky's Russian term, *osviatit'*, can be translated as "to consecrate," to "sanctify," or in some contexts even as "to bless" (as when a priest blesses a home). What is sanctified at one level both points to and hides what is at a level above. The "veiling" protects worshippers from being overwhelmed by a holiness that they are not yet able to receive because of their sinfulness. The "revealing" enables them nevertheless to see something of God's glory even now in the world around them. They can gradually take in more and more of God's glory, although some—the saints, the "holy" ones—because of their extraordinary ascetical deeds make more progress than the rest of us.[25] In any case, as long as we are still on earth, our encounter with God will always be mediated through the cult and its objects.

22. Florenskii, *Filosofiia kul'ta*, 221.

23. Florenskii, *Filosofiia kul'ta*, 212.

24. Florenskii, *Filosofiia kul'ta*, 213.

25. See Florensky's chapter on "The Witnesses," who help us see more of the holy beyond our personal spiritual limitations, in Florenskii, *Filosofiia kul'ta*, 354–77.

Florensky understands this hiding and revealing to be the function of the "symbol." Insofar as a symbol participates in the higher reality to which it points, it unites the finite and the infinite, meaning and reality. As Florensky later writes, "A symbol can mean any reality that contains in its energy the energy of another reality higher in value and hierarchy; the lower reality is a window into the higher reality, and if the lower reality is destroyed, the light of the higher one fades, not in itself but insofar as the window is closed."[26] As we shall see, blessed loaves of bread, such as the *prosphora* and the *artos*, are not simply *like* the Eucharistic bread. Rather, they share in its holiness, though to a lower degree—and thus more accommodated to our physical being.

Eucharistic Hierarchies

Florensky relates the hierarchical character of holiness to the sacraments. Although reluctant to define a precise number of sacraments—all of reality is potentially "sacramental," even as Christ is the one true sacrament—Florensky nevertheless concludes that the traditional delineation of seven is philosophically fruitful.

All seven sacraments flow from the cross, but each relates Golgotha to a different aspect of ordinary human existence, such as what we eat, what we wear, or how we live within the social-political order: "Like a white ray that a prism dissolves into seven … the mystery of Golgotha divides into separate sacraments, as it enters the multidimensionality of human existence. Their number is determined not by Golgotha but rather by human nature—by the presence of a certain number of dimensions of human existence, each of which is distinct and irreducible to the other."[27] The Eucharist—in which we most fully receive Christ's blood and, therefore, his "life force"—is at the "center" of the others, but we need the others to help us rightly receive the Divine Mysteries.[28]

26. Florenskii, *Filosofiia kul'ta*, 137.
27. Florenskii, *Filosofiia kul'ta*, 156.
28. Florenskii, *Filosofiia kul'ta*, 147.

The greater part of *Philosophy of the Cult* explicates the structure and interrelationship of these different sacramental hierarchies. In relation to the Eucharist, Florensky assigns different kinds of meals to different ranks in a hierarchy. One step below receiving the Eucharist is consumption of a *prosphora* that has not been consecrated for the Eucharist, or of a piece of the *artos*—breads that have been blessed during the liturgy. The next step down is the meal that a Christian family or a monastic community partakes together. One step beneath it are other meals over which the participants have prayed. Still lower are meals that are received reverently but without prayer. The most worldly kind of meal is that which a person eats on the run.[29] Each meal from below prepares us to receive a higher degree of holiness in the meal above; each meal from above reminds us that the meal below is also God's holy gift.

Another hierarchy to and from the Eucharist relates to the status of grain. At the most basic level, grain is a gift of nature. A step up, grain is cultivated by humans for their use. Here, Florensky notes how Orthodox rituals extend holiness not only upward but also outward. When Orthodox believers sow grain, they bless not only the seed but also the granaries in which they will store its fruits and the ovens in which they will bake bread from it. Other rituals further intensify bread's holy character. An Orthodox believer makes the Sign of the Cross over the dough that is being kneaded; holy water is added to the dough for *prosphora*; the oven in which the bread or *prophora* is baked is lit from a lamp whose flame came from Easter's holy fire; the Sign of the Cross is cut or stamped into the surface of a freshly baked loaf.

In the fall, loaves baked in the shape of the cross are placed in bins of grain to protect the grain from mice and insects; in the spring, these loaves are brought out into the ripening fields and fed to horses. The cult, says Florensky, has "numberless threads by

29. Florenskii, *Filosofiia kul'ta*, 174.

which animals and plants and the heavenly energies commune. These creatures are younger members of the church."[30] Bread in the shape of the cross is also shared with people on holy days or on the day of a person's patron saint.

A step up from everyday bread are the *prosphora*, loaves specially prepared for liturgical use. Some *prosphora* will be blessed in commemoration of deceased persons; some will be used for the Eucharist; and some (the *antidoron*) will be divided up and offered to worshippers after they commune and at the end of the liturgy (when non-communicants may also receive it).

A step up from the *prosphora* are the loaves of bread that the priest blesses in the all-night vigils (*litya*) before a church feast day. Yet a step higher is the *artos*, a special loaf that the priest blesses at Pascha in front of the icon of the resurrection. Florensky notes that the priest carefully guards the *artos* because it is understood to offer healing; in certain circumstances, it may even be received in place of the Eucharist. *Kulich*, the special Easter bread that believers prepare and bring to the church to be blessed on Holy Saturday, is similar to the *artos* but lower on the holiness scale. Grain attains its highest status in the pieces of *prosphora* that are consecrated for the Eucharist.[31]

These ritualistic acts lead us back into our original ontological state, and the creation back into its. By blessing grain or bread, we reactivate its proper nature; the grain or bread becomes transparent to God's energies again. At the same time, we recover our proper nature; we are able to receive these energies and to grow in *theosis* (deification, sanctification).[32] This restoration of the creation's true "objectivity," and of the human's true "subjectivity," that the cult effects is best understood as initiating not two separate processes but rather one, which reunites subject and object. Through the cult,

30. Florenskii, *Filosofiia kul'ta*, 275.

31. Florenskii, *Filosofiia kul'ta*, 274–78.

32. Alexander Schmemann refers to humans' priestly vocation in Alexander Schmemann, *For the Life of the World* (Crestwood, NY: St. Vladimir's University Press, 1973), 11–22.

the analytic rationality that separates adults from the creation is replaced by a childlike sense of oneness with reality.

Wine is defined by a similar hierarchy. As the most basic level, wine is a product both of what nature (and God) gives and of what humans cultivate. Moreover, argues Florensky, all cultures have regarded wine as a symbol of blood and therefore of life. Wine enjoys a "natural" status of holiness. Orthodoxy, however, brings wine into the cult, beginning with various blessings for vineyards. A step up is the ordinary table wine for which believers give thanks at a meal. Another step higher is the wine mixed with warm water (*zapivka*) that communicants drink after receiving the Eucharist.

A yet higher degree of holiness inheres in the wine that along with loaves of bread is consecrated during vespers at the *litya*. Believers will receive this bread and wine as an agape meal (love feast) during matins in preparation for receiving the Eucharist in the Divine Liturgy that follows. The priest has prayed that these gifts of bread and wine be multiplied (he refers to the Gospel story of Jesus's feeding of the five thousand) and that, in faith, they will satisfy us spiritually, even though we see with our earthly eyes how little there is. We need just enough that we recognize the bread and wine as nourishment but not so much that they fill us up, as though they would constitute just another earthly meal.

Another step up the hierarchy is the wine that is blessed, though not sacramentally consecrated, in a common cup at a wedding. Above that is the wine that is mixed with oil for the sacrament of the anointing of the ill and dying. Still higher up the ladder is the wine that is used in the liturgy of the Presanctified Gifts, which is celebrated only during Lent. Here, consecrated bread that has been reserved from the Sunday liturgy is placed in the cup with the wine. According to Florensky, the church has generally taught that this wine does not become the blood of Christ. Only at the highest level, the Eucharistic consecration of the elements in the regular Divine Liturgy, does this transformation occur.

Although here we have traced the hierarchy of wine from below to above, the same two-way dynamic holds as with bread. The cult blesses the basic gifts produced by the interaction of nature and culture—ordinary bread and wine—in order to lead us to the cross and Christ's life-giving sacrifice, while the downward steps of the cult and its many acts of blessing direct Christ's energies into nature and culture. Each level prepares us to rise to the next, even as it sanctifies what is below it.

Oil and Water

Through the cult, God's glory permeates the world, yet in a way that preserves rather than violates the many unique forms of reality in which humans may take delight, as did Florensky in his childhood. Rather than overwhelming people with God's glory, the cult trains us gradually to see it in all things. Florensky adds that each step of blessing has corresponding rituals of purification. What is activated by the cult to show forth God's glory is simultaneously exorcised of what is evil.[33]

Florensky develops two other sacramental hierarchies in considerable detail. In each, the same dynamic holds as with the hierarchies of bread and wine. Through faith, humans climb the ladder; by grace, divine energies descend it. In one direction, the cult makes the sanctification of humans possible (*theosis*). In the other, the cult makes culture possible—God's energies penetrate into and sustain humans' everyday existence.

The first hierarchy is related to oil and "anointing," which Florensky associates with "covering" and protection. At its most "earthly" level, oil, like bread and wine, is a product of nature and culture. Humans work with natural, divine gifts—certain plants—to make oil for fuel and nourishment. A level higher on the "anointing" ladder is the oil that is blessed for use in prayer and worship. At the all-night vigils, a priest sanctifies oil (along

33. Florenskii, *Filosofiia kul'ta*, 233–34.

with bread and wine), places it in a lamp before an icon of the saint of the day (Florensky remarks on instances of such oil miraculously lighting itself), and takes some of it to anoint the worshippers (he makes the Sign of the Cross on their foreheads). This oil communicates God's grace almost "substantially or substantially-spiritually," says Florensky.[34]

At the crown of the hierarchy is the sacramental use of oil: in chrismation, to anoint the eyes, ears, mouth, throat, hands, and feet of one who has just been baptized; and in the sacrament of the anointing of the ill and dying. In these instances, the oil is understood to seal a person with the Holy Spirit and to draw that person into communion with the Holy Trinity. One's body becomes a temple of God; it is clothed in immortality.[35]

The second hierarchy that Florensky explicates is organized around water and flows to and from baptism. In Florensky's (and Orthodoxy's) perspective, water is never "naturally" neutral. It has a living will of its own; Florensky notes that icons of the baptism of Christ depict sea creatures in the waters of the Jordan. Water can rebel against God and threaten human existence. Through the cult, however, water is redeemed to show forth God's energies. Florensky sets forth five steps of sanctification, while adding that he has not exhaustively included all of the church's blessings of water in his scheme.[36]

At the first step are the church's prayers over water for our everyday use. A second step is the church's blessing of springs and waters that have miraculous powers of healing. At a third level occurs the Lesser Blessing of Water, a ritual that a priest can perform at any time during the church year. Believers drink this water in church and at home, as they pray for spiritual and physical protection. At the fourth rung of the ladder is the Great Blessing of Water at Theophany (Epiphany). In both the lesser and great

34. Florenskii, *Filosofiia kul'ta*, 240.
35. Florenskii, *Filosofiia kul'ta*, 247–48, 287–88.
36. Florenskii, *Filosofiia kul'ta*, 233.

blessings, the priest dips a cross three times into the water, reciting the Trinitarian persons' names, but the prayers for the great blessing are more complex and powerful. Filled to a higher degree with divine energies, the water is objectively changed. It acquires a special taste and does not spoil.

Florensky asserts that one's body immediately experiences the blessed water's life-giving power, almost as though one were receiving the Eucharist. Now, the water is no longer simply "natural"; rather, it has become "a new being, a spiritual-physical being."[37] Fifth and at the top of the hierarchy is the sacrament of baptism, whose waters deliver us from an old self of sin and raise us up with Christ to a new life in God.

Intersecting Hierarchies

Florensky delineates other hierarchies, noting, however, that many of the blessings associated with them are no longer familiar to people.[38] Each hierarchy has both a vertical and a horizontal trajectory. There are both different levels and broadening spheres of sanctification. Moreover, each sacramental hierarchy intersects with the others. A complex network of relationships weaves itself through reality. As Florensky states, "The cult is a holy, many-sided, and differentiated unity, permeated by reflections, interrelationships, and mutual resemblances."[39] Just as the basic needs of human existence—food, drink, clothing, shelter, healing, and protection—overlap and intersect, so, too, do the cultic rituals that sanctify them.

Florensky notes the significance of grain not only for the Eucharist but also for communion with the dead. The Orthodox service for commemorating the dead, the *panikhida*, includes a blessing of *kolivo*, a mixture of boiled wheat kernels and honey. The association of wheat with commemoration of the dead is

37. Florenskii, *Filosofiia kul'ta*, 231.
38. Florenskii, *Filosofiia kul'ta*, 216.
39. Florenskii, *Filosofiia kul'ta*, 263.

also evident in the blessing of five small loaves of bread in the all-night vigils, a worship service whose original purpose was to commemorate the church's martyrs and saints. Florensky argues that in European cultures, wheat has been regarded as symbolizing, more fully than other grains, death and resurrection: its seed "dies" in the ground in order to bring forth new life. Similarly, the cult blesses grain mixed with honey because these cultures have traditionally regarded a bee as "revealing" the soul of a deceased person—indeed, in Orthodox practice, there is a special blessing of bees.

In honoring the dead, we cannot substitute other foods, and those who try to feed the dead with other foods are engaging in black magic. Only the church's blessing of wheat grain (or bread) rightly activates the two-way movement that characterizes the cult as a whole: our prayers and ritual actions feed the dead with Christ's life energy (we lift them up to heaven), and they become present to us on earth (they move from above to below).[40]

The deceased also "assert their presence" and come closer to us when the priest commemorates them by name during his preparation of the Eucharistic elements. In a letter to Rozanov, Florensky reports on his own experience as a priest: "With each memorializing of a name of a deceased person ... [I feel in me] a certain poke in the heart, a certain physical-spiritual touch upon the heart."[41]

In *Philosophy of the Cult*, Florensky tells of a similar experience associated with bees. Sergei Troitskii, Florensky's closest friend in seminary, had been murdered by a disgruntled pupil soon after he married Florensky's sister and moved to Tbilisi to teach school. On the anniversary of his death, Florensky was serving the liturgy in the chapel of the sisters of the Red Cross in Sergiev Posad. The chapel was almost completely sealed off from the outdoors. To get to it, one had to climb several sets of stairs and pass through

40. Florenskii, *Filosofiia kul'ta*, 278–79.

41. Pavel Florenskii to V. V. Rozanov, September 9, 1912, in V. V. Rozanov, *Literaturnye izgnanniki* [Literary exiles], vol. 2 (Moscow: Respublika, 2010), 76.

long corridors and closed doors. Moreover, the chapel windows were shut tight and could not be opened. As Florensky prepared the Eucharistic elements, he was astonished to find a bee buzzing around the altar. He suddenly remembered that he had forgotten to memorialize Troitskii. Florensky insists that this realization was not merely "psychological" or subjective. The bee was Troitskii's soul, objectively present again to Florensky.[42]

Just as Orthodox rituals for grain and honey intersect both with celebration of the Eucharist and with prayers for the dead, so too the sacramental hierarchy related to anointing with oil projects itself into other dimensions of worship, such as "smell." As we have noted, Florensky himself had an extraordinarily sharp sense of smell and was interested in developing a science of smell. Now, he notes that odor, like oil, can serve as a protective coating, as with plants whose "vapors" ward off animals.

At a basic level, oil for everyday use has a naturally "pure" smell that pleases us. At the next level up is the especially fragrant oil that the church blesses and uses in the cult. Further up the hierarchy is the pleasant smell that emanates from the corpses of extraordinarily holy people, such as that of Fr. Isidore. An even sweeter smell emanates from holy relics, something that Florensky claims to have experienced when the Bolsheviks unwrapped the body of Sergius of Radonezh.[43] This odor, too, serves as a protective clothing; because of the fragrance, believers approach the relics with particular reverence and care. In contrast, tobacco smoke—perhaps, in Florensky's thinking, the typical smell (stench) of the modern, disenchanted world—is repulsive and screens people from reality.[44]

Like oil and odor, incense serves to cover and consecrate people and things, and the church's use of it can also be delineated hierarchically. The censing at vespers leads a step up to that at matins.

42. Florenskii, *Filosofiia kul'ta*, 285–86.
43. Florensky, *At the Crossroads*, 46.
44. Florenskii, *Filosofiia kul'ta*, 237, 175.

Still higher is the censing of the *prosphora*, when the priest prepares the Eucharistic elements during the *proskomedia*, the first part of the Divine Liturgy. Above that is the censing of the Eucharistic elements, as the priest prays for them to be transformed into the body and blood of Christ. Each step upward teaches us that the incense has significance ontologically and not merely aesthetically. The incense rises into the heavenly, noumenal world and returns to us as divine grace. When the priest censes the table at which the dead are commemorated, we are able to sense their presence, even as we become present to them.[45]

Florensky extends "covering" to different kinds of clothing, means of transportation, dwelling places, church buildings, weapons, and even pots, pans, and utensils. The church has rituals of blessing for each. The most basic things and activities of human culture flow in and out of the cult.

Similarly, the cult sanctifies time (the church calendar). The natural seasons become transparent to God's energies, as the church celebrates holy days. Pagan celebrations of spring offer one example. Florensky argues that "the [pagan] celebration of flowers is a celebration of the Earth, and celebration of the Earth, celebration of the departed, and celebration of the departed, the anticipation of their final and complete revealing, when the whole world will flow with 'honey and milk.'"[46] For Florensky, Orthodox Pascha does not so much replace these celebrations as fulfill the deep human longings that each of them expresses. At Pascha, Orthodoxy declares that Christ not only rises from the dead but also descends into the depths of the earth. As he releases the Old Testament saints from their imprisonment in hell, he pours his divine energies into the very earth.[47] In renarrating these events,

45. Florenskii, *Filosofiia kul'ta*, 244–47.

46. Florenskii, *Filosofiia kul'ta*, 305.

47. A "dual faith" that venerates both heaven and earth is a larger theme in Russian thought. See Caryl Emerson, "Love as an Act of Rebellion: Orthodoxy and Literary Culture," *Christian History* 146:21–25.

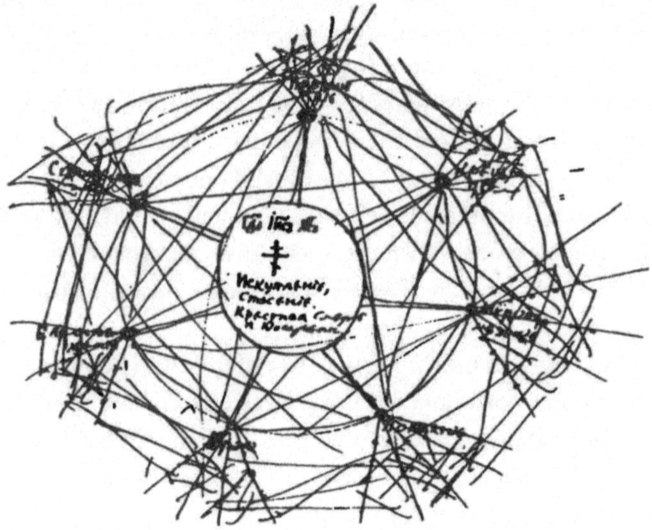

Figure 6.1. Intersecting Hierarchies, *Philosophy of the Cult* / Public domain. By courtesy of the Florensky family archive, from P. A. Florenskii, *Filosofiia kul'ta* (Moscow: Akademicheskii proekt, 2018).

the Orthodox cult unites earth and heaven and thereby places the chronological cycles of the seasons within God's eternity.

A pen sketch that Florensky prepared for *Philosophy of the Cult* captures the intricacies of the cult perhaps more fully than his words alone.[48] A circle at the center of the page is labeled "Jesus Christ, Atonement, Salvation, Beauty." Strings of black thread fly outward from it, crisscrossing and winding themselves around one another. Seven nodules (the seven sacraments) emerge on the periphery. The cult, for Florensky, is not a static set of rituals but rather a dynamic movement of energies that sweep up all of creation into their arc. Humans have the privilege of participating in—indeed, of helping to activate—this cosmic drama.

48. Florenskii, *Filosofiia kul'ta*, 264.

Political Hierarchies

In light of the political turmoil of the time, one other hierarchy is of particular interest. Florensky delivered his lectures only a few months after the October Revolution. He clearly rejects the Bolshevik conviction that history has evolved to where revolutionary power is given to the proletariat and its party to overthrow the bourgeoisie and to create a new, higher, more just social order.[49] Instead, Florensky orders political power sacramentally and, in particular, in relation to the sacrament of ordination: "The priesthood is the ground of the function of power."[50]

Ordination, says Florensky, removes a person from society; one is sacrificed to God. There is a parallel between the church's act of ordination and the Old Testament cult of animal sacrifice—in both cases, there is a laying on of hands (on the ordinand, on the bull or ram), signifying that those who exercise power, whether in church or state, are given over to God and God's purposes.

Similarly, according to Florensky, society is constituted by "a hierarchy of transcendent powers" that come from God and direct themselves back to God, who alone has absolute power.[51] Like an icon or a sacrament, those who exercise power unite heaven and earth. Although human authorities are merely mortal (Florensky notes that at the enthronement of a tsar, the patriarch hands him a bag of earth), they become transparent to God's glory, if they are faithful to God.[52] God has established every rank within society, as in the church, to serve him.

In *Philosophy of the Cult,* Florensky delineates only the first and the last rungs of a hierarchy of civil power. At the base level is the ritual of cutting a boy's hair (for the first time since his birth) immediately after his baptism. This "sacrifice" represents

49. Florensky, *At the Crossroads*, 77.
50. Florenskii, *Filosofiia kul'ta*, 177.
51. Florenskii, *Filosofiia kul'ta*, 289.
52. Florenskii, *Filosofiia kul'ta*, 296–97.

his "transference into another realm."[53] The boy is now marked as a citizen of the state. He is recognized as having the power, when he grows up, to make decisions for himself. Nevertheless, he fully becomes a person (*lichnost'*) only as this principle of self-determination is balanced by a principle of sociality, for a "person" is both independent and dependent. One maintains one's individuality, yet enters into relationships of mutual care and service.[54]

At the top of the hierarchy is the anointing of the tsar, a ritual that sets him apart uniquely as an icon of Christ. Florensky regards the tsar's power as absolute on earth. It must not be limited even by a "secular, juridical constitution." Nevertheless, as representing Christ, the tsar stands beneath Christ and his laws. Moreover, the (worldly) obedience that the tsar demands does not deny the citizen of his capacity for "spiritual freedom" within himself. No matter what the tsar commands, the citizen must live and act according to the truth, a truth that the citizen knows only through the Orthodox Church and its worship.[55]

This way of delineating and balancing different kinds of power characterizes Florensky's understanding of society as a whole. On the one hand, society depends on a principle of unity, which Florensky sees represented by the monarchy. On the other, social life requires a principle of mutuality—in Orthodox terminology, *sobornost'* (conciliarity)—which, for Florensky, is represented by the church.[56] Florensky rejects other ways of ordering political power, whether caesaropapism, where a secular ruler controls church affairs; Catholicism, where spiritual power is concentrated in a pope, rather than in the church as a whole; or republicanism, where secular power is exercised collectively.

To be sure, Florensky seems not to escape the charge of advocating "theocracy." He regards all legitimate power as derived

53. Florenskii, *Filosofiia kul'ta*, 289.
54. Florenskii, *Filosofiia kul'ta*, 181.
55. Florenskii, *Filosofiia kul'ta*, 294.
56. Florenskii, *Filosofiia kul'ta*, 291.

from God and therefore as "holy." Nevertheless, in *Philosophy of the Cult*, Florensky clearly rejects church control of secular affairs. A godly society needs both church and state, both conciliarity and unity, and both individuals' capacity for inner, spiritual freedom and their commitment to worldly obedience. As in his other writings, Florensky does not know how to think theologically except in terms of antinomies.

Coordination, Cooperation, and Communion

Throughout *Philosophy of the Cult*, Florensky emphasizes that the cult has objective force. Religious ritual does not simply change us subjectively by giving us a sense of peace or by making us more aware of our dependence on God. Rather, the cult does something objectively, ontologically, to reality; it sanctifies our world and us. As Florensky says elsewhere, "The one essential thing is to transform all of reality," "first in one's consciousness and then outside oneself."[57] Through the cult, the world and we ourselves become more transparent to God and God's energies. The sacramental hierarchies ensure that this transformation takes place by steps, so that God's glory destroys neither our world nor us.

However, Florensky argues against the Catholic notion of *ex opere operato*—that is, that the sacrament has objective force regardless of the recipient's inner state. For Florensky, we must cooperate with God—what Orthodoxy calls "synergy"—by bringing our will into correspondence with God's, as we know it from his past deeds in Scripture and among the saints. The priest and the people together activate the power of the ritual by speaking the words that accompany the ritual. We speak them rightly only as we make use of the freedom that God has given us: "The divine energies help us only when we open ourselves to their power, removing the interior wall of the self, repudiating our focus on

57. Florensky, *At the Crossroads*, 21.

ourselves."[58] By praying the verbal formulas of the ritual, we realize its sacramental potential.

These words demand a concentration of our whole being. They are nothing less than an "appeal" to God. When we call upon God, especially by his Trinitarian name, we move outside of ourselves, acknowledging our dependence on God. Florensky calls this movement an act of "self-sacrifice," a kind of martyrdom.

When we pray over the ordinary things of nature and culture that sustain our lives—oil, water, bread, wine—we set aside our selfish interests and give these things and our very selves over to God.[59] We abandon our efforts to understand God rationally and according to human categories of thought and analysis. Instead, we enter into the cult and experience its power. Indeed, says Florensky, "If you are to know yourself, you must touch otherworldly manifestations, you must go beyond your own manifestations.... And then you will find in yourself the ground of the Supreme Being."[60]

To step out of self-enclosure is, for Florensky, to risk "faith."[61] To be sure, none of us, not even the greatest saint, has enough faith. None of us is personally worthy of calling upon God. Nevertheless, when we appeal to God by his name, God enables us to do something of eternal significance. We are able to manifest and guard the truth about all of reality's capacity to show forth, like an icon, the divine glory.[62]

On that May afternoon, as he moved from grave to grave, Fr. Ephrem called on God again and again by his triune name:

> Give rest, O Lord, to the souls of thy servants, and establish them in Paradise, Where the choirs of the Saints, O Lord, and of the Just, shine like the stars of heaven, give rest to thy servants who have

58. Florenskii, *Filosofiia kul'ta*, 395–96.
59. Florenskii, *Filosofiia kul'ta*, 408.
60. Florensky, *At the Crossroads*, 75.
61. Florenskii, *Filosofiia kul'ta*, 207.
62. Florenskii, *Filosofiia kul'ta*, 404.

> fallen asleep, regarding not all their temptations.... Devoutly do we hymn the triune Effulgence of the one Godhead, crying aloud: Holy art thou, O Father who art from everlasting, O Son coeternal, and Spirit divine! Illumine us who, with faith, do worship thee and rescue us from fire eternal.[63]

As people quietly departed, some left small wrapped pieces of candy, or even a shot glass of vodka, at the gravesite, a further act (though not endorsed by the church) of communion with the dead.

As a Protestant, I may not receive the Orthodox Eucharist or have a *panikhida* performed for my deceased loved ones. However, when he had finished blessing the graves, Fr. Ephrem did invite me to have lunch with him in the parish fellowship hall. He told me how, over many years and with numerous difficulties, he had rebuilt the parish and its life.

Yes, I would always remain an outsider to him and his world. But for a few precious moments, there really was "communion," a mysterious yet glorious, fearful yet loving, presence of God between the two of us, Orthodox and Protestant, Russian and American.

Fr. Ephrem drove me in his car back into the city.

63. See "The General Panikhida or Requiem Service," in *Service Book of the Holy Orthodox–Catholic Apostolic Church*, trans. Isabel Florence Hapgood, 7th ed. (Englewood, NJ: Antiochian Orthodox Christian Archdiocese, 1996), 566.

7

SERGIEV POSAD AND THE LAVRA

"The heart of Russia . . . the guardian angel of Russia"

As I walk from the train station into the town of Sergiev Posad ("Sergius's town"), the Holy Trinity–St. Sergius Monastery, like a heavenly apparition, rises up before my eyes on the other side of the valley. Onion domes—some glistening with gold, others blue and studded with silver stars—a massive bell tower, and the monastery's tall, white fortress walls float in the air.

The last book of the Christian Bible, the Revelation of St. John, tells of a New Jerusalem that comes down from heaven, like a bride prepared for her bridegroom. It is a place in which there is no longer sorrow or suffering, and all tears are wiped away. The Holy Trinity–St. Sergius Monastery invites me, as it has millions of Russians over the centuries, to imagine for a moment this heaven on earth.

In the early fourteenth century, Sergius and his elder brother

Stephan, desiring to live an intensely ascetical life, traveled into the remote forested wilderness north of Moscow and west of Rostov (an ancient city on Russia's Golden Ring). On a low rise (the Makovets Hill), the brothers cleared the trees and built a cell and a small wooden church. Stephan soon returned to Moscow, but as Sergius became renowned for his holiness and spiritual wisdom, other monks joined him. Some of them would eventually journey even farther into the Russian wilderness to found new monastic communities; Florensky attributed a quarter of the church's existing monasteries to Sergius's spiritual children and grandchildren.[1]

After Sergius's death, his relics reposed at the monastery. They were reputed to be incorruptible and miracle-working, thereby enhancing the monastery's reputation as a pilgrimage site. Over the next centuries, a large monastery complex developed, with churches, bell towers, monastic living quarters, and a holy spring. A town, known until 1919 as Sergievskii Posad, grew up outside the monastery walls.

Sergius was particularly devoted to the Trinity—the one God, who is Father, Son, and Holy Spirit—and had several mystical visions of it. The first church that he built in his clearing was dedicated to the Trinity. A successor church, the Trinity Cathedral, would hold Sergius's relics. The monastery became known as the Holy Trinity–St. Sergius Lavra. For generations of Russians, it has represented the spiritual heart of their nation.

A small seminary, founded within the monastery walls in the eighteenth century, eventually became the renowned Moscow Theological (literally, Spiritual) Academy. As we have seen, Florensky enrolled here in 1904, completed the basic course of study in 1908, defended his master's thesis in 1914, and that same year was called to be its professor of the history of philosophy. In

1. Pavel Florenskii, "Troitse–Sergieva lavra i Rossiia" [The Trinity–Sergius Lavra and Russia], in Pavel Florenskii, *Istoriia i filosofiia iskusstva* [History and philosophy of art] (Moscow: Akademicheskii proekt, 2017), 141.

1915 he bought a house with a large garden near the Lavra. Although by the 1920s he was working most of the time in Moscow, the family continued to live in Sergiev Posad, and he joined them as often as he could. He regarded Sergiev Posad as "beneath the veil [i.e., protection] of St. Sergius," and he pleaded with his children to keep the house, no matter what happened to him.

Florensky's Sergiev Posad

Others, too, seeking a place of beauty and calm, settled in Sergiev Posad. Moscow, about fifty miles to the southwest, was easily accessible by rail, but Sergiev Posad retained the atmosphere of an older, more holy Russia. Its population was only twenty-one thousand. One could easily walk into the surrounding countryside. Besides the Lavra, several other, smaller monasteries and sketes lay nearby: the Bethany Monastery, the Paraclete Skete, Zosimova Pustyn', the Gethsemane Skete, and the Chernigovskii Skete. In the aftermath of the Bolshevik Revolution, the town and its environs offered refuge to a number of prominent personalities and families, often interrelated by marriage.

Count Yurii Olsuf'ev, an expert on ancient Russian art, abandoned his country estate and moved his family to Sergiev Posad soon after the March 1917 revolution that brought about Nicholas II's abdication of the throne. St. Sergius had appeared to Olsuf'ev's wife Sofia (neé Glebova), a pious Orthodox believer, in a dream and had commanded her to move close to his tomb in the Lavra.[2]

Sergei Mansurov and his wife Maria (neé Samarina), both of noble origins, came to Sergiev Posad in the summer of 1917 and moved into the first floor of the large Olsuf'ev house; the two families had long been acquainted. Mansurov was a scholar of Russian history. Maria's sister Varvara was married to Vladimir

2. T. V. Smirnova, *"... pod pokrov Prepodobnogo": ocherki o nekotorykh izvestnykh sem'iakh zhivshikh v Sergievom Posade v 1920-e gody* [Beneath the protective veil of the Saint: notes about several famous families living in Sergiev Posad in the 1920s] (Sergiev Posad: Sviato-Troitskaia Sergieva Lavra, 2008), 10.

Komarovskii, a talented painter and iconographer. When the Bolsheviks seized their country estate in 1923, they moved into the second floor of the Olsuf'ev house.

Vladimir Derviz, an artist and agriculturist, was descended from a prominent German family. He married Nadezhda (neé Simonovich), whose sister Nina (in marriage, Simonovich-Efimova) was an artist and a director of the famous puppet theatre that Florensky so enjoyed. As children, the Simonovich sisters and their mother Adelaida had lived with Derviz on his country estate. When the revolutionary government seized it late in 1917, the Simonovich family moved to Sergiev Posad; Derviz joined them two years later to live with his daughter Maria (his wife Nadezhda had passed away in 1908). Maria was married to Vladimir Favorskii, whose father, a member of the Duma, had moved his family to Sergiev Posad in 1919, after state authorities expropriated his large, prosperous farm.

Mikhail Shik, son of a wealthy Moscow merchant and a convert to Orthodoxy from Judaism, moved with his wife Natal'ia (neé Shakovskaia), who was of noble origins, to Sergiev Posad in 1918, in part because of his close friendship with Vladimir Favorskii. Petr Istomin, also of nobility, was a jurist. After the March revolution, Komarovskii, a longtime friend, invited Istomin and his family to live on the Komarovskii estate outside of Moscow. In 1923, Istomin and family, like Komarovskii, were forced off the estate, and they moved to Sergiev Posad.

Anna Khvostova bought a house in Sergiev Posad, after her husband Sergei, a civil servant in the Ministry of Interior Affairs in St. Petersburg, was killed by a terrorist bomb in 1906. She settled there permanently with her children after the October Revolution and, along with her daughter Ekaterina, secretly took monastic vows. Other prominent families in the town included Vladimir Golitsyn, the governor of Moscow until 1905, and Vladimir Trubetskoi, a decorated army officer in World War I and a talented musician.

Not all of Sergiev Posad's new residents had such distinguished family pedigrees, but some, like Florensky, had equally prominent reputations. Vasilii Rozanov, the famous publicist, moved with his wife and daughter to Sergiev Posad in September 1917, after he fell seriously ill and was no longer able to support himself financially in St. Petersburg. Florensky and Sofia Olsuf'ev helped care for him and his family.

When state authorities closed Zosimova Pustyn' in 1923, the Great Monk Aleksii (Solov'ev), a renowned holy elder, was taken in by two of his spiritual daughters in Sergiev Posad. At the 1917 Local Church Council, Aleksei had drawn lots to determine which of three candidates would become patriarch. Fr. Sergii Sidorov came to Sergiev Posad in 1923 to serve the Peter and Paul Church, just across the street from the Lavra; Shik became his deacon.

These intellectuals, artists, and former high-ranking government officials socialized with one another, stimulated one another's thinking, and assisted one another materially through the trying years of cold, hunger, and political repression that followed the Bolshevik Revolution. Not only their close social relationships but also a common spiritual world united them. Most lived near the Lavra and, like Florensky, believed in its protective veil, even after the state closed the monastery. Fr. Sidorov and Mansurov had at various times turned to the holy elder Aleksii for spiritual guidance; Shik and Anna Khvostova counted themselves among his spiritual children. When the regime closed Zosimova Pustyn', Ekaterina Khvostova helped to resettle its monks and to save its icons and liturgical implements.

Others in Sergiev Posad drew spiritual strength from the nearby sketes. The Manusurov and Khvostova families loved the Chernigovskii Skete, and Rozanov was buried there in 1919. When authorities closed Chernigovskii in 1921, the remaining monks moved to Gethsemane, their sister skete, where Florensky as a seminarian had known the holy elder Isidore. In the 1920s, as other churches were closed, the skete became the area's spiritual center, and by 1924 it had opened its worship services to all visitors, including women. Florensky regularly walked there with his children. One of the monks, Fr. Porfirii, became a spiritual father to Olsuf'ev and his wife. Istomin helped the skete's abbot, Izrail, with legal matters, and the Istomin family regularly attended the skete's services. Istomin's daughter Ksenia and Golitsyn's grandson Sergei later wrote of the monks' beautiful singing and liturgical garments.

Florensky had close friendships with many of these figures. He had corresponded with Rozanov for years. Fr. Sidorov had attended lectures that Florensky had given in Moscow. Mansurov had been so deeply moved by Florensky's *The Pillar and Ground of the Truth* that he had briefly considered becoming a monk. Favorskii was godfather to Florensky's daughter Ol'ga, and Favorskii's son Nikita and Florensky's son Kirill loved exploring the surrounding countryside together. In 1921, Favorskii invited Florensky to give lectures on space and perspective at the Higher State Art–Technical Studios in Moscow, where Favorskii taught and briefly served as rector.[3]

Florensky interacted closely with Sergiev Posad's other artists. He praised Simonovich-Efimova's paintings: They "are always symbolic. In addition to what they depict, there is another meaning, of which you may not even be aware."[4] Florensky also thought very highly of Komarovskii's art—and especially of his iconography. Komarovskii made several portraits of Florensky; though

3. For more about the Higher State Art–Technical Studios (Vysshie gosudarstvennye khudozhestvenno-tekhnicheskie masterskie, VkhUTEMAS), see Nicoletta Misler, "Pavel Florensky as Art Historian," in Pavel Florensky, *Beyond Vision: Essays on the Perception of Art*, ed. Nicoletta Misler (London: Reaktion Books, 2002), 73–83; and Yve-Alain Bois, "School," in *Revoliutsiia! Demonstratsiia! Soviet Art Put to the Test*, ed. Matthew S. Witkovsky and Devine Fore (Chicago: Art Institute of Chicago, 2017), 44–49.

4. Smirnova, *"... pod pokrov Prepodobnogo,"* 168.

Figure 7.1. Portrait of Florensky, by Vladimir Komarovskii
Public domain. Wikimedia Commons. Florensky P. by Komarovsky, V. A.

not icons, they capture something of Florensky's unusual spiritual concentration.

The Commission for the Preservation of the Lavra

Perhaps the most significant interaction between Florensky and these talented personalities took place through the Commission for the Preservation of the Artistic and National Monuments of the Trinity–Sergius Lavra. Founded in the fall of 1918, after state authorities closed the monastery, the Commission reported to Trotsky's wife Natalia Sedova in the Ministry of Education and had the task of inventorying the monastery's holdings and of converting the monastery complex into a museum. Florensky, Olsuf'ev, and Mansurov were among the Commission's first members. Florensky headed up its work in scholarly research. Olsuf'ev prepared publications about the Lavra's treasures, restored its ancient icons, and organized exhibitions of its notable objects. Mansurov studied the collection of materials in the monastery library. Rozanov's daughter Tat'iana served as a typist.

In April 1919, Shik joined the Commission and dedicated himself to preserving the Lavra's musical heritage, including its ancient manuscripts of musical notations and its renowned bells. In 1920, Favorskii became the Commission's bookkeeper. That same year, Derviz joined the Commission, assumed various administrative duties, and in 1922 became its chairman. When the Bolshevik regime began confiscating church treasures (claiming that it needed to sell them to raise money to feed victims of the famine), Derviz worked closely with Olsuf'ev to save the Lavra's most valuable and historically significant items. Soon after his arrival in Sergiev Posad in 1923, Komarovskii, too, joined the Commission. He painted views of the Lavra and some of its interiors.

This concentration of the "old guard" in Sergiev Posad—the "has beens," as their opponents dismissively labeled them—could not but draw the worried attention of the regime. Mansurov was briefly imprisoned in 1920, as the authorities searched for his father Pavel, a prominent diplomat. In 1924, when the state was seeking to break the church's political influence, Fr. Sidorov invited Patriarch Tikhon to celebrate the liturgy in Sergiev Posad, an act of defiance, for which the authorities detained Sidorov.

In 1925, arrests accelerated. Mansurov and Komarovskii were briefly imprisoned. Olsuf'ev, Shik, and Istomin, were interrogated after they had met to drink tea; an informant suspected that they were discussing opposition to the government. Anna and

Ekaterina Khvostova were sent to prison camps because they refused to disclose the location of the treasures that they had removed from Zosimova Pustyn'. In the fall of 1925, Mansurov, Istomin, Fr. Sidorov, and Shik, among others, were imprisoned for supporting Metropolitan Petr, Patriarch Tikhon's successor, when he refused to yield to state demands to rid the church of "counter revolutionaries."[5] Even when these people's sentences expired, few were allowed to return to Sergiev Posad.

The heaviest blow fell in May 1928, when eighty people in the town were rounded up: several members of the Commission, other "has beens," and fourteen monks who had been working as museum guards and guides. All were suspect because of their association with the pre-revolutionary order. Florensky and Istomin's wife and eighteen-year-old son were among them. Olsuf'ev and Komarovskii narrowly escaped but would later be arrested and executed.

Among the items found on Florensky was a photograph of Nicholas II. Under interrogation, Florensky acknowledged his sympathy for the tsar but declared that he had a "good" relationship with the Soviet government and noted his work on its behalf in Moscow's Electro-Technical Institute. Although he admitted that he did not agree with every government measure, he emphasized that he was categorically opposed to those who wished to take military or economic measures against the Bolsheviks.[6]

Thanks to connections in high places, Florensky spent only three months in internal exile (in the city of Nizhnii Novgorod). He returned to his work in Moscow and continued to see his family in Sergiev Posad. But the town had changed. Its population

5. See A. Mazyrin, "'Sergievskaia' ('Samarinskaia') tserkovnaia gruppa i Patriarshii mestobliusitel' mitropolit Petr (Polianskii) v 1925 g." [The Sergiev (Samarin) church group and the patriarchal locums tenens metropolitan Petr (Polianskii)], in *Podvigom dobrym podvizalsia* [Having attained spiritual victory by means of spiritual achievement], ed. S. N. Chernyshev and Dimitrii Sazonov (Kostroma: Kostroma Metropolia, 2017), 162–76, http://bibl-kostroma.ru/wp-content/uploads/2018/07/Podvigom-dobrym_block-2017-web.pdf.

6. Smirnova, "*. . . pod pokrov Prepodobnogo*," 100.

had more than doubled since he studied there. Many of his friends were gone. The museum that he had hoped would preserve Russia's religious heritage had been reorganized to advance antireligious, "scientific" work. The churches had been closed, and the town had been renamed Zagorsk, in honor of a Bolshevik revolutionary hero. The street on which the Florensky house was located also had a new name, Pionerskaia, in honor of the communist youth organization, the Pioneers.

The last photograph of Florensky in his priestly cassock dates from his short exile in Nizhnii Novgorod in 1928. Looking straight at the camera, he stands on a platform above the banks of the Volga River. The wind blows against him and his cassock. He had faithfully worn that cassock for many years, even when working at the Electro-Technical Institute. Now, a new chapter of his life had begun. He would no longer wear a cassock or serve the church.

Five years later, Florensky was sentenced to the gulag and immediately shipped off to Siberia. He never saw his beloved Sergiev Posad again. But his family remained there, and whenever he wrote home, he remembered the town and the house that meant so much to him.

Florensky's Lavra

As Florensky began his work with the Commission to preserve the Holy Trinity–St. Sergius Monastery, he articulated his understanding of the monastery's significance historically and for the future. Florensky delivered his thoughts verbally to the Commission on the first anniversary of the 1917 Bolshevik "world revolution." The next year, 1919, they appeared in print and in essay form as "The Trinity–Sergius Lavra and Russia," part of a brochure published by the Commission. Florensky's essay is key to understanding his thought as a whole.

Florensky sees the Lavra as embodying, summarizing, and synthesizing all of Russian history and identity. It is "the heart of Russia," "the guardian angel of Russia," the place where one feels most "at home"—indeed, where one is "more at home than in one's own home." Here, he says, are the prototypes, the purest realizations, of Russian culture, art, and architecture and of the distinctive Russian way of life. The Lavra is the spiritual center out of which the rest of Russia has developed and to which the rest of Russia refers. In Florensky's words, "In order to understand Russia, one has to understand the Lavra."[7]

Florensky's high claims had practical relevance. Although the Bolshevik government had nationalized the monastery in early 1918, it had not immediately dissolved its monastic community. In desperately trying to save both the monastery complex and its monks, Florensky was implicitly making a case to government authorities: they needed to preserve the monastery if they were to unite the Russian people behind them.

In Florensky's view, the monastery was inseparable from its founder. Not only had St. Sergius established monasticism as a permanent and central feature of Russian life, but he had also articulated the unique calling of Russia and its Orthodoxy. Florensky notes that Sergius lived just as Byzantium was experiencing its final blossoming. Through Sergius, Byzantine culture with its synthesis of Greek antiquity and Christian faith had now passed into the trusteeship of Russia. Sergius did not know Byzantium directly; he had never traveled there. But he had received from God a spiritual insight that crystalized the legacy of Byzantium; Sergius had peered into the mystery of the Trinity.

Florensky argues that culture in its truest sense is possible only where two ideological extremes are overcome and synthesized. At one extreme is an overemphasis on God as monotheistic and transcendent, typified for Florensky by Judaism. At the other is an overemphasis on God as pantheistic and immanent, represented by paganism. Christian heresies, too, have veered in one direction

7. Florenskii, "Troitse-Sergieva lavra," 130, 132, 141. For key passages of the essay translated into English, see Scott Kenworthy, *The Heart of Russia: Trinity-Sergius, Monasticism, and Society after 1825* (New York: Oxford University Press, 2010), 310.

or the other. What Byzantium long guarded—and what Russia has now been called to protect—is the truth that unifies these antinomies, the truth that is set forth by the Orthodox doctrine of the Trinity and its accompanying affirmation of the Incarnation of the Son.

The doctrines of the Trinity and the Incarnation establish, on the one hand, the absoluteness and otherness of God and, on the other, the spiritual value of the world that he has created.[8] The communion that characterizes God's innermost character (Father, Son, and Holy Spirit) is the basis for God's communion with the world and for humans' communion with one other and with the natural world. When related to the triune God, human culture as an organic harmony of different parts becomes possible.

Florensky argues that Sergius's experience of the mystery of the Trinity shaped the life of the Lavra and, thereby, the existence of the Russian people as a whole. For Florensky, it is significant that Sergius dedicated his small church to the Holy Trinity. Florensky argues that up to that time few churches bore that name; after Sergius, many of Russia's most prominent churches would.

Sergius's plain wooden church was eventually replaced by a magnificent stone edifice. In the tradition of Orthodox Christianity, the new church required an icon on the iconostasis in honor of the church's protector, the triune God. Andrei Rublev, a monk in the Lavra who perhaps even knew the elderly Sergius, completed a Trinity icon that uniquely captured Sergius's spiritual insight. Earlier icons had depicted the persons of the Trinity in the three angels who visit Abraham and Sarah and promise them a son (see Gen. 18:1–18). Rublev, says Florensky, was the first to paint an icon that did more than depict the event as biblical history; he "drew back the curtain" and invited worshippers to look into heaven itself.[9] The Trinity was now more than abstract church

8. Florenskii, "Troitse–Sergieva lavra," 134.
9. Florenskii, "Troitse–Sergieva lavra," 139.

dogma; it was an ontological reality that one could experience by worshipping and venerating it.

A Trinity icon in a Trinity Cathedral required a liturgical celebration dedicated to the Trinity. Originally conducted at the Lavra in front of Rublev's icon, this "Trinity Day" soon spread throughout Russia. It fell on Pentecost, whose liturgy includes prayers to the Holy Spirit. Eventually, the next day (the Monday after Pentecost) was dedicated in Russia to the Holy Spirit, whom Florensky associates with joy, beauty, and "the eternal feminine."[10]

Here, Florensky makes a connection to the Orthodox understanding of Sophia, the Wisdom of God, who together with the Trinity has been entrusted to Russia. The honoring of Sophia by naming churches after her and by depicting her in iconography characterized ancient Kievan Rus' and, for Florensky, expresses the Russian people's "feminine" principle—that is, its capacity through the Holy Spirit to receive God. In contrast, the Rus' of Moscow and St. Petersburg, from the time of Sergius on, has been characterized by the "masculine" principle of the Trinity and the Incarnation—that is, of the God who enters into the world. For Florensky, these two principles have given birth to Russia's unique artistic achievements, form of government, and national identity.

According to Florensky, the communion among humans that flows out of the Trinity shaped the first Christian communities. It gave birth to and has regularly renewed monastic communities ever since, and it was Sergius's ideal for his monastery on the hill. For Sergius, "life together" would mean perfect love, oneness of mind, and the sharing of goods, such that one person would no longer say, "That is mine," or "That is yours." Florensky notes that this way of life is a "communism." As realized in the Lavra, this is the genuine communism that shines forth into all of Russia. It has always been "close to the Russian spirit," its driving force.[11]

In a particularly moving passage, Florensky writes, "Amidst

10. Florenskii, "Troitse-Sergieva lavra," 140.
11. Florenskii, "Troitse-Sergieva lavra," 143.

the turbulent circumstances of time; amidst discords, internecine feuds, generally wild conditions, and Tatar raids; amidst this profound agitation of a decaying Rus', an eternal, untroubled, indestructible world, a world 'from above,' a heavenly world, opened itself [to Sergius and Rublev]."[12] Florensky saw his own time of revolutionary change as equally troubled and therefore as needing the same light of eternity to guide the Russian nation.

Florensky ends his essay by calling for the Lavra to renew this historic vision of Russia and its distinctive cultural accomplishments. The Lavra should have workshops and schools for icon painting, the sewing and embroidery of liturgical garments and objects, popular crafts, church architecture, and religious education. At its center should be, as before, the holy relics of Sergius, the Lavra's "founder, builder, and angel," whose spiritual energy still flows across the Russian lands.[13]

The Lavra as Synthetic Vision

Two other essays that Florensky wrote for the Commission at about the same time complement his understanding of the Lavra and Sergius. In "Church Drama as a Synthesis of the Arts," Florensky argued for turning the Lavra into a living museum, where visitors would see the monks at prayer and work. The Lavra's synthesis of dramatic elements, especially in worship, creates a special spiritual atmosphere. The clouds of incense, the darkened space pierced by burning candles, the chanting of prayers, and the movements of the priests and deacons through the doors of the iconostasis—all this is a unique historical, artistic, and spiritual achievement of the Russian people that deserves protection.[14]

The second essay, "The Prayer Icons of St. Sergius," describes the two icons that Sergius had in his cell: one of the Mother of

12. Florenskii, "Troitse–Sergieva lavra," 139.

13. Florenskii, "Troitse–Sergieva lavra," 144.

14. See Pavel Florensky, "The Church Ritual as a Synthesis of the Arts," in Pavel Florensky, *Beyond Vision: Essays on the Perception of Art*, ed. Nicoletta Misler, trans. Wendy Salmond (London: Reaktion Books, 2002), 95–111.

God with the Christ child (in the iconographic tradition known as the Hodegetria), and one of St. Nicholas, Russia's patron saint. Florensky argues that both icons came from Byzantium at the time of its flowering in the thirteenth century. As in his Lavra essay, he sees this as evidence that Sergius and Russia had become the heir of Hellenic and Byzantine culture.

Florensky interprets the Hodegetria as combining elements of the Syrian mother-earth goddess with those of the Athenian Pallas, the goddess of wisdom. The other icon represents Nicholas as the prototype of saintliness. In his essay on the Lavra, Florensky had lifted up the antinomy between Sophia (the world's capacity to receive the divine) and the Trinity (the divine that enters into the world). In "The Prayer Icons of St. Sergius," he identifies an antinomy between heaven coming down to earth (the Hodegetria) and earth reaching up to heaven (St. Nicholas).[15] The movement between heaven and earth that the two icons set forth shaped Sergius's capacity to see the truth of the Trinity. Conversely, Sergius's vision of the Trinity enabled him to see the spiritual truth embodied in his two icons.

Florensky's essays demonstrate his deep knowledge of—and ability to synthesize insights from—antiquity, church history, and specifically Orthodox theology, liturgy, architecture, and iconography. Just as the Lavra is the "heart of Russia," Florensky's essays about the Lavra distill themes and ideas that are at the heart of his other religious-philosophical writings. Three matters receive particular emphasis.

First, Christianity does not contradict but rather more fully expresses the beauty and harmony that the ancient Greeks cultivated. Hellenic culture was preserved and deepened by Byzantium and its Orthodoxy. Preservation and development of this legacy has now passed to Russia and its church and saints. Through

15. See Pavel Florenskii, "Molennye ikony prepodobnogo Sergiia" [The prayer icons of St. Sergius], in Pavel Florenskii, *Istoriia i filosofiia iskusstva* (Moscow: Akademicheskii proekt, 2017), 145–63.

St. Sergius, the Lavra has become the spiritual center of Russian history and identity. His relics have a spiritual energy that pervades the Lavra, the surrounding town of Sergiev Posad, and the rest of Russia, especially by way of the monasteries that his followers founded.

Second, culture is the cultivation of communion—the communion of humans with the divine, the communion of humans with one another ("communism"), and the communion of humans with the natural world—and this communion flows out of the cult, because it is there that humans become most fully aware of the presence of God in their midst. The performance of the liturgy transforms finite earthly things and activities—iconography, chanting, words, and dramatic movement—into windows into the infinite. Through the cult, we learn to see all of reality as reflecting the glory of God. God remains other, yet near; unknowable, yet revealed. The genius of the early church's resolution of the Trinitarian and Christological controversies lay in the insight that humans can know God only through ideational antinomies that are nevertheless not contradictions but rather dynamic tensions.

Third, the particular spiritual wisdom of Russian Orthodoxy lies, first, in relating Sophia and the Trinity to each other and, second, the Mother of God and the saints to each other. In each pair of terms, we find a principle of heaven reaching toward earth and a principle of earth ascending toward heaven. Florensky's central concern is the synthesis of these dynamic tensions: the right relationship of the divine and the human, of the transcendent and the immanent, and of the infinite and the finite. He wants to avoid two theological dead ends: preserving God's otherness by making him inaccessible to humans and affirming God's immanence by collapsing him into the created world.

Florensky's three spiritual insights failed to persuade the Bolsheviks. They sought, instead, to desecrate the Lavra, Sergiev Posad, and, indeed, all of Russia by closing, destroying, or converting churches into antireligious museums; dissolving monasteries; confiscating icons; and exposing relics, including those of St. Sergius, to public ridicule. Florensky and other members of the Commission would be arrested; most would be executed.

The fate of Florensky's essay on "The Trinity–Sergius Lavra and Russia" is indicative of the fate of Florensky personally and of his religious vision. Soon after publication of the brochure that included the essay, an article appeared in the Soviet press, denouncing Florensky and the Commission. The author, a former priest who had renounced his office, accused Florensky of being closely allied with Patriarch Tikhon, who was defending the church against Bolshevik efforts to control it. The Commission was supposedly intent on preserving the church and religious life under the pretense of "historical and artistic value."

State authorities intervened. Of the initial run of two thousand copies, only a handful were distributed. The rest were destroyed, as was the type set. Although a few specialists during the Soviet period were familiar with the essay, they did not openly refer to it until the 1980s. But by the end of that decade, as communism fell, no other piece by Florensky had been more often published.[16]

Today, pilgrims again crowd into the Lavra's churches and draw water from its holy well. Long lines stretch from the Trinity Cathedral into the monastery courtyard, as believers patiently wait to venerate the relics of St. Sergius. Few of them have heard of Florensky. But just a few blocks away, his house still stands, a modest wooden structure that over the years has begun to lean in the shifting soil. As I walk by, I pause. I look around and see the towering, magical domes of the Lavra. St. Sergius still casts his protective veil over Florensky and his legacy.

16. Florenskii, "Troitse–Sergieva lavra," 550–51.

8

ICONS

"If there is the Rublev Trinity, then there is God."

On a wintry December day, I step into Moscow's famous Tretiakov Art Gallery. It is my very first visit. Famous works of both Western and Russian artists fill the rooms. I have only one goal, however. I proceed to the lower level and into a large room with an icon beneath protective glass. A woman is crossing herself in front of it. Another visitor seems uncertain about how close to approach it.[1]

The icon is more than four and a half feet high, and more than three and a half feet wide—the size of a large window. Its background is white with suggestions of gold. Three large figures, with identical-looking angelic faces, sit around an altar-table and gently bow their heads toward one another. The predominant color of

1. As I write, the icon has been transferred, by presidential decree, to the church, which intends to return it to its original place in the Trinity Cathedral in the Holy Trinity–St. Sergius Lavra. See Sophia Kishkovsky, "Putin Now Orders Return of Russia's Most Precious Icon to the Church," *The Art Newspaper* (May 18, 2023), https://www.theartnewspaper.com/2023/05/18/putin-now-orders-return-of-russias-most-precious-icon-to-the-church.

the robes of the figure to the left is a light, nondescript brown. The figure on the right is in green. The figure in the middle is clothed in scarlet and blue and makes a sign of blessing over a chalice in which a bloody sacrifice lies.

For a moment, the noise and commotion of the big city fade. Another world is beckoning. I am standing in front of what today is the world's best-known Orthodox icon, Andrei Rublev's Trinity. Here, in a secular museum, I am encountering something that evokes holiness.

In traditional Orthodox iconography, only the Son may be represented as a human figure, since only he of the three Trinitarian persons became incarnate. But early Church Fathers saw in the three angels who visited Abraham and Sarah a prefiguration of the Trinity, and this way of depicting the Trinity became an established iconographic theme. Rublev's unique achievement was to interpret the scene as something more—indeed, as a revelation of God's glorious presence with us on earth. Earlier icons often included Abraham and Sarah on opposite sides of a long table at which the angels were seated; Rublev does not depict them at all. Moreover, the angels no longer enjoy an earthly feast; rather, they gather around the Eucharist. Objects in the background have been reduced to the outlines of a building, a rocky cliff, and an oak tree.

The icon invites the viewer to complete the circle, to stand at the fourth side of the altar-table, and to enter into the eternal fellowship, the *koinonia*, of Father, Son, and Holy Spirit, which the Orthodox liturgy declares to be "the Trinity one in essence, and undivided." The icon exudes peace, calm, and harmony. It points to a different dimension of life, that which Christians call eternal.

Rediscovering Rublev

Florensky does not discuss the Trinity icon in *Pillar and Ground*. There, he focuses, instead, on historic icons of Sophia, the Wisdom of God. The Trinity icon came to interest Florensky only later, as he served on the Commission to save the Lavra and its historic treasures from the Bolsheviks.

Florensky's work for the Commission included cataloging the monastery's numerous icons. As we have noted, of particular interest to him were St. Sergius's Hodegetria and St. Nicholas, and Rublev's Trinity, the icon that in Florensky's view most powerfully communicated St. Sergius's insight into the meaning of the Trinity for the Russian Church and the Russian people.

The new government nationalized the monastery on January 20, 1918, less than three months after the October Revolution. The Lavra's future was now uncertain. On August 21 of that year, Florensky acquired a photograph of the Rublev icon, perhaps so that he would still be able to venerate it, in the event that the icon had to be concealed from the Bolsheviks, who had begun to confiscate church treasures.[2]

The Rublev icon, like many other ancient church icons, had become scarcely recognizable over the years. A gold and silver cladding studded with jewels covered the greater part of the icon, and the aging paints and the soot from the candles that burn perpetually in Orthodox churches had darkened what had been left exposed, the faces and the hands of the three figures. Familiarity with Rublev and other iconography of the Russian Middle Ages had been further obscured by styles that became popular after Peter the Great's turn toward Western Europe. Influenced by the Baroque religious art of Catholic Italy and France, newer icons tended toward emotionalism and sentimentality.

Early in the twentieth century, Russian historians and religious scholars, seeking to reassert their country's unique Orthodox cultural identity, began restoring these medieval icons to their

2. See Igumen Andronik Trubachev, "Prilozhenie: khronologiia zhizni sviashchennika Pavla Florenskogo, 1918–1922" [Appendix: chronology of the life of Fr. Pavel Florensky, 1918–1922], in Igumen Andronik Trubachev, *Put' k Bogu: lichnost', zhizn' i tvorchestvo sviashchennika Pavla Florenskogo* [The way to God: the person, life, and work of the priest Pavel Florensky], vol. 4 (Sergiev Posad: Gorodets, 2016), 376.

original condition.[3] Florensky's Commission report on "The Trinity–Sergius Lavra and Russia" was intended to draw further attention to what Florensky and his colleagues considered a national treasure, the Rublev icon.

A first—and unsuccessful—cleaning of the Trinity icon had taken place in 1904. Now, on November 26, 1918, Commission members invited a group of experts to conduct tests on the Trinity icon, as well as on other icons on the iconostasis in the Trinity Cathedral (some of which were also attributed to Rublev). In December, the experts removed the Trinity icon from the iconostasis, cleaned it, and studied it. Presumably, however, Commission members were nervous about what might happen to the icon if it remained for long apart from the iconostasis. On January 4, 1919, Florensky and others were present, as the icon was returned to its place in the cathedral.[4]

As these events were taking place, Florensky was already working on what would become his major work on iconography, *Iconostasis* (he would not complete it until 1922, after the Commission had been formally dissolved).[5] Originally, the piece would have been part of his treatise on the *Philosophy of the Cult*. A complementary essay is "Reverse Perspective," which Florensky prepared for the Commission at about the same time.[6]

As Florensky wrote, two tendencies in Orthodox believers' relation to icons were apparent. On the one hand, believers ascribed miracle-working properties to certain historic icons and made pilgrimage to them to pray for divine intervention and healing; interestingly, Rublev's Trinity icon, though glorified in the seventeenth century as miracle-working, was not as renowned as others

3. Irina Yazykova, *Hidden and Triumphant: The Underground Struggle to Save Russian Iconography*, trans. Paul Grenier (Brewster, MA: Paraclete Press, 2010), 45–46, 52.

4. Trubachev, "Prilozhenie: khronologiia," 381, 385, 389.

5. See Igumen Andronik Trubachev, "Primechaniia" [Notes], in Pavel Florenskii, *Istoriia i filosofiia iskusstva* [History and philosophy of art] (Moscow: Akademicheskii proekt, 2017), 550.

6. For an insightful analysis of this work, see Clemena Antonova, *Visual Thought in Russian Religious Philosophy: Pavel Florensky's Theory of the Icon* (New York: Routledge, 2019).

(such as the Kursk Root icon, featured in a famous 1883 painting by Iliia Repin).[7]

On the other hand, believers often regarded the "ordinary" icons in their homes as little more than decorative or illustrative pictures.[8] In earlier centuries, people had often acquired only two or three icons, each of which had special personal associations. Florensky speculates that Sergius had received his two icons from his parents, when they blessed him to become a monk.[9] As late as the second half of the nineteenth century, the young Lev Tolstoy had only three icons, each of which a close family member had given him.[10] Soon, however, workshops began mass production of icons; people could easily acquire them for private use and according to personal taste.

Florensky wants to recover a proper theological understanding of icons. He agrees that they have spiritual power, but in a different sense from "miracle-working." For him, they are essential aids to personal prayer, but not because of their emotional or aesthetic content. Icons are most at home in the context of the church's worship. It is in the liturgy that they most fully realize their function. There, they mediate the presence of the divine; they teach us, as does the liturgy as a whole, how to enter into God's life.

For Florensky, Rublev's Trinity icon connects us to St. Sergius and his vision of the Trinity; similarly, the icon of a particular saint opens us to the living reality of that saint and the saint's

7. Regarding its glorification, see Natalya Sheredega, "Andrei Rublev: Image of the Holy Trinity," *The Tretiakov Gallery Magazine* (2013), https://www.tretyakovgallerymagazine.com/articles/%E2%84%963-2013-40/andrei-rublev-image-holy-trinity.

8. Pavel Florenskii, "Ikonostas," in Pavel Florenskii, *Istoriia i filosofiia iskusstva* (Moscow: Akademicheskii proekt, 2017), 75. See Pavel Florensky, *Iconostasis*, trans. Donald Sheehan and Olga Andrejev (Crestwood, NY: St. Vladimir's Seminary Press, 1996), 134.

9. Pavel Florenskii, "Molennye ikony prepodobnogo Sergiia" [The prayer icons of St. Sergius], in Pavel Florenskii, *Istoriia i filosofiia iskusstva* (Moscow: Akademicheskii proekt, 2017), 149.

10. See Pavel Basinskii, *Sviatoi protiv L'va: Ioann Kronstadtskii i Lev Tol'stoi, istoriia odnoi vrazhdy* [The holy man versus the Lion: John of Kronstadt and Lev Tolstoy, the history of an enmity] (Moscow: ACT, 2016), 18–19.

continuing witness to God. As Florensky would write a few years later, an icon sets forth "not a thought or 'idea' conceived through the abstraction of a representation, but a spiritual reality, that spiritual essence which makes a saint himself, that power which forms his spiritual personality and organism, shines in his countenance, and is visible through the coverings of his body. The icon is, first of all, the energy of the saint's body and, secondly, that which the artist understands the saint's essence to be."[11]

Even the title of Florensky's treatise, *Iconostasis*, suggests key dimensions of his thinking. His interest is not limited to explicating the historical development or theological meaning of particular icons, such as Sergius's personal icons or Rublev's Trinity. Rather, he wishes to examine the special role that icons play on the iconostasis. What in early Christian churches began as a low barrier to keep the priests and the worshippers from bumping into each other during worship, became in fourteenth-century Russia a tall barrier reaching from floor to (high) ceiling, completely obscuring worshippers' sight of the murals or mosaics that fill the walls and ceiling of the altar area.

A general plan for ordering icons on the iconostasis evolved. Specific tiers (rows), five (or more), came to be devoted to particular kinds of saints. The top tier typically consists of renowned Old Testament prophets and kings. The tier below presents great saints of the Orthodox Church. The middle tier, known as the *deisis*, places Christ the Pantocrator (World Ruler) in the center; he is venerated at his right hand by Mary, and by John the Baptist, the Forerunner, at his left. Below the *deisis* are icons of the major church holy days. The bottom tier has central doors (called the "royal doors"), on which the Annunciation and the Gospel writers are depicted, and two side doors, on which angels or deacons appear. To the left of the royal doors (as worshippers face them)

11. Pavel Florensky, *At the Crossroads of Science and Mysticism*, trans. Boris Jakim (Kettering, OH: Semantron Press, 2014), 140.

is an icon of Mary the Mother of God holding the Christ child; to the right, an icon of the risen Christ as the Pantocrator, usually holding an open Gospels book. The first icon to the right of Christ (again, from the worshipper's point of view) is often the "local icon," which honors the saint or holy event after which the church is named. During the Divine Liturgy, the central and side doors open or close at particular moments, as the clergy go in and out of the altar area.[12]

Some historians believe that the first church to have a tall, multistoried iconostasis was the Trinity Cathedral in the Holy Trinity–St. Sergius Lavra.[13] Its iconostasis follows the general plan that we have described, with several exceptions—for example, the local icon, Rublev's Trinity, rather than the Pantocrator, is to the immediate right of the royal doors. On the right side of the iconostasis as a whole is the reliquary with St. Sergius's body. To this day, it is the practice of the monks to end evening prayer, as did Florensky and his fellow seminarians, by chanting a hymn to Sergius and going up individually to the reliquary, prostrating themselves, and venerating the relics by kissing the glass plate above the saint's head, which is wrapped in liturgical cloths.

Understanding *Iconostasis*

Florensky's writing style makes much of *Iconostasis* difficult to follow. His sentences are long and grammatically complex; his English translators suggest that he wanted his words to be like icons, which both reveal and hide truth.[14] As likely, he deliberately used poetically and philosophically rich and evocative language in order to contrast his thinking with that of the

12. See Leonid Ouspensky, "The Iconostasis" and "The Holy or Royal Door," in *The Meaning of Icons*, ed. Leonid Ouspensky and Vladimir Lossky (Crestwood, NY: St. Vladimir's Seminary Press, 1989), 59–69.

13. Trubachev, "Primechaniia," 537 n. 102.

14. Donald Sheehan, "Introduction," in Pavel Florensky, *Iconostasis* (Crestwood, NY: St. Vladimir's Seminary Press, 1996), 3.

scientific, mechanistic, and positivistic language that he saw infecting Russian society, as in the revolutionary propaganda of that time.

The fact that *Iconostasis* was written in stages may contribute to its unevenness. It is repetitive, and sometimes Florensky makes sweeping generalizations that do not stand up to careful historical analysis. Nevertheless, the essay brilliantly synthesizes insights about Orthodox iconography that Russian scholars of that day were developing, and the essay remains a landmark study to which scholars continue to refer. Indeed, Florensky's work has generally shaped the way Orthodox believers today understand icons and the iconostasis.

Iconostasis has four major sections. Florensky begins with reflections on sleep and dreams. The second section explicates what he takes to be an Orthodox understanding of icons and the iconostasis. The third (and longest) section is structured as a dialogue between the author and an interlocutor; here Florensky draws contrasts between Orthodox iconography and Western art. The last section draws parallels between Orthodox iconography and ancient Egyptian masks. In what follows, I will explicate Florensky's train of thought and relate it to the worldview that he develops more fully elsewhere.

Dreams Florensky opens his treatise with a reference to the first verse of the Bible—God created the heavens and the earth—and then adds words from the opening line of the Nicene-Constantinopolitan Creed, recited in every Orthodox liturgy, "Maker of all things visible and invisible." The theme of two worlds, central to his thinking in *Pillar and Foundation*, also becomes a leitmotif of *Iconostasis*. Florensky turns to the phenomenon of sleep, because it represents to him a preliminary stage of moving from the sphere of visible reality to that of the invisible, spiritual world.

Of particular interest to Florensky are dreams, because they seem to combine, yet rearrange, impressions from waking life. Perhaps, he says, you are dreaming about a man climbing a church tower to ring the bells; you hear the bells, only to wake up and discover that your alarm clock is ringing. In another dream, you are sitting in a winter sled, and when the horses start up, their bells jingle. You wake up, again to discover that your alarm clock is ringing. Or you dream about a waitress carrying a pile of dishes. You warn her that they are about to come crashing down; a minute later, you hear them breaking on the floor—and again you wake up to your alarm clock. In each instance, a future occurrence in everyday (what Florensky calls "Kantian") time (the ringing alarm clock) sets in motion a sequence of events that lead up to it. Time has been reversed, turned "inside out." The future has determined the past.

Florensky examines one more scenario. A man dreams that he participated in the French Revolution, was arrested, and was sentenced to die by the guillotine. He awakens from his dream just as the blade falls, only to discover that an iron spring from the bed is poking into his neck. The iron spring, concludes Florensky, has been symbolized in the dream by the guillotine. The blade in the dream has represented an event (the poky spring) in "this world."

From this example, Florensky argues that dream symbolism moves in two directions. Early in the night, he says, our dreams are still mostly working with impressions from the day. As with the man and the iron bedspring, our dreams create symbols for these earthly impressions. In contrast, early in the morning, right before we wake up, things from this world become symbols for spiritual realities ("ideas," in the Platonic sense) that we have glimpsed in our sleep (like the man's dream of ringing bells, which turn out to have been his alarm clock). Here, Florensky does not give a concrete example, but we can suggest one: a good person about whom we dream is actually a symbol of the pure goodness that is God alone.

What dreams teach us, Florensky concludes, is that an "other," invisible world exists next to our ordinary, visible world. At the boundary of these two worlds (in what today we sometimes call "liminal" spaces), time no longer flows in a linear direction; symbols appear that mediate between the two worlds.

Florensky sees human creativity, like dreams, operating in this liminal space. The proper calling of the artist is to create symbols that draw us out of this world into that other reality. However, human creativity easily goes awry. Here, Florensky explicates the Orthodox understanding of "seduction" or "charm." We sinfully latch on to images generated by our imagination that divert us from, rather than direct us to, God. We create our own picture of what is good and lovely; we elevate things of this world to ideals that we worship. "Ordinary" sin is checked by reality (the robber is confronted by the police; the liar is refuted by the truth-teller), but "seduction" and "charm" are less easily corrected. They close us in upon ourselves. We live in a fantasy world shut off from reality.

Florensky sees much of Western art as succumbing to this temptation. Things of this world are projected into an imaginary space, as though they were realities that could be understood on their own terms (what Florensky calls "naturalism"), without reference to God. In contrast, Orthodox iconography crystallizes spiritual realities into symbols that draw the viewer into the spiritual world.

Icons and the Iconostasis As we have noted, Florensky in his childhood was fascinated with natural phenomena that seem to lie on the boundary between two modes of existence. Water plants exhibit characteristics of both fluidity and solidity; tunnels lead a person from one space to another. Likewise, he was fascinated by moments in which natural phenomena become "revelations" of the mystery at the heart of all existence. Like dreams, the natural world can draw a person into another dimension of time and space.

As we have also noted, no less important for shaping Florensky's worldview was his relationship with Fr. Isidore. In Fr. Isidore, Florensky experienced how not only natural phenomena but also certain human beings live at the boundary of the two worlds. This kind of holy man, like the church's canonized saints, is able to see the love and glory of God in every created thing and to reflect that love and glory back to those things and to God. The holy man has spiritual freedom; he knows that he belongs wholly to God. Someone such as Fr. Isidore allows nothing and no one to divert him from God's presence.

Behind Florensky's understanding of the holy man lies a particular theological anthropology. As in *Pillar and Ground*, Florensky argues here that humans have been created in both the "image" and the "likeness" of God. The "image" is an ontological reality that we cannot lose; we bear the image of God, no matter what we do with our lives. The "likeness" is our empirical person, which we shape by living either in correspondence, or in contradiction, to the "image."

In making these distinctions, Florensky, again as in *Pillar and Ground*, plays with different but related words in the Russian language for "face." The ordinary word for a person's face is *litso*; for Florensky, *litso* designates the "empirical" face that we present to the world around us, the face that "reveals" who we are. Our personality, by which we relate to that world, is our *lichnost'*. When our *lichnost'* develops our *litso* to align with the image of God that we bear, we become a *lik*, a face that is transparent to the glorious light of God, as was Christ's on the Mount of Transfiguration. If our *lichnost'* falls into sin, our *litso* is distorted and darkened. It becomes a mere *lichina*, a mask that hides our inner emptiness from others. What Kant takes to be our natural human condition—our inability to rise above the phenomenal to the noumenal—is for Florensky the mark of our fall into sin. The saints and holy elders, such as Fr. Isidore, have a *lik*, whereas when Florensky the young seminarian had fallen into despair and decadence, he had become a mere *lichina*.

Further reflecting on the *lik*, which shines with light, Florensky refers to Matthew 5:16, "Let your light so shine before men, that they may see your good works and give glory to your Father who is in heaven." Florensky argues against understanding this verse as a mere moralistic demand, as had Tolstoy. The spiritual warrior (*podvizhnik*)—the ascetic, the saint—may do good works but, more importantly, the *podvizhnik* points beyond himself to God. In doing so, his entire self is transformed and becomes beautiful—again, not because of its moral achievements but rather because it has become a witness to God by becoming transparent to God. Florensky notes that when the first Christian martyr Stephen met angry resistance to his declaration of what God had done in Jesus Christ, "his face was like the face of an angel" (Acts 6:15)—and so, too, has been the face of other spiritual warriors up to the present day. In this regard, as in *Pillar and Ground*, Florensky is influenced by Palamas and hesychasm, and by the account of St. Seraphim of Sarov's transfiguration into sheer light.

Florensky believes that the church and its liturgy, not admirable moral deeds (contra Tolstoy), are the principal means by which we become aware of God's presence with us and enter into his life. The very arrangement of an Orthodox church is a "Jacob's ladder," "a means of heavenly ascent."[15] The nave represents the visible world; the altar area behind the iconostasis, the invisible, heavenly realm. Each space retains its symbolic integrity only insofar as it is clearly separated from the other; to have no partition between them would reduce the altar area to just another part of the visible world.

However, this partition, the iconostasis, not only separates the two spaces but also mediates between them. It both hides and reveals the spiritual mysteries that belong to the altar area.

15. Florenskii, "Ikonostas," 26. See Florensky, *Iconostasis*, 59.

An iconostasis is like our dream life; it straddles the boundary between the two worlds. It leads us from an ordinary state of consciousness into a higher; conversely, that higher state of consciousness penetrates into our ordinary. An iconostasis opens us to invisible, spiritual realities; it draws us into God's mystery.

This mediation occurs, again as in our dream life, through symbols. In the case of icons, the symbols are the saints, each of whom has an angelic face (*lik*) that looks at both earth and heaven—using Platonic language, Florensky also calls them living "ideas" of spiritual realities. Were our spiritual vision strong enough, the Mother of God and Christ, as living, spiritual presences, would suffice to mediate for us between the two worlds. However, because we are spiritually weak, we need an additional aid: a material iconostasis. The iconostasis "punches a window" into the spiritual world and its hierarchy of witnesses.[16] Its tiers of icons—again, like a ladder—witness to the saints, who, in turn, witness to the Theotokos and her Son, the resurrected Christ. Material icons do not replace the holy people whom they represent; rather, icons draw us into their living presence, and these saints draw us into the very life of God as Trinity: Father, Son, and Holy Spirit.

As symbols, icons are "revelations." They are inseparable from what they reveal.[17] They are "ontologically" related to the "First Form" (in Platonism, the "idea") that they represent.[18] Florensky compares them to a window. When light streams through a window, the window itself becomes light. It is no longer mere glass within a wooden frame. So, too, an icon, when it leads us into the spiritual realm, is more than a wooden board with colors on it. The icon makes witness to a saint, one in whose personality (*lichnost'*) shines forth the very "Name" of God. Because, for Florensky,

16. Florenskii, "Ikonostas," 28. See Florensky, *Iconostasis*, 63.

17. Florenskii, "Ikonostas," 29. See Florensky, *Iconostasis*, 65. See also Paul Tillich, *Theology of Culture* (New York: Oxford University Press, 1959), 53–67. For Tillich, as for Florensky, a symbol participates in the reality to which it points.

18. Florenskii, "Ikonostas," 33. See Florensky, *Iconostasis*, 69.

names, too, are revelatory, opening us to a deeper dimension of reality, the Name of God takes us yet another "rung" up a ladder toward God himself, whose energies we experience and whose essence is revealed to us, yet who exceeds our understanding and cannot be reduced to his Name.

The God toward whom we ascend is also the God who descends toward us. Like a window or a ladder (or a "door," says Florensky), an icon is two-way. From one side, we pass through it into the spiritual realm; from the other, spiritual realities flow into our material, sensual world.[19] Florensky therefore concludes that the icon offers "proof" of the existence of God: "If there is the Rublev Trinity, then there is God."[20] We can also translate Florensky's phrase as, "The Rublev Trinity exists, therefore God exists."

Florensky insists that the iconographer serves the church, which alone is the "pillar and ground of the truth." The church has established and preserved the canonical forms that orient the iconographer. Even an icon of "lesser" quality witnesses to the spiritual world, if it faithfully preserves the church's iconographic traditions.[21] Similarly, a faithful copy of a "revelatory" icon has the same spiritual content as the original.[22]

Rather than constraining the iconographer, the church's canonical forms free the iconographer to seek the truth and even to create new forms that penetrate even more deeply into the truth.[23] Rublev's Trinity is again exemplary. Born out of St. Sergius's distinctive insight into the heavenly mysteries of Father, Son, and Holy Spirit, Rublev's icon departed from traditional iconographic depictions of the biblical motif of the three angels visiting Abraham and Sarah. The church nevertheless affirmed that his

19. Florenskii, "Ikonostas," 34. See Florensky, *Iconostasis*, 71.
20. Florenskii, "Ikonostas," 31. See Florensky, *Iconostasis*, 68.
21. Florenskii, "Ikonostas," 34. See Florensky, *Iconostasis*, 72–73.
22. Florenskii, "Ikonostas," 35. See Florensky, *Iconostasis*, 74.
23. Florenskii, "Ikonostas," 40. See Florensky, *Iconostasis*, 81.

icon complemented, rather than contradicted, existing iconographic and dogmatic canons.

The icon's double movement means that there is a revelation from outside ourselves—the world as it is in God—as well as a revelation from within ourselves—our true identity before God.[24] Drawing again on Platonic thinking, Florensky asserts that the icon helps us "remember" ourselves. It awakens us to the self that God made us to be. The icon becomes a window into our innermost being as the image of God.

Indeed, the icon reveals the fundamental truth of all human reality. Insofar as an icon is "canonical," it is "ecclesiastical." Insofar as it is "ecclesiastical," it is "conciliar." Insofar as it is "conciliar," it is "universally human."[25] Those icons that most fully realize the spiritual vision of the great ascetics utilize simple earthly forms—such as fathers and sons, seed and grain, or bread and wine—whose meaning is universally recognizable.[26]

To illustrate his point, Florensky refers to the icon of the Mother of God, "The Multiplier of Loaves" (more literally, "The Bread Winner"). During a time of famine in the late nineteenth century, the great holy elder of Optina Pustyn', Amvrosii, had a vision in which the Mother of God appeared in the sky and blessed a field of wheat below her. Afterward, Amvrosii commissioned an icon of the revelation.[27] Florensky criticizes the iconographer for an overly naturalistic style. Nevertheless, says Florensky, the icon succeeds in depicting the Mother of God as the "earth goddess," a motif in every human culture. "The Multiplier of Loaves" especially resembles Demeter, the Greek goddess of agriculture, in whom, asserts Florensky, the Greeks anticipated the Christian Mother of God.[28]

24. Florenskii, "Ikonostas," 42. See Florensky, *Iconostasis*, 85.
25. Florenskii, "Ikonostas," 43. See Florensky, *Iconostasis*, 87.
26. Florenskii, "Ikonostas," 43. See Florensky, *Iconostasis*, 87.
27. Florenskii, "Ikonostas," 43, 535 n. 91. See Florensky, *Iconostasis*, 87.
28. Florenskii, "Ikonostas," 43–44. See Florensky, *Iconostasis*, 88.

That icons emerge out of the life of the church is further evident for Florensky in the Orthodox practice of "naming" them. An icon becomes an icon not when the iconographer has completed painting it, but rather only after the church recognizes that it corresponds faithfully to its "First Form." The bishop then blesses the iconographer to write the name of the icon on its backside (in contrast to Western artists who complete a painting by signing their name on the front).[29] Once again, we see the importance of names in Florensky's thinking.

As a servant of the church, the iconographer prays while painting. Because the prayers of iconographers were especially intense during the Russian Middle Ages, when all life revolved around the Eucharist, Florensky believes that their witness to heavenly beauty was more Spirit-filled than that of later iconography.[30] An icon such as Rublev's Trinity has most fully directed Russian believers—today, too—to God's energies, as they permeate the land and people of Rus'. We can understand why Florensky and his colleagues so desperately wished to protect the Lavra, the relics of St. Sergius, and Rublev's Trinity icon. These treasures were, indeed, the very heart of Russia, and to lose them would be to lose Russia itself.

In sum, for Florensky, Christianity collects the greatest spiritual insights of all the ages and brings them to their fullest expression, as when one of the church's holy people is granted deeper vision into the spiritual realities and truths revealed in Christ, the Mother of God, or the Trinity. Guided by the church's canons, the iconographer depicts simple material forms in such a way that they point beyond themselves to these spiritual realities and truths. The forms become symbols, and the icon becomes a window that mediates between the spiritual and material realms. By means of this window, we look toward God, and God looks toward us. We see

29. Florenskii, "Ikonostas," 47. See Florensky, *Iconostasis*, 91.
30. Florenskii, "Ikonostas," 51. See Florensky, *Iconostasis*, 98.

ourselves and the world around us as filled with divine energies. Every person, every created thing, becomes an icon of God's glory.

Dialogue about Orthodox Iconography and Western Art Florensky composed this section of *Iconostasis* several years prior to the others and then integrated it into the larger treatise. Originally entitled "Platonism and Iconography," it differs in style from the other three sections by taking the form a dialogue between the author and an interlocutor. Like a Socratic dialogue, the interlocutor sets up the author to make his points. Florensky's basic thesis is that the art of the (Orthodox) East and that of the (Catholic, Protestant) West reflect contrasting mentalities and metaphysical foundations.

Florensky argues that an artist's very choice of materials has spiritual significance. At the time of the European Renaissance, oil paints applied to a stretched canvas became the principal materials for painting. The rich colors and the flexible, pliable surface gave the artist the freedom to depict earthly sensuality and luxuriousness, which Florensky regards as typical of Catholic art.[31] In contrast, the Protestant Reformation favored engravings. Black and white lines on fragile paper reflect a logical rationality (*rassudok*), a dialectic of assertion and negation. An imaginary rationalistic scheme, as in Hegel's logic of history, was imposed on reality.[32] Both artistic approaches, Catholic and Protestant, seem to regard the artist as an individual with creative genius.

In contrast, Eastern iconography uses a hard surface, either a church wall or a specially prepared wooden board, from which all accidental properties have been removed. The goal is to express the unchanging essence of the spiritual world, in which sin and death are no more. Florensky repeats that icons are symbolic and revelatory. One cannot understand them by reducing their subject

31. Florenskii, "Ikonostas," 54–55. See Florensky, *Iconostasis*, 102–5.

32. Florenskii, "Ikonostas," 56–61. See Florensky, *Iconostasis*, 106–13.

matter to something "naturalistic," "decorative," or "earthly." Rather, an icon reflects and points to the heavenly world.[33]

In "Reverse Perspective," Florensky contrasts Western art and Orthodox iconography in yet another way. The Enlightenment West has insisted on the use of "natural" perspective in painting. Parallel lines should come closer to each other as they approach the horizon. Florensky argues that this kind of "perspective" rests on the Euclidian assumption that space is consistent and unchanging. The artist asserts both a privileged point of view and a right to organize space as he wishes. The artist depicts reality as though photographing it.

For Florensky, in contrast, Western perspective is hardly "natural." It is not the way children draw, and, historically, there have been other ways of organizing space, as in ancient Egyptian art or in Western art prior to the Renaissance. Even great Western artists since the Renaissance have not used it consistently. And recent mathematics (as Florensky knew from his mathematics professor, Bugaev) had explored non-Euclidian geometry and noncontinuous space. The "reverse perspective" of the iconographer is not simply a matter of how spatial relations are organized. Iconographic perspective opens us to a different reality—a "third," spiritual dimension—beyond the "two-dimensionality" of the Western artist. Western perspective is "abstract." It misses the concrete phenomenon that is constantly changing and revealing different sides of itself to us.[34]

However, if the church's spiritual condition is unhealthy, its iconography will be distorted, as in the iconography that began to predominate in Russia from the late sixteenth century on (and in French and Italian religious art of that era).[35] A healthy Church

33. Florenskii, "Ikonostas," 61–63. See Florensky, *Iconostasis*, 113–16.

34. Pavel Florenskii, "Obratnaia perspektiva," in Pavel Florenskii, *Istoriia i filosofiia iskusstva* (Moscow: Akademicheskii proekt, 2017), 208–25. See Pavel Florensky, "Reverse Perspective," in Pavel Florensky, *Beyond Vision: Essays on the Perception of Art*, ed. Nicoletta Misler, trans. Wendy Salmond (London: Reaktion Books, 2002), 246–72.

35. Florenskii, "Ikonostas," 42, 63–66. See Florensky, *Iconostasis*, 85–86, 117–20. The

affirms canonical iconography instead. Of particular importance is differentiation of the *lichnoe* (what belongs to the face) and the *dolichnoe* (what surrounds the face, such as the body with its clothing, the buildings, and the natural landscape). As Florensky noted earlier in the treatise, the iconographer seeks to depict the face, *litso*, as the *lik*, the image of God cleansed of sin and earthly decay. The *lik* secondarily includes the hands and the feet. The *dolichnoe* situates the *lik* and its divine light in the visible, material world. In a canonical icon, the *lichnoe* and the *dolichnoe* are in harmony, although the focus is on the *lik*.[36] Interestingly, Florensky's discussion reflects actual Orthodox practice. When worshippers venerate an icon, they kiss the figure's hands and the feet (though not the face) where they protrude from the garments (the *dolichnoe*).

Florensky asserts that Western art since the Renaissance has set humans and the creation in opposition to each other. The result is the painting either of pure landscapes or of pure portraits, with the latter becoming increasingly "abstract," insofar as they express the emotional character rather than the spiritual essence of an individual.[37]

Perhaps the most important contrast between Western art and Eastern iconography is in the use of light. Some Western artists depict objects as illuminated from a source outside the painting. Shadows and darkness help to individualize forms. This approach, according to Florensky, is "rationalistic." For other Western painters, such as Rembrandt, light emanates out of a primordial darkness, an approach that Florensky associates with Jakob Böhme's pantheism.[38] In contrast, the iconographer depicts things and people as radiating light. They have a light from beyond themselves that shines through them: "The iconographer regards light not as something external in relation to things, nor as a self-existing

English translation omits Florensky's remarks about the decay of Russian iconography after the Petrine reforms.

36. Florenskii, "Ikonostas," 76. See Florensky, *Iconostasis*, 135.

37. Florenskii, "Ikonostas," 76. See Florensky, *Iconostasis*, 136.

38. Florenskii, "Ikonostas," 84. See Florensky, *Iconostasis*, 149.

property of a thing. For the iconographer, light sets forth and creates things. As their objective cause, it cannot be understood in relation to them as something merely external. Rather, it is their transcendental, creative beginning, manifesting itself through them but by no means exhausting itself in them."[39]

The Western artist moves from light to darkness (or shadows), whereas the iconographer moves from darkness (shadows)—the unprepared board or wall—to light. The iconographer's figures emerge into reality insofar as they begin to light up. This light sets forth life over and against the darkness of nonexistence.[40] Florensky therefore asserts that iconography is nothing less than a "metaphysics of light."[41]

In this regard, the use of gold is essential. Gold, says Florensky, is pure light. Strictly speaking, it has no color. The first thing that the iconographer applies to the prepared board is gold leaf. It is the background out of which the figures emerge, and it washes them with the divine energies.[42] The gold that remains visible behind the figures represents the sky, which, says Florensky, is not blue, but rather, like gold, pure light.[43] The last thing that the iconographer applies to the icon is gold along the folds of the figures' clothing (*razdelka*). For Florensky, these gold lines represent God's unseen energy penetrating the visible world, just as an unseen magnet exerts power over a nearby line of iron filings.[44] "The gold light of unconditioned being," he asserts, "surrounds the emerging silhouettes, manifests them, and allows what is abstract to be transformed into what is concrete and filled with potency."[45]

Florensky concludes that Platonism and Christianity agree that light, being, and God are a unity. For Florensky, Ephesians 5:13—

39. Florenskii, "Ikonostas," 85; See Florensky, *Iconostasis*, 150.
40. Florenskii, "Ikonostas," 81–82. See Florensky, *Iconostasis*, 144–45.
41. Florenskii, "Ikonostas," 86. See Florensky, *Iconostasis*, 153.
42. Florenskii, "Ikonostas," 76–77. See Florensky, *Iconostasis*, 138.
43. Florenskii, "Ikonostas," 69. See Florensky, *Iconostasis*, 125–26.
44. Florenskii, "Ikonostas," 70. See Florensky, *Iconostasis*, 127.
45. Florenskii, "Ikonostas," 77. See Florensky, *Iconostasis*, 138.

"when anything is exposed by the light, it becomes visible, for anything that becomes visible is light"—means, "Everything that appears [we can also translate, "reveals itself"], or, to put it differently, the content of every experience, that is, of every existent thing, is light."[46] Things exist only as they exist in God, who is light. In bringing figures out of light and into light, the iconographer imitates God, who calls a people into existence (Eph. 1:4) and names them "children of light" (Eph. 5:8). Ephesians "witnesses to the ontological reality of another world, which the Apostle has seen with his own eyes. He wants his witness to be the seed that brings forth the same way of seeing" among the faithful, whom he is addressing.[47]

Ultimately, Western (Catholic and Protestant) and Eastern (Orthodox) artistic approaches represent two contrasting metaphysics and worldviews. For the Enlightenment West, reality is self-sufficient, closed in upon itself, whereas Orthodoxy sees it as God's creation and therefore as transparent to God.[48] Western metaphysics is "abstract"; it tries to understand the world by imposing human-created categories upon it. In contrast, Orthodoxy has a "concrete metaphysics." Says Florensky, "The Church denies spiritual meaning to thinking that does not base itself on something concrete in experience. The Church asserts the metaphysical character of life and the living character of the metaphysical."[49]

Here, we again see the Aristotelian twist to Florensky's Platonism. The Platonic "idea" is simultaneously Aristotle's concrete "form." Iconography penetrates to the inner, spiritual reality of the holy ones whose forms it depicts, and in seeing those forms, we ourselves are transformed. Their light shines into us, and we discover the light that is already in us by virtue of our being the image of God that reflects his light.

46. Florenskii, "Ikonostas," 87. See Florensky, *Iconostasis*, 154–55.
47. Florenskii, "Ikonostas," 91. See Florensky, *Iconostasis*, 159.
48. Florenskii, "Ikonostas," 82. See Florensky, *Iconostasis*, 146.
49. Florenskii, "Ikonostas," 85. See Florensky, *Iconostasis*, 151–52.

Egyptian Masks The last section of *Iconostasis* functions as an addendum that nicely demonstrates Florensky's interest in antiquity as a source of spiritual insight. Florensky notes that Christianity has typically regarded the Egyptian mask as a *lichina* (the face of the fallen, sinful human). It is part of a pagan cult. However, Florensky believes that the Egyptian mask should be understood differently. For him, it realizes genuine spiritual insights that Orthodox iconography does not reject but rather purifies and perfects.

The portrait placed over a mummy divinizes the deceased by representing him in his ideal humanity. Similarly, in Christianity, the church venerates deceased saints, their pictures, and their remains, over which it has celebrated the Eucharist since the first centuries. Egyptian masks and Christian icons alike seek to reveal the spiritual essence of the deceased person, to depict the person's *lik*.[50]

Iconography Today

Today, one can easily purchase a high-quality reproduction of Rublev's Trinity icon right off the internet. Icons are everywhere. Catholics and Protestants are increasingly fascinated by icons; they now hang not only in their homes but also in some of their churches. Whether aware of Florensky's thinking or not, many people sense something intriguingly "spiritual" or "otherworldly" about an icon.

In *Iconostasis*, Florensky acknowledges that such massive proliferation of icons represents a theological truth: God's holiness seeps into every corner of everyday life.[51] But if he is right that artistic materials and methods reflect metaphysical foundations and worldviews, mass production and sale of icons inevitably reflect the dominant consumerist mindset of contemporary society.

50. Florenskii, "Ikonostas," 93–94. See Florensky, *Iconostasis*, 161–63.
51. Florenskii, "Ikonostas," 75. See Florensky, *Iconostasis*, 134.

Florensky may seem excessively elitist. After all, an Orthodox believer—or, for that matter, a Catholic, a Protestant, or even a vaguely "spiritual" person—may treasure and venerate even a printed, paper icon. One might argue that if the icon is canonical, it still communicates something of that other, divine world that Rublev glimpsed. But Florensky insists that icons are most fully themselves in Orthodox churches and worship. They belong within a liturgical complex of prayer, hymnody, and feast and fast days.

Florensky idealizes the Russian Middle Ages and hopes to recover their intense realization of this liturgical network. Today, however, Orthodox life no longer permeates even traditionally Orthodox societies. Few Orthodox inhabit a "holy world" for more than a couple of hours each week. One of Russia's most renowned contemporary iconographers, Fr. Zinon (Teodor), therefore contends that in our situation less may be more.[52] If the church is to cultivate an alternative ethos to the dominant consumer culture in which it finds itself, its iconographers may, paradoxically, need to become a bit more iconoclastic.

This kind of iconography would simplify and focus its subject matter for our time, as Rublev did for his. A church with two icons—Christ the World Ruler and Mary the Mother of God—may better open a window into the spiritual world than a church covered from floor to ceiling with dozens of saints and festal events that simply call attention to themselves, rather than pointing beyond themselves.

Or is that putting things backward? Perhaps iconography will make sense again only when Christians recover the sacramental view of all creation that Florensky himself so deeply experienced.

52. See Arkhimandrit Zinon (Teodor), *Besedy ikonopistsa* [Conversations with an iconographer] (St. Petersburg: Bibliopolis, 2017), 116. For an English-language introduction to Zinon's thinking and iconography, see Yazykova, *Hidden and Triumphant*, 132–40. See also John P. Burgess, "A Visit to Fr. Zinon," *First Things* (January 2024): 47–52; and John P. Burgess, "Iconography as Alternative Social-Religious Vision: Fr. Zinon (Teodor)," *Orthodox Arts Journal* (February 14, 2024), https://orthodoxartsjournal.org/iconography-as-alternative-social-religious-vision-fr-zinon-teodor/.

In the disenchanted world that we have inherited, sacramentality may seem, at most, an isolated moment that we encounter in certain ritual actions, such as the Eucharist. For most Christians, church and world are two separate spheres of existence, sealed off from each other, each with its own rules and coordinates.

Nevertheless, standing quietly before Rublev's Trinity icon on that cold December day—in a secular museum, not even a church—I sensed that it still has power to awaken us to that "other, third dimension" that inheres in all reality. To be sure, when I walked back into the "real" world, the vision quickly faded. But I have not forgotten. I have not forgotten the possibility of seeing something more.

9

THE GULAG

"Nothing passes away entirely, nothing gets lost. . . .
What is of value lives on."

In the early fifteenth century, two intrepid monks—German and Savvatii—sailed across Russia's treacherous White Sea to Solovki, only sixty miles south of the Arctic Circle, to live as hermits on the uninhabited island.[1] A few years later, Savvatii died, but another monk, Zosima, joined German. They soon attracted other monks, and the community began to grow into one of the church's major monasteries.

At the tsar's command, thick, high walls composed of huge boulders were constructed around the complex at the end of the sixteenth century, to protect it from foreign invaders, and to assert Russian imperial control of these far northern, sometimes disputed territories. In the seventeenth century, the word "Solovki" acquired a new association, when its monks rebelled against the

1. For a history, beautifully written, of the island, see Roy R. Robson, *Solovki* (New Haven, CT: Yale University Press, 2004).

liturgical reforms that Patriarch Nikon introduced. They were driven from the island and had to go underground on the mainland with those other "dissidents" who would become known as the Old Believers.

In the 1920s, the Bolsheviks dissolved the monastery and turned the complex into one of their first labor camps, where they tested out methods of prison administration and punishment that would serve as models for the gulag as a whole. In 1939, however, the Soviet authorities abruptly closed the camp and transferred the last prisoners to the mainland. A few workers—guards, cooks, repairmen, and fishermen—and their families remained behind. The monastery buildings were stripped down—leaving only their lathes and floorboards within—and were abandoned.

In the late Soviet period, historians and archaeologists rediscovered the island and began working to conserve the area and restore the monastery complex. In the 1990s, after the fall of communism, the church regained access to the site, and a monastic community reestablished itself. Today, the monastery churches have been restored to their former glory, and tens of thousands of pilgrims and tourists make their way there annually.

In the summer of 2006, I was among them. Fr. Evlogii, abbot of a skete on the island of Anzer, across from the main island, had invited me to visit. The journey entailed a twenty-four-hour train trip from Moscow and an overnight boat ride from the town of Kem' to Anzer. The island's vast silence, the sky's ever-changing play of thick clouds and intense sunshine, and the natural world's sheer rawness immediately awed me. Here were thick pine forests and swamps, but no cars or machinery, and if there were birds or animals, they had managed to hide themselves.

On a hilltop known as Golgotha stands a small church dedicated to Christ's crucifixion. At the base of the hill is the Church of Christ's Resurrection. During the 1930s, both churches had served as holding pens for prisoners with typhoid. The men had slept on the bare wooden floor and were so crowded together that

Figure 9.1. Solovki / Public domain. Wikimedia Commons. Photo by Aleksandr Baidukov, Creative Commons Attribution-Share Alike 4.0 International license.

they could not roll over. When monks returned in the 1990s, there were still bloodstains in the planks. Now, for seven days, I regularly gathered here with Fr. Evlogii, three other monks, and their several helpers. Our prayers sometimes lasted all the way through the "white nights" of that July.

One afternoon, Fr. Evlogii led me to a birch tree on the side of Golgotha. During the years of Soviet persecution, the tree had grown into the shape of a cross. We paused before it in silent veneration. Like an icon or a relic, it was transparent to God, the God who had never abandoned the island or his suffering people.

All too soon, it was time for me to take a boat to the main island, where I would stay for a few days before returning to Moscow. Fr. Evlogii and I had grown close; he had honored me by inviting me into his world. Now, I stumbled about, not quite sure how to say goodbye. But Fr. Evlogii knew what to do. He reached his arms out, hugged me tightly, lifted me off the ground, blessed me, and sent me on my way.

Enigmatic Last Years

Much about the last years of Florensky's life remains unclear. The details of his arrest and interrogation in 1933 are murky, and we have only fragmentary information about his physical, emotional, and spiritual well-being during the following four years in the gulag. Although Florensky was able to conduct extensive correspondence with his family, we cannot be sure when he is speaking in code, perhaps in order to protect himself or the family from political repercussions, and when he is accurately describing the camps and his personal condition.

As we have noted, Florensky had always been something of a curiosity to others. In his youthful correspondence with Rozanov, his boundless curiosity and impulsive nature had led him to speculate about Jewish blood sacrifice and ritualistic killings, and about the superiority of same-sex friendships to marriage and family. In his early adulthood, he had moved easily in disparate circles: among Bolshevists and monarchists, Orthodox priests and holy elders, avant-garde artists and iconographers, spiritualists and theosophists, and research scientists and technical experts. He made an odd impression in public, looking downward and a bit cross-eyed when he lectured, and his words were soft and almost indistinct, even while he radiated a charisma that attracted large audiences.

Florensky's religious philosophy was equally unusual. He believed that one arrives at the truth only by embracing pairs of antinomies, such as self-renunciation and self-discovery, outer form and inner reality, and the Trinity's oneness and threeness. But as Prince Evgenii Trubetskoi wrote in an analysis of *The Pillar and Ground of the Truth*, Florensky did not always clarify which antinomies were productive of truth, and which were genuine contradictions that demanded a decision for one of the opposing principles over the other.[2]

In all that he did, Florensky seemed driven by competing, sometimes opposing, principles: mystical apprehension of the world versus scientific observation of it; a naïve belief in luck and good fortune versus a religious faith that purified reason and committed it to truth; and a longing for a return to the Middle Ages versus a conviction that one had to live wholly in the present, rather than in a golden past or future. Indeed, these antinomies defined his thinking to the end. What is not always clear is where they opened him to God, and where they led him down dead ends.

In the last decade of his life, Florensky refused to abandon his priestly status, yet devoted his life entirely to scientific-technical work on behalf of the Bolshevist state. Upon his arrest in 1933, he confirmed that he was the chief ideologist of a counterrevolutionary, monarchist group—what was, in fact, a false confession from one who had once noted in his diary that any compromise of the truth just leads to new compromises.[3] The man who in *Philosophy of the Cult* had called for a society in which the tsar's centralized authority would be complemented and balanced by the church's conciliarity now composes for his interrogators a political tractate in which he extols Hitler and Mussolini and suggests that the Soviet Union needs a heroic leader whose authoritarian power exceeds even theirs.

Some commentators have been tempted to smooth out these contradictions. They argue that Florensky's thinking remains roughly consistent to the end. He holds to an organic vision of beauty, truth, and harmony that offers humans a vision of divine glory even in the midst of personal loss and social confusion.

2. Avril Pyman, *Pavel Florenksy: A Quiet Genius* (New York: Continuum, 2010), 250.

3. Natalino Valentini, *Pavel Florenskii* (Moscow: Bibleisko-bogoslovskii institut sv. apostola Andreia, 2015), 6–7. Valentini cites an entry from Florensky's diary from the early 1920s.

Other scholars question whether his thought really has any value at all. For them, his sparks of brilliance cannot hide what appears to be reactionary political and social positions.[4]

There is a third possibility. As we look at Florensky and especially at the last years of his life, it may be that we simply cannot come to firm conclusions about all of his intentions in his "confession" and prison correspondence. We may have to accept that disturbing questions remain. We can do only what Trubetskoi had asked of him: try to sort out where the antinomies of Florensky's life and thought help illuminate the truths to which he was committed, and where the antinomies pose genuinely irresolvable and even troubling contradictions.

Florensky's Arrest

Florensky's arrest in 1933 was not his first brush with the law. Already as a student at the Moscow Theological Academy, Florensky had incurred the government's wrath. It was a time of high political tension in the Russian Empire. Strikes and protests had forced Nicholas II in March 1905 to agree to political reforms that limited his power. Not all opposition figures felt, however, that he had gone far enough. In December, Lieutenant Petr Schmidt, a popular naval commander, led a mutiny of sailors belonging to the Black Sea fleet in Crimea. When Schmidt was put on trial, he offered an eloquent defense, but the court condemned him to death before a firing squad. Florensky preached a sermon at the Academy in which he lamented the shedding of blood and called for national repentance.

Many of the students and professors at the Academy were sympathetic to Florensky's position, and the sermon was soon published and distributed. However, tsarist officials were not impressed; Florensky was arrested and sentenced to three months in prison. Only the intervention of the rector won him freedom after

4. See my discussion in chapter 10.

a few days and the right to return to his studies at the Academy.

Florensky's second run-in with government authorities took place in 1928. As we have noted, antireligious propagandists had conducted a smear campaign against prominent cultural figures in Sergiev Posad, including those who like Florensky had tried to save the Lavra and its historic treasures. Florensky was accused of involvement in a counterrevolutionary plot to restore the monarchy and was sentenced to internal exile for three years. As before, however, prominent officials made interventions on his behalf, arguing that the state needed him for his scientific work. After three months, he was allowed to return to Moscow.

The third arrest, five years later, came as Stalin was increasingly resorting to terror to consolidate his power. Under pressure from government interrogators, a professor of canon law gave a detailed but imaginary account of a clandestine counterrevolutionary organization whose aim was, in the words of Florensky's English biographer, "to help Nazi Germany take over Moscow and ... establish a neo-Slavophile, anti-Semitic, crypto-monarchist government."[5] Moreover, the man accused Florensky, whom he did not even know personally, of serving as the organization's chief ideological propagandist.

We can only speculate as to why Florensky played along and admitted that he was guilty. Was he trying to save himself from unintentionally incriminating other, innocent figures? Did he hope that a quick resolution to the case would allow friends in high places to intervene on his behalf, as in 1906 and 1928? There is evidence that he was subjected to sleep deprivation and perhaps harsher measures—did he simply break under the psychological pressure?

When he was arrested in 1928, a photograph of Nicholas II had been among his personal possessions—now, in 1933, did he imagine to himself that he could have played the part of which he

5. Pyman, *Florensky*, 154.

was accused, even if the case itself had been fabricated?[6] According to an informant, Florensky later claimed that the authorities had arrested him prophylactically—that is, because he was indeed capable of that to which he had confessed.[7]

Also puzzling, as we have noted, is the political tractate that he wrote during the time of his interrogation.[8] This expansive, handwritten, ten-thousand-word manuscript, marred by torn edges and splotches of ink, remained in Florensky's KGB file until 1990, when the file was turned over to his family.[9] Entitled "A Proposal for the Construction of a Future Government," the tractate sketches out a utopian society in which centralized political control is perfectly integrated with decentralized cultural, educational, and economic activity. Florensky claims that such a political order would avoid the extremes of either bureaucratic absolutism or democratic anarchism. Citizens would reach their full creative potential, in large part because they would be shielded from politics. Management of government would be left to experts.

Such a government would be organized from above to below and would be headed by a man with remarkable powers of intuition. This leader would be able to anticipate what society needs in order to develop its powers, and would therefore know how to direct it. High intelligence would be less important than a powerful, creative will. Hitler and Mussolini represent only a preliminary stage of such leadership. In Florensky's words, we do not yet find in them "genuine creativity." A truly heroic leader will

> not be of human origin. Rather, he will deserve the name of that which is divine. Regardless of how we label such a creator of culture—

6. Vitalii Shentalinskii, "Khranit' vechno" [Preserve eternally], *Ogonek* 45 (November 1990): 23.

7. Sviashchennik Pavel Florenskii, *Vse Dumy—o Vas* [All my thoughts are about you] (St. Petersburg: Satis'/Derzhava, 2004), 142.

8. Pavel Florenskii, "Predpolagaemoe gosudarstvennoe ustroistvo v budushchem," in Pavel Florenskii, *Sochineniia v chetyrech tomakh* [Collected essays in four volumes], vol. 2, ed. Andronik Trubachev et al. (Moscow: Mysl', 1996), 647–81.

9. Pyman, *Florensky*, 157.

> dictator, ruler, emperor, or something else—we will regard him as one who is truly all-powerful (*samoderzhets*), and we will submit to him not out of fear but rather in strength, having the awed awareness that before us stands a miracle, a living revelation of the creative power of humanity.[10]

Some of these statements are consistent with the few points that Florensky makes elsewhere in his writings about politics.[11] Like other religious intellectuals of the time, he was suspicious of democracy and regarded strong, centralized government as an essential element of Russia's unique national identity.[12] Moreover, he agreed with many of his fellow Orthodox believers that political rulers are appointed by God; they are to be obeyed, whether one agrees with them or not, unless they ask you to renounce your faith.[13]

Nevertheless, Florensky's political "confession" leaves out major elements of his sacramental worldview. He makes no mention of the church as a counterweight to the ruler, nor does he discuss the church's practice of anointing the ruler, placing him beneath Christ's authority and thereby requiring the ruler to serve God and the people. Instead, Florensky calls for a temporary separation of church and state, foresees a collapse of the Orthodox Church, and anticipates the emergence of a new, vital, self-organizing religious movement that the government will value and protect.

10. Florenskii, "Predpolagaemoe gosudarstvennoe ustroistvo," 652. The term *samoderzhets* can also be translated as autocrat.

11. See Igumen Andronik Trubachev, "Filosofsko-politicheskie vzgliady sviashchennika Pavla Florenskogo" [The philosophical-religious views of the priest Pavel Florensky], in Igumen Andronik Trubachev, *Put' k Bogu: lichnost', zhizn' i tvorchestvo sviashchennika Pavla Florenskogo* [The way to God: the person, life, and work of the priest Pavel Florensky], vol. 4 (Sergiev Posad: Gorodets, 2016), 7–36.

12. See the discussion of the "Russian idea," in Arsenii Gulyga, *Tvortsy russkoi idei* [Makers of the Russian idea] (Moscow: Molodaia gvardiia, 2006).

13. See, for example, the protocol of Maria (Tseitlin), as cited in John P. Burgess, *Holy Rus': The Rebirth of Orthodoxy in the New Russia* (New Haven, CT: Yale University Press, 2017), 149: "As a believer, I understand every government to be from God." The allusion is to Romans 13:1: "For there is no authority except from God."

How are we to understand Florensky's intentions? Is it possible that he had truly renounced his Orthodox faith? Or is he using coded language? Has he composed a parody, issuing a hidden warning about Stalin and about what happens to political power when it is not subject to God or blessed by the church? Alternatively, did Florensky believe that he could give his interrogators what they wanted, while remaining "spiritually free" within himself?

Florensky seems trapped in contradictions from which he cannot extract himself. In his last professional years, he expressed no reservations about his scientific-technical work on behalf of the Bolshevik government, even though he must have been deeply troubled by its persecution of the church. His writings occasionally allude to the difficult political and social circumstances of the time but never rise to direct accusation of the regime. According to the informant to whom we referred earlier, Florensky went so far as to suggest that the Bolsheviks were making the same mistakes as the tsarist regime. Nevertheless, he never issues a public criticism of political conditions or even a call for national repentance, as he had in 1906.

Here, the antinomies that Florensky otherwise so embraces do not work together to point to the God to whom Florensky had given his life. The contradictions seem irresolvable. As careful a thinker as he could be in *Pillar and Ground* and *Philosophy of the Cult*, Florensky in his political thought leaves us with troubling questions about his enthusiastic glorification of autocracy and with few clear answers about what he really meant.

Journey to Solovki

Florensky received a ten-year sentence and was shipped by train with other prisoners to Russia's Far East. The trip took the entire month of September 1933. For the next two months, he lived at a camp called Ksenevskaia, beyond Lake Baikal. In late November, he was moved another seven hundred miles to the east, to a labor camp near the town of Svobodnyi. In February 1934, he was transferred three hundred miles to the north to Skovorodino, where he worked at a research station investigating the properties of permafrost.

Florensky threw himself into his work enthusiastically. The research interested him, and he felt confident that he could make new, significant discoveries. To his surprise and delight, a fellow exile to the research station was Nikolai Kapterev, an old friend from Sergiev Posad, who had served with him on the commission to save the Lavra. A high point for Florensky was a visit from his wife and their three youngest children from early July until mid-August. But just as the family began the arduous journey back to Sergiev Posad, the authorities ordered Florensky to return to Svobodnyi and then shipped him back across the continent, from east to west and from south to north, to the infamous labor camp on Solovetskii Island, a trip of nearly five thousand miles.

Here, Florensky would spend the last three years of his life, constantly being transferred from one place on the island to another, sometimes living in relative peace and quiet but at other times crowded together with other prisoners. His work assignments varied, but some, to his delight, drew on his scientific skills. Much of the time, he worked for a factory on the island that extracted iodine from seaweed.

From the time of his sentencing until a few weeks before his death, Florensky was able to carry on regular correspondence with his family. Family members could write to him as often as they wished; he was limited to one, sometimes two, letters a month. Termination of navigation between Solovki and the mainland during the winter months delayed delivery. Florensky sometimes had only scraps of paper available, which he filled out to the very edges with his tiny script. Most of the letters were directed to his wife Anna, but he also wrote to his mother and to each of his children. Anna occasionally sent him small packages with food, tobacco, watercolor paints, and brushes, and he sent her several packages with dried plants and minerals, portraits of him that artistically gifted prisoners had executed, and his own drawings, sometimes in color, of the island's water plants.

Florensky had once asserted that letters were the genre of writing that he valued most highly.[14] The correspondence with his family reveals an intimate, tender side of him that we do not find in his lectures or treatises. One published collection of his letters is appropriately entitled (in Russian), *All My Thoughts Are about You*. Florensky constantly emphasizes how much he misses his family, how each member is constantly in his thoughts, and how he wishes to share his life experience, so that each may live a good, strong life, despite the many difficulties that each faces.

The prison correspondence, like Florensky's political "confession," is not easy to interpret. His letters do not allow us to make clear judgments about his personal condition or religious faith. Because all the letters had to pass muster with a censor, Florensky could not openly criticize conditions in the prison. Moreover, he knew that touching on matters of religious belief risked further repercussions for him and his family; by the time he was transferred to Solovki, the authorities had already confiscated his personal libraries in Sergiev Posad and Moscow, removing even Pushkin's writings.[15]

Nevertheless, nothing in the correspondence, not even between the lines, suggests that Florensky still prayed or observed other basic Orthodox religious practices. Moreover, no prisoners report that he secretly served the liturgy or offered pastoral care, in contrast to some priests in the camps.[16] Indeed, in his letters from Solovki, Florensky goes out of his way to emphasize his disinterest in religious matters. He writes that the island's ancient churches repel him and that he has not even bothered to step into them.[17]

14. V. V. Rozanov, *Literaturnye izgnanniki* [Literary exiles], vol. 2 (Moscow: Respublika, 2010), epigraph.

15. To Anna Florenskaia, March 18, 1934, in Florenskii, *Vse Dumy*, 61 n. 1.

16. See *Father Arseny, 1893–1973: Priest, Prisoner, Spiritual Father*, trans. Vera Bouteneff (Crestwood, NY: St. Vladimir's Seminary Press, 2002).

17. To Vasilii Florenskii, December 14, 1934, in Florenskii, *Vse Dumy*, 357.

What, however, does Florensky mean to communicate by such assertions? Is it true, as he claims in one letter, that even in his childhood he disliked what he read about Solovki, notwithstanding its antiquity and historical significance?[18] If so, why does he not explain himself? Does he associate the island and its monastery with the tragic schism of the seventeenth century and the repressive measures of the government and the church against the Old Believers? Alternatively, is he so uniquely at home in Sergiev Posad with its Lavra and relics that he cannot imagine venerating Solovki?[19] Or is he staying away from the Solovetskii churches because the Bolsheviks have desecrated them, insofar as they now serve as warehouses rather than as places of worship and prayer? But if so, why then does he bother to mention the churches at all?

We do know that Florensky was deeply affected by his arrest in 1933. His prison mug shot shows him disheveled and disoriented. In his letters from the gulag, he bitterly complains that society has not appreciated his scientific work, and that unfortunate circumstances have prevented him from ever bringing any of his projects to successful completion. Whereas in his memoirs for his children he writes that tobacco disgusts him, he now, like most of the prisoners at Solovki, smokes (although, most of the time, they had no tobacco and had to be content with grasses and weeds). Matters of religious faith seem far away.

Nevertheless, next to these moments of despair and of seeming absence of religious faith, Florensky's prison letters movingly express his sacramental vision of the "other" world that reveals itself in this world. He returns to lessons from his childhood: the importance of knowing one's family heritage, of immersing oneself in humanity's greatest cultural achievements, and of cultivating a sense of wonder in the natural world. Plants and minerals again fascinate him, and he describes his longing to enter into the mystery of each unique form of existence that he encounters.

18. To Vasilii, December 14, 1934, in Florenskii, *Vse Dumy*, 357.

19. To Kirill Florenskii, December 24–25, 1934, in Florenskii, *Vse Dumy*, 377.

In an odd way, his life has come full circle. As a child, he was particularly drawn to the mystery that he sensed in water plants; now, at Solovki, he studies the properties of seaweed. In his letters home, he takes a child's delight in observing and describing different kinds of seaweed and their properties.[20]

Florensky's Testament

Florensky's first effort to pass on his worldview to his children was his "Testament." In the first portion, composed in 1917, Florensky asks that on the day of his burial they receive the Eucharist and, thereafter, commune as often as possible. He will be comforted, he says, if they refuse to be sad and, instead, live joyfully and actively. He promises always to be near them spiritually and to watch over them.

Moreover, Florensky directs his children not to seek power or wealth, but rather to remain true to what he believes is the family's calling to spiritual, intellectual work. Things for the family will not go awry if one member of each generation becomes a priest. Florensky appeals to his children to keep in their possession the family home in Sergiev Posad, which is under the spiritual protection of St. Sergius. They should not sell Florensky's library except in the most extreme of circumstances—which further underlines the blow that the entire family felt when the authorities seized the books after his arrest and, despite the family's pleas, refused to return them.

Two years later, in 1919, Florensky adds to the "Testament." He acknowledges the hardships that have come in the wake of the Bolshevik Revolution: epidemic disease, hunger, runaway inflation, lawlessness, and the constant threat of violence. He instructs the family to pray for mercy to God, the Mother of God, St. Sergius, St. Nicholas, St. Seraphim of Sarov, and the angels. The

20. Rachel Carson had a similar fascination with different kinds of seaweed and their properties. See Rachel Carson, *The Edge of the Sea* (New York: Houghton Mifflin, 1955).

family should also appeal to the special protectors of their home, the men, now deceased, who had been Florensky's spiritual fathers: Bishop Antonii and Fr. Isidore.

Other, short entries in the "Testament" date from 1920 to 1923. The lines from 1921, the year in which Florensky largely had to abandon his work and life in Sergiev Posad and began spending most of his time in scientific research in Moscow, are especially poignant. He writes of how his heart aches for his each of his children and for his ill mother, but also of how little time and energy he now has for them. The one thing that will sustain them, he asserts, is careful and clear thinking: "Thinking is God's gift and requires you to get out of yourself.... Thinking is the guarantor of spiritual freedom."[21]

A year later, Florensky commends an additional source of spiritual support: "When you feel down, look at the stars or at the azure of the afternoon [sky]. When you are sad, when others offend you, when things do not go your way, when spiritual turmoil comes over you, go out into the [open] air and stand alone with the sky. Then your soul will calm itself."[22] The color azure had special significance to Florensky. In *Pillar and Ground*, he had asserted, "sky-blue attunes the soul to contemplation, to detachment from the earthly, to quiet longing for peace and purity. This blue of the heavens ... is a profound image of heavenly creation, ... an image of the Intelligent World" (which Florensky associates with Sophia, the mediator between the two worlds).[23] The heavenly beauty of the natural world and especially of the sky heals body and spirit.

21. Pavel Florenskii, "Zaveshchanie" [Testament]. in Florenskii, *Vse Dumy*, 29–30. The entry is dated, Moscow, March 19–20, 1921.

22. Florenskii, "Zaveshchanie," in Florenskii, 30. The entry is dated August 14, 1922.

23. Pavel Florensky, *The Pillar and Ground of the Truth*, trans. Boris Jakim (Princeton, NJ: Princeton University Press, 1997), 271–72. For the Russian, see Pavel Florenskii, *Stolp i utverzhdenie istinny*, 2nd ed. (Moscow: Akademicheskii proekt, 2017), 380. For Florensky's understanding of color, see Nicoletta Misler, "Pavel Florensky as Art Historian," in Pavel Florensky, *Beyond Vision: Essays on the Perception of Art*, ed. Nicoletta Misler, trans. Wendy Salmond (London: Reaktion Books, 2002), 37.

Passing on Life Experience

Florensky's correspondence from the gulag a decade later develops these themes, but now without explicit reference to God or religious life. As in his "Testament," he wants his family to live with joy and confidence. "That all of you be happy and joyful—that is my only wish," he writes, after arriving at Solovki.[24] Later, in a letter to his son Vasilii, he says, "I want you to have as much joy as one can on earth."[25] He tells his wife Anna, "How I wish that our children would gather up positive experiences and joy."[26]

Florensky feels increasingly desperate to pass on his life experience to his children during these "tumultuous" and "momentous" times.[27] Indeed, he feels guilty that he had not earlier given them the attention that they needed. He writes his wife, "Please tell all of [our children] how much I love them and how much I suffer, because I am unable to help them with life."[28] In a letter to his son Kirill, Florensky apologizes for having been insufficiently sensitive to him as he was growing up.[29] Florensky says that he always did his own work selflessly, but because he was so busy, his children suffered deprivations, including his frequent absence.[30] If he is ever allowed to return home, he will devote himself entirely to them.[31]

Despite his regret that he can no longer help his children directly, Florensky seems resolved to do what he can for them through his correspondence. True to his conviction in *Pillar and Ground* that one knows another person only by going out from oneself and entering into the other person's unique personality, Florensky

24. To Anna, October 24, 1934, in Florenskii, *Vse Dumy*, 72.
25. To Vasilii, July 15, 1935, in Florenskii, *Vse Dumy*, 362.
26. To Anna, June 18, 1937, in Florenskii, *Vse Dumy*, 249.
27. To Anna, January 3–4, 1937, and to Anna, January 16–17, 1937, in Florenskii, *Vse Dumy*, 210, 222.
28. To Anna, October 24, 1934, in Florenskii, *Vse Dumy*, 72.
29. To Kirill, January 24–25, 1935, in Florenskii, *Vse Dumy*, 83–84.
30. To Kirill, January 24–25, 1935, in Florenskii, *Vse Dumy*, 358.
31. To Anna, November 30, 1934, in Florenskii, *Vse Dumy*, 78–79.

patiently addresses the particular needs and circumstances of each family member..

Florensky uses his letters to his eldest sons, Vasilii (twenty-two to twenty-six years old during Florensky's imprisonment) and Kirill (eighteen to twenty-two years old), to guide them into adulthood and their professional work. He tells them that they are free to use his books and experimental chemicals, and he refers them to scientific articles that he believes will interest them.[32]

When Vasilii returns from a geologic expedition in Central Asia, Florensky shares his convictions about the nature of scientific observation. Vasilii should pay attention to his first impressions of a geologic site, including the surrounding landscape. Before drawing any conclusions, he should allow these impressions gradually to form themselves into a general picture.[33] Moreover, he should take a few minutes each day for quiet reflection, so that he remains focused on what is essential to life and is not distracted by trivialities. Only then will he be ready to analyze what he has observed. "The whole is prior to its parts," Florensky reminds him.[34]

Florensky also directs Vasilii to care in Florensky's place for the rest of the family. Vasilii should be a loving support to his mother Anna, who suffers from ill health and carries the burden of caring for the children.[35] He should teach the younger children about the natural world. Further, after Vasilii's marriage in 1935, Florensky advises him to care for his wife by entering into her interests and "inner life."[36] The relationships that keep one rooted in family life help secure one's place in the larger world.

Florensky's letters to Kirill make similar points. Despite the many successes of the contemporary natural sciences, they impose an abstract scheme on reality, rather than entering into it and

32. To Vasilii and to Kirill, November 23, 1933, in Florenskii, *Vse Dumy*, 347, 340.
33. To Vasilii, November 23, 1933, in Florenskii, *Vse Dumy*, 344.
34. To Vasilii, December 16, 1935, in Florenskii, *Vse Dumy*, 375.
35. To Vasilii, July 15, 1935, in Florenskii, *Vse Dumy*, 364.
36. To Vasilii, December 16, 1935, in Florenskii, *Vse Dumy*, 375.

understanding it from the inside: "I fear that they have lost what is most important: a living sense of the reality of their object."[37] Florensky shares his own extended scientific interests, including the distinctive geographic characteristics of different places that he has visited and the derivation of Russian mineralogical terms.[38] In another letter, Florensky lists the most important mathematical, philosophical, art historical, and scientific questions that he has investigated over his lifetime and expresses the hope that Kirill might someday make use of, and build on, this work.[39]

Florensky's correspondence with his eldest daughter Ol'ga (fifteen to nineteen years old) is especially detailed and poignant. As she goes through adolescent struggles and rebelliousness, Florensky tells her (like the other family members) to stay focused on what is most important: her health (he recommends that she combat her headaches by getting plenty of fresh air and watching what she eats), family relationships, and clear thinking.[40]

Ol'ga, he notes, wants to go off by herself with her friends, but he warns her that these relationships are temporary and fleeting. Nothing can replace the stability that her own home and family provide.[41] Her mother is the most precious person she has.[42] Moreover, Ol'ga needs to pay attention to her family heritage. Young people often think that they can do whatever they like, but if Ol'ga ignores her family inheritance, tragedy will inevitably befall both her and her descendants.[43]

Ol'ga's frustrations with school must not become an excuse for her to abandon disciplined learning. Florensky notes that his own

37. To Kirill, November 11–12, 1936, in Florenskii, *Vse Dumy*, 382.

38. To Kirill, November 5–6, 1935, and December 24–25, 1935, in Florenskii, *Vse Dumy*, 368, 377.

39. To Kirill, May, 13, 1937, in Florenskii, *Vse Dumy*, 241–42.

40. To Ol'ga Florenskaia, June 13–14, 1935, and May 13, 1937, in Florenskii, *Vse Dumy*, 302, 337.

41. To Ol'ga, June 1936, in Florenskii, *Vse Dumy*, 322.

42. To Ol'ga, September 16, 1935, in Florenskii, *Vse Dumy*, 307.

43. To Ol'ga, March 10–11, 1936, in Florenskii, *Vse Dumy*, 315.

intellectual development came primarily by his own efforts and not in school.[44] He underlines what he had written earlier in his memoirs for his children. He wants Ol'ga, like his other children, to embrace humanity's highest values, regardless of what others think.[45] He advises her to learn foreign languages, play the piano, and study mathematical ways of thinking. Attention to physics, the natural sciences, drawing, music, and literature is essential. She should read foreign-language literature aloud, taking wonder in the very sound of each word.[46] She should study the structure of musical pieces and how the whole brings forth its different parts (here, again, he refers to the Aristotelian principle that the whole is prior to the parts).[47]

Florensky writes her that history is "the higher judge" of what will endure of humanity's works. At the same time, his letters do not conceal his own judgments. To his thinking, Dostoyevsky, like much of Russian literature, is too dark, introspective, and inattentive to the natural world.[48] Balzac, who knows his characters from the inside, is better than Zola, who sets forth ghostly abstractions.[49] Shakespeare and Beethoven explore the full range of human emotions but embody Renaissance culture, which reduces humans to drives and impulses and fails to recognize what is holy.[50] The world would be better without Scriabin and Tchaikovsky. Neither penetrates to the depths of being; rather, both wish to remake reality, rather than to recognize, and be creative within, their limited powers.[51]

In contrast, the world is brighter because of Bach, Mozart, and

44. To Ol'ga, December 27, 1933, in Florenskii, *Vse Dumy*, 295.

45. To Ol'ga, May 13, 1937, in Florenskii, *Vse Dumy*, 337.

46. To Ol'ga, November 12, 1933, in Florenskii, *Vse Dumy*, 291–93.

47. To Ol'ga, November 1–4, 1935, in Florenskii, *Vse Dumy*, 309–10.

48. To Ol'ga, September 16, 1935 in Florenskii, *Vse Dumy*, 306.

49. To Ol'ga, June 1936, in Florenskii, *Vse Dumy*, 323. See also to Kirill, February 29–March 1, 1936, in Florenskii, *Vse Dumy*, 379.

50. To Ol'ga, January 1936, in Florenskii, *Vse Dumy*, 311.

51. To Ol'ga, March 23, 1937, in Florenskii, *Vse Dumy*, 334–35.

Schubert.[52] Their attention to order, harmony, and form transports Florensky back to the lost paradise of his childhood: "Right order gives freedom; arbitrariness results in necessity."[53] For the same reason, Pushkin and Goethe are real poets.[54] They know the importance of form; creativity takes place within limitation.

In all of these reflections, Florensky is making a more basic point. In *Pillar and Ground*, he had defined sin as self-enclosure, an unwillingness to abandon oneself in order to enter into the reality of the other. Now he is concerned that Ol'ga is too turned in on herself. He warns her that those who get lost in their own subjectivity slowly die. She should engage the world actively and realize her possibilities. In one of his rare allusions to Christian faith in the letters, he tells her, "Only through Realization (his capitalization; the Russian word *voploshchenie* can also be translated as "incarnation" or "embodiment") can one assess one's own authenticity and worth."

If Ol'ga actively encounters the world, she will discover its revelatory quality. Appealing to Goethe, Florensky says, "What I want above all is that you cultivate in yourself a vital attitude toward life, and that you be able to perceive reality symbolically."[55] Our passions, he adds, blind us to the beauty that shines through the creation. If we know how to look, what is highest and most precious reveals itself to us here and now. We will take joy in what we have, rather than seeking happiness in what we do not.

Florensky's letters to his two youngest children, Mikhail (nicknamed Mik, twelve to sixteen years old during his father's imprisonment) and Mariia-Tinatin (Tika, nine to thirteen), are shorter and more playful, as when he describes Solovki's animals and birds, especially its seagulls. In a more serious tone, Florensky laments to Mik that humans are destroying the natural world that Florensky so wants his children to discover and experience.

52. To Ol'ga, March 23, 1937, in Florenskii, *Vse Dumy*, 333.
53. To Mariia Veniaminovna Iudina, April 19–20, 1936, in Florenskii, *Vse Dumy*, 175.
54. To Ol'ga, June 1936, in Florenskii, *Vse Dumy*, 324.
55. To Ol'ga, September 16, 1935, in Florenskii, *Vse Dumy*, 307.

Industrial civilization provides humans with various conveniences but undermines their sense of the poetic and of home.[56] The rural-like Sergiev Posad that Florensky once knew is becoming just another suburb of Moscow.[57] While in the Far East, Florensky begins a long poem, "Oro," about a Siberian tribe and its closeness to the land and the natural world, and he dedicates it to Mik.

Florensky tells Tika that a seagull brings him messages from Sergiev Posad about what she is doing. He wonders how her piano playing and German lessons are coming along, asks about her dolls, and tells her to find plants in the forest that she can transplant into the family garden. When he first arrives at Solovki, he invites her to pick out an ancient coin from his collection. Three years later, he tells her to choose a photograph from his album of the Caucasus, or to hang in her window a specimen of seaweed that he has sent home.[58] Florensky so wants his children to remember him and his love for them, but in a letter to his wife, he sadly concedes that they will begin to forget who he is.[59]

Florensky's Spiritual Condition

Florensky's correspondence with Anna, with his mother, and later with Nataliia, his daughter-in-law, reiterates his fundamental convictions about life wisdom. A family needs to know its history; the past has entrusted its members with a specific legacy to preserve and pass on. For the Florensky family, this legacy includes attention to literature and music that embody the highest humanistic values.

Moreover, family members should spend as much time as possible in the natural world. It provides for their physical and emotional well-being and teaches them how to think. Each child should gather concrete, sensory impressions of the world—colors,

56. To Mikhail Florenskii, October 11–12, 1936, in Florenskii, *Vse Dumy*, 281.

57. To Mikhail, December 4, 1937, in Florenskii, *Vse Dumy*, 214–15.

58. To Mariia-Tinatin Florenskaia, June 19, 1937, in Florenskii, *Vse Dumy*, 290.

59. To Anna, January 24–25, 1935, in Florenskii, *Vse Dumy*, 82.

tastes, smells, sounds, and observations of landscapes and plants—and then allow time for them to form themselves into ideas.[60]

"Facts," he writes in a letter, "say more than theories."[61] Concrete thinking receives the world as it reveals itself to us, whereas abstract thinking imposes dead schemes on it. As we have noted, Florensky believes that when we carefully observe the natural world's unique forms and allow them to show forth their inner life, we discover their symbolic, revelatory character. The "other" world shines into and through this world, lifting us up to God.

For Florensky, these three commitments—to knowing one's family heritage, to guarding the greatest achievements of human culture, and to receiving the creation's "revelations"—are pillars of stability for children as they grow up. In a letter to his daughter-in-law about her newborn son, Florensky emphasizes the importance of a child's first impressions. It is not too early for his grandson to hear classical music or to be shown plants, flowers, water, the sky, clouds, and the dawn. Even if a baby can receive these impressions only subconsciously, they lay down foundations of personality that will manifest themselves later on.[62]

Perhaps Florensky succeeded in instilling in his children a sense of wonder in the creation; all five eventually went into scientific-technical professions. Vasilii would become a petrographer; Kirill, a planetologist; Ol'ga, a botanist; Mikhail, a specialist in drilling wells; and Mariia, a chemist. Besides keeping them close to the natural world, such scientific-technical work had the advantage during the Soviet era of being less burdened ideologically than professions in the humanities or social sciences.

Florensky tries to take his own advice. Even in the gulag, he commits himself to his family and to its spiritual-intellectual calling. His letters home recall his childhood memories of the Caucasus. He records dreams that he has been having about his

60. To Anna, November 22, 1936 in Florenskii, *Vse Dumy*, 196.

61. To Ol'ga P. Florenskaia (mother), March 23, 1937, in Florenskii, *Vse Dumy*, 235.

62. To Nataliia Florenskaia, July 7–8, 1936, in Florenskii, *Vse Dumy*, 412–15.

(and their) ancestors.[63] His scientific curiosity is unabated. At Solovki, he thinks about inventing an apparatus for extracting iodine from seaweed.[64] He participates in geologic expeditions to nearby islands.[65] He asks his wife to send him books about the Siberian tribe that his poem for Mik will feature.[66] Moreover, he discovers that the academics among the island's prisoners have organized various intellectual events, and he attends and gives lectures on mathematical questions.[67]

Florensky continues to surround himself as best he can with great literature and music. Despite the difficulty of obtaining books, he reports from Ksenevskaia that he reads Pushkin for fifteen minutes after lunch every day.[68] In letters from Solovki, he mentions Balzac, a book on mineralogy, and a history of the ancient Russian city Ostrogozhsk.[69] On a radio (as much as he hates radios, he says), he listens to performances of Mozart and Bach.[70]

Florensky's attention to the natural world remains alive. He fills many of his letters home with precise, detailed descriptions of the Solovetskii landscape and its plants and animals. When he first arrived, he found the island and its features peculiar and even repulsive. Nothing here is "at home," he writes; everything (and everyone) has come from somewhere else, the result of glaciation (and exile). Eventually, however, he discovers the island's beauty and compelling mystery. He becomes captivated by the northern lights, by the colors of the morning sky, and by how the sea breaks up reflected sunrays into intensely bright sparkles of light.[71]

63. To Kirill, January 8–9, 1937, in Florenskii, *Vse Dumy*, 217.

64. To Vasilii, February 17, 1935, in Florenskii, *Vse Dumy*, 217.

65. To Anna, July 20–21, 1936, in Florenskii, *Vse Dumy*, 179.

66. To Anna, September 5–6, 1935, in Florenskii, *Vse Dumy*, 138.

67. To Mikhail, December 4, 1937, in Florenskii, *Vse Dumy*, 216.

68. To Ol'ga, October 13–14, 1933, in Florenskii, *Vse Dumy*, 291.

69. To Ol'ga, April 27–28, 1936, and to Vasilii, June 24–25, 1936, in Florenskii, *Vse Dumy*, 316, 410.

70. To Mariia Veniaminovna Iudina, April 19–20, 1936, and to Ol'ga, November 25, 1936, in Florenskii, *Vse Dumy*, 175, 331.

71. To Vasilii, February 17, 1935, to Vasilii, January 7, 1937, and to Anna, June 18, 1937, in Florenskii, *Vse Dumy*, 157, 390–92, 247, 249.

Now, the steely gray color of the White Sea no longer irritates him. Instead, he remembers his love of the sea in his childhood, when it represented eternity to him. The other prisoners have come to fascinate him too. They have come from all parts of the Soviet Union. He feels a special bond to the Muslims. And when a Persian prisoner tells him about his ancient religion, Florensky concludes that their two faiths mostly agree.[72]

As Florensky experiments with seaweed and water plants, his curiosity grows. He remarks in a letter to Anna that these plants originated in the Precambrian Age, just as life was beginning on earth.[73] Fascinated by their intricate structure, he prepares (and sends to Anna) beautiful ink and acrylic paintings that reflect his wonder in their inner life. One commentator says, "[In these drawings, Florensky] enters into immediate communion with the mystery of Nature. Straight through the organic forms of the created, earthly world flows Light.... [The drawings] allow us to glimpse the boundary between the earthly and the heavenly."[74] They are nothing less than "icons."

Family heritage, humanity's great cultural achievements, and nature's mystery clearly sustain Florensky spiritually after his arrest and imprisonment. Nevertheless, his letters also suggest just how trying the conditions in the gulag were. Life in the Far Eastern camps had been relatively comfortable. Solovki was different. At Kem', he is robbed of money and belongings, and once he arrives on the island, he has to sell his leather coat.[75] At first, he is bored and despondent, fearful of what will come next.

Thankfully, the next days prove better. He is able to settle into a routine and soon reports that he feels relatively content, especially after he is assigned to a laboratory. The work interests him; he

72. To Kirill, May 19, 1937, in Florenskii, *Vse Dumy*, 393. The implication is that the Persian is a Zoroastrian.

73. To Anna, January 3–4, 1937, in Florenskii, *Vse Dumy*, 207.

74. Florenskii, *Vse Dumy*, 385.

75. To Anna, November 30, 1934, in Florenskii, *Vse Dumy*, 77.

is living and working in a natural setting, outside the monastery walls; he enjoys a good deal of peace and quiet; and he shares a room with just one other person, a pleasant coworker. In his letters home, he claims that he is healthy and warm and has plenty to eat. He is happy that he is able to live on vegetables; he gives away anything with meat. His wife need not send him money or food. Instead, she should ensure that she and the children eat better and guard their health, about which he constantly worries.

Nevertheless, Florensky's reassurances to Anna are so insistent that one wonders whether he is actually writing in code about how bad things are. We know from other sources that most prisoners suffered from malnourishment and physical exhaustion, and it is hard to imagine that Florensky was an exception.[76] Indeed, he complains that his memory is getting weaker and that he is losing his sense of time.[77] He typically works until 4 a.m. or later, seven days a week, and sleeps only three hours before going to breakfast. He writes that he has no time left to be creative—or to fall into despair.[78]

By early 1937, Florensky admits that he has had many sleepless nights. When he does sleep, he dreams of his childhood and of his children when they were small.[79] The iodine factory closes in May, leaving him without intellectually stimulating work. The prison regime becomes harsher. Through the winter, he complains that his fingers are cold and numb, and that he is lonely and unable to concentrate. His lament that he has been a professional failure intensifies: "With my whole being, I sense the nothingness of man, his work, his efforts."[80] Peace, quiet, and natural beauty are now

76. See Anne Applebaum, *Gulag: A History* (New York: Doubleday, 2003), 23, 104, 109, 111.

77. To Anna, October 24, 1934, to Ol'ga (mother), February 20, 1937, and to Ol'ga (mother), March 23, 1937, in Florenskii, *Vse Dumy*, 72, 232, 234.

78. To Anna, February 28–March 1, 1936, in Florenskii, *Vse Dumy*, 162–63.

79. To Kirill, January 8–9, 1937, and to Kirill, May 19, 1937, in Florenskii, *Vse Dumy*, 217, 393.

80. To Anna, June 4, 1937, in Florenskii, *Vse Dumy*, 246.

Figure 9.2. Florensky with Daughter Mariia, 1926, Sergiev Posad / Public domain. By courtesy of the Florensky family archive, from *P. A. Florenskij e la cultura della sua epoca* (Marburg: Blaue Horner Verlag, 1995).

far away; he has been transferred to the monastery and shares a large room with forty other prisoners.[81]

In a letter to Anna in June, he shares his uneasiness that something is changing for the worse.[82] The letter proves to be his last.

What Lives On

The trying conditions of the gulag evoked contradictory responses in prisoners.[83] Some became like their guards, mean-spirited and abusive. A few, despite their experience of dehumanization, discovered a capacity to do good: to share rations, to offer encouragement to other prisoners, or even to accept a punishment due to another. Still others did whatever they could just to survive, even if it meant tricking or cheating another prisoner or the guards. Some even mutilated themselves so that they would be sent to the camp hospital, where they hoped to rest and recover their strength.

The antinomies that Florensky experiences spiritually at Solovki—hope and despair, wonder and indifference, faith and lonely isolation—seem to deepen his faith in what Christians call "providence" (Florensky says "history," the "higher judgment"), rather than to lead him into the dead end of his political confession. Citing Pushkin, Florensky writes his wife, "The more selfless one's gifts [for humanity], the severer the persecution and the harsher the suffering. It is a law of life."[84] To his son Kirill, he writes that life inevitably brings us difficulties, but "if we bear them consciously and in the light of life as a whole, they nourish and enrich us, and bring forth good fruit later."[85]

Especially moving are Florensky's reflections on remembering

81. To Anna, June 4, 1937, in Florenskii, *Vse Dumy*, 242, 244.

82. To Anna, June 18, 1937, in Florenskii, *Vse Dumy*, 249.

83. See Solzhenitsyn's documentation in *Gulag Archipelago*. See also Tzvetan Todorov, *Facing the Extreme: Moral Life in the Concentration Camps*, trans. Arthur Denner and Abigail Pollak (New York: Henry Holt, 1996); and Applebaum, *Gulag*.

84. To Anna, February 13, 1937, in Florenskii, *Vse Dumy*, 228.

85. To Vasilii, November 23, 1933, in Florenskii, *Vse Dumy*, 347.

the past. Even as he complains that his memory has grown weaker, such that he often cannot think of anything new to write home, he reports that he remembers the distant past more vividly than ever. He writes his mother that each of us is a collection of layers of memory. At any given moment, we remember only those things at the top; other things remain subconscious. But as we grow older, we descend through these layers, and the interests and thoughts of long ago return to us.[86]

Florensky recalls a place near the Black Sea where his parents had taken him and his siblings when he was a child. He and his sister had their own rooms in a guardhouse apart from the main house, and the young Florensky felt like a prince on his own estate. Now, in 1935, his mother writes that his two older sons have just made a trip to the place, but that it made no particular impression on them. "Everything passes away," Florensky concedes. But then he adds:

> And, yet, everything remains. I cherish the sense that nothing passes away entirely, nothing gets lost, it somehow and somewhere preserves itself. What is of value lives on, even if we no longer perceive it. And [our] good achievements, even if we have completely forgotten them, somehow live on and bear fruit. So, although we are sad about what passes away, there is nevertheless a living sense of its eternity.[87]

Later that year, in a letter to his wife, Florensky recalls an incident when their son Vasilii was seven years old. Vasilii had vowed to give up his stamp collecting, if only a fire that was sweeping through the Lavra would die out. Swept up into this memory, Florensky writes, "Dear Anya [his preferred name of endearment for her in the correspondence], the past is not past but rather preserves itself to eternity. We forget it and leave it behind, but in the right circumstances, it discloses itself again, as an eternal

86. To Ol'ga (mother), July 28–29, 1937, in Florenskii, *Vse Dumy*, 186.
87. To Ol'ga (mother), April 6–7, 1935, in Florenskii, *Vse Dumy*, 95.

present."[88] A year later, Florensky writes his mother, "To remember the past is a duty and a support of life. It is impossible to value the present and make use of it, unless it is rooted in the past."[89]

To memorialize what we have experienced: this theme runs throughout Florensky's thinking. In *Pillar and Ground*, he memorializes the Trinity, its inner life, and its relation to the world. He writes *Salt of the Earth* to memorialize Fr. Isidore. Florensky sought to preserve the Lavra, to memorialize it as an essential element of Russia's identity past and present. He understood icons as memorials to the saints, who are with us still, whether we are aware of their presence or not. In his letters, he memorializes his and his family's past in order to preserve it for his children.

Florensky's understanding of ritual and worship offers additional insight. In performing ritualistic blessings, which come to their fullest intensification in the celebration of the sacraments, the church activates two capacities: reality's capacity to reveal divine glory, the very light of Tabor, and the human capacity to draw out and perceive that glory. For Florensky, the activating power that lies in the act of blessing always depends on an act of "naming." In prayer, the priest and the people lift up the things of nature and culture by name, asking that those things be as they truly are in and for God. We call the bread "bread," as we bless it, the wine "wine," but in such a way that they are no longer ordinary bread and wine but rather bread and wine that mediate human communion with Christ.

This naming is an invoking. It involves something more than the recitation of a bare word, such as "bread" or "wine." For Florensky, to name something is to enter into its life, to describe it and to honor it in its unique particularity—and, therefore, to commemorate it, to memorialize it, or, we could even say, to "eternalize" it.

88. To Anna, May 27, 1935, in Florenskii, *Vse Dumy*, 119.
89. To Ol'ga (mother), July 28–29, 1936, in Florenskii, *Vse Dumy*, 185.

Florensky had always been fascinated by names. *In Pillar and Ground* and *Philosophy of the Cult*, he conducts extended etymological investigations of particular words, in order to tease out all of their nuances. Earlier, he had been sympathetic to the position of a group of monks on Mt. Athos who claimed that their invocation of the name of God in the Jesus Prayer made God present (*imiaslavie*).[90] In the early 1920s, he completed a treatise on given human names (not published during his lifetime), in which he associates particular personality characteristics with different names: an Aleksandr does not easily share his inner life, while an Anna is naturally sensitive to artistic beauty.[91]

In his letters from the gulag, the question of names arises again, when Vasilii and Nataliia ask him what name they should choose for their son. Florensky is hesitant to select, but he does insist that naming is not a matter of indifference or of arbitrary signification. Florensky compares a name to a musical form. In order to create a composition successfully, one must respect the limitations and possibilities of the form with which one is working.[92] Similarly, while a name does not wholly determine a person's personality, it does establish parameters within which one develops one's unique self. A name influences how one perceives oneself and how others perceive one.

To call a person by name is therefore to invoke that person's unique being. As we saw, Florensky makes the same point in his discussion of the Orthodox liturgy. When the priest recites a deceased person's given name aloud, that person somehow becomes present to us again. The ritual activates an objective disclosure, a revelation, while at the same time enabling us to perceive it subjectively.

90. Pyman, *Florensky*, 99–102. See also Scott M. Kenworthy, "The Name-Glorifiers (*Imiaslavie*) Controversy," in *The Oxford Handbook of Russian Religious Thought*, ed. Caryl Emerson, George Pattison, and Randall A. Poole (New York: Oxford University Press, 2020), 327–42.

91. Pyman, *Florensky*, 87.

92. To Anna, April 8–9, 1936, in Florenskii, *Vse Dumy*, 401.

We have no way of knowing whether Florensky prayed for those to whom he wrote, or whether he recited formal Orthodox blessings of the natural world around him. Nevertheless, his sacramental worldview remains steady. He implicitly prays for, and blesses, his family and the things of creation around him, whenever he calls them by name and attends to them with loving care and consideration. In addressing each family member, he invokes that person's personal presence. He empties himself in order to enter into their unique personalities and circumstances. Similarly, he names the plants, animals, landscapes, and skies that he sees around him by describing each, so as to call forth its unique mysterious being.

In the end, we again encounter enigmas. We just cannot say whether the imprisoned Florensky still regards himself as an Orthodox believer, or whether he now embraces a universal religiosity that includes yet goes beyond Christianity. In his early studies, he had found genuine religious impulses in Greek antiquity, and now, perhaps, he has discovered them again in the faith of the Persian prisoner at Solovki. Moreover, as Florensky approaches death, he descends through the layers of his personality and returns to his childhood experience of the world's revelatory character, a reality for him before his conversion to Christ. The circle back to a "natural" religion seems complete.

Nevertheless, as Florensky says, nothing is lost. What has value lives on. Florensky's way of memorializing reality clearly derives from the sacramental worldview that he as a young, confused man had discovered in Orthodoxy and into which he later immersed himself as a priest. We do not have to speculate about whether Florensky's gulag letters are written in code. Perhaps there is no code to break. Just as they are, the letters powerfully testify to that "other," mysterious world within this world.

For a few days, I had the privilege of seeing the same magical landscapes and skies that once captivated Florensky. Whether I will ever be able to return to Solovki is unclear; as I write, U.S.-Russian relations are at a historic low point. But I often think of Fr. Evlogii and the tree-cross. I commemorate them in my thoughts and prayers. In the mystery of God's ways, we are somehow still present to each other.

10

FLORENSKY TODAY

"The truth is not knowledge about life; rather, it is true life."

My path to Florensky has been unusual. Many years ago, I had looked at his book *Iconostasis*, but I was never able to make headway with it. The dense, iconic-like language, as his translators describe it, put me off.[1] However, during a sabbatical year at a Russian university in 2018–19, I met a philosopher who regarded Florensky as the most important religious philosopher of the twentieth century.[2] Under his guidance, I returned to *Iconostasis*, but now in the original Russian, and then took up *Pillar and Ground*. I began to make slow but steady progress in comprehending Florensky.

One other factor was key. Because of my years of immersing myself in Orthodoxy in Russia—during two previous sabbaticals—Florensky's attention to the liminal, to those places where

1. Donald Sheehan, "Introduction," in Pavel Florensky, *Iconostasis*, trans. Donald Sheehan and Olga Andrejev (Crestwood, NY: St. Vladimir's Seminary Press, 1996), 3.

2. See my acknowledgments in the preface.

Orthodox Christians believe that the transcendent and the immanent meet, began to make sense to me. I still remember the time and place—a small hotel room in Moscow on a chilly January evening—when I read "To the Reader," the opening pages of *Pillar and Ground*. Something suddenly clicked in me: "[Only] living religious experience … [opens one to] the spiritual treasures of the Church.… Orthodoxy is shown, not proved.… It is necessary to immerse oneself all at once in the very element of Orthodoxy, to begin living in an Orthodox way. There is no other way."[3]

These words helped me understand that the more I entered into Orthodoxy—experiencing its liturgy, iconography, pilgrimages, seasons of fasting and feasting, rituals of blessing, and monasteries and parishes—the more I would grasp Florensky's vision of a world transparent to God's light, energy, and glory. Indeed, that is the best advice that I can give my own readers: if you want to understand Florensky, experience living Orthodoxy—even if you, like I, may enter only so far if you remain non-Orthodox.

One might also reverse the dictum. If you really want to understand Orthodoxy, read Florensky. For Florensky beautifully explicates the life, rituals, and sacraments of the Orthodox Church. He helps us understand what Orthodox believers feel, more than understand, when they say that the liturgy lifts them up into heaven.

If Florensky's language is difficult, it is because he is writing to the intellectual, "cultured despisers" of religion of his time, who are dabbling in occultism, theosophy, and various Western philosophies. Their language is not ours. A patient reader will nevertheless learn much not only about Florensky's thinking but also about other theological-philosophical currents and debates of his time.

Throughout this book, I have tried to let Florensky speak for himself. However, readers who have come this far may find it

3. Pavel Florensky, *The Pillar and Ground of the Truth*, trans. Boris Jakim (Princeton, NJ: Princeton University Press, 1997), 5, 9. See Pavel Florenskii, *Stolp i utverzhdenie istinny*, 2nd ed. (Moscow: Akademicheskii proekt, 2017), 9, 13, 14.

helpful to know how scholars have regarded Florensky—where they have praised or criticized him. Florensky evoked strong reactions during his lifetime and evokes them still today, perhaps reflecting the complexity of his thinking, as well as its hard, controversial edges. Occasionally, I will add my own brief comments about where I think Florensky got things right or wrong.[4]

Memorializing Florensky

As we have seen, Florensky constantly memorialized his past, trusting that what had been good and valuable would not die but rather would live on and continue to bear fruit. Today, he himself is being memorialized as one of Russia's great religious philosophers.

In his foreword to Avril Pyman's biography of Florensky, Geoffrey Hosking, the eminent scholar of Russian history, notes, "Florensky has been called the twentieth-century Russian Leonardo da Vinci so great was his erudition in very diverse scientific fields: he published serious studies in mathematics, physics, electrodynamics, folkloristics, philology, art history and theory, philosophy and theology."[5] In *The Gulag Archipelago*, Aleksandr Solzhenitsyn comes to a similar conclusion: Florensky was "one of the most remarkable men devoured by the Archipelago. . . . He was a scholar rare for the twentieth century, who had attained a professional mastery of a multitude of knowledge."[6]

When in April 1943 Sergei Bulgakov, friend and colleague, received word of Florensky's death, he wrote a glowing tribute. In contrast to Bulgakov, Florensky had chosen not to leave Russia after the Revolution, but rather to make a Christian witness under the new, trying political circumstances. "Among my contemporaries,"

4. For important summaries and assessments of Florensky that I have consulted, see my bibliography.

5. Geoffrey Hosking, "Foreword," in Avril Pyman, *Pavel Florensky: A Quiet Genius* (New York: Continuum, 2010), xviii.

6. Aleksandr I. Solzhenitsyn, *The Gulag Archipelago*, vol. III-IV, trans. Thomas P. Whitney (New York: Harper and Row, 1975), 670.

asserts Bulgakov, "he was the greatest." He was a "confessor" and a "martyr." Bulgakov particularly admired Florensky's capacity to retain an "inner freedom" during revolutionary times, a "theological freedom" sustained by life in the church and service as a priest.[7]

Like Bulgakov, Florensky's namesake, grandson Pavel Vasil'evich Florensky (b. 1936), emphasizes his grandfather's "inner freedom." He was "spiritually free," even under outer conditions of political repression, and this freedom gave him the strength and determination to "carry his cross to Golgotha."[8]

According to Pavel Vasil'evich, it was fitting, ironically, that Florensky had been given a cross to bear—undeserved arrest and condemnation, suffering in the gulag, and arbitrary execution. Florensky, in fact, had belonged to a counterrevolutionary organization, just not the one of the fabricated 1933 case. Rather, he had conspired with others in 1919 to hide the head of St. Sergius from desecration, something that the authorities never learned.[9] Florensky had accepted suffering by remaining in Russia, in order to guard Russia's mission to show forth God's beauty and truth to the rest of the world. In a similar vein, Natalino Valentini, an Italian scholar, argues that Florensky understood himself to be taking Bolshevik Russia's guilt upon himself as an act of expiation.[10]

True to their family heritage, of such importance to Florensky, his children and grandchildren rescued his life and work from obscurity after his imprisonment and death—and at considerable risk to themselves. As Solzhenitsyn notes, "In that awful time, when in apprehensive loneliness precious photographs, precious letters and

7. S. N. Bul'gakov, "Sviashchennik o. Pavel Florenskii" [The priest Fr. Pavel Florensky], in Bul'gakov, *Sochineniia v dvukh tomakh: filosofiia khoziaistva/tragediia filosofii* [Essays in two volumes: philosophy of economy and the tragedy of philosophy], vol. 1 (Moscow: Nauka, 1993), 538, 544.

8. P. V. Florenskii, "Predislovie" [Foreword], in Sviashchennik Pavel Florenskii, *Vse Dumy—o Vas* [All my thoughts are about you] (St. Petersburg: Satis'/Derzhava, 2004), 16.

9. Florenskii, "Predislovie," 14.

10. Natalino Valentini, *Pavel Florenskii*, trans. Ol'ga Khmelevskaia (Moscow: Bibleisko-bogoslovskii institut sv. apostola Andreia, 2015), 9.

diaries, were burned, when every yellowed piece of paper in the family cupboard all of a sudden gleamed out like a fiery fern of death … what great heroism was required *not* to burn things up night after night … and to preserve the archives of those who had been sentenced (like Florensky)."[11] Thanks to Florensky's family, writings that could not be published in his lifetime began to appear in a slow but steady trickle after the Khrushchev thaw.

Another grandson, Archimandrite Andronik (Aleksandr Sergeevich) Trubachev (1952–2021), devoted his life to editing and explicating his grandfather's thinking. His five volumes, *Put' k Bogu: lichnost', zhizn' i tvorchestvo sviashchennika Pavla Florenskogo* (The Way to God: The Person, Life, and Work of the Priest Pavel Florensky), collect passages from Florensky's letters, diaries, lectures, and occasional writings; memories and reflections from his contemporaries; and Trubachev's own commentary.[12] Trubachev paints a glowing picture of his grandfather, even lauding his political thought, including the controversial tractate that Florensky wrote while under interrogation in 1933.[13]

Already the subject of considerable scholarly attention in Russia, Italy, and Germany, Florensky is now becoming better known in the English-speaking world. *Pillar and Ground*, *Iconostasis*, key essays on art and the Lavra, and some of his early theological writings are available in fine translations. Other key

11. Solzhenitsyn, *Gulag*, 641.

12. See Pavel Florenskii, "Predpolagaemoe gosudarstvennoe ustroistvo v budushchem" [A proposal for the construction of a future government], in Pavel Florenskii, *Sochineniia v chetyrech tomakh* [Collected essays in four volumes], vol. 2, ed. Andronik Trubachev et al. (Moscow: Mysl', 1996), 647–81.

13. Trubachev goes so far as to call the tractate a "classic" alongside the political works of Ivan Il'in and Aleksandr Solzhenitsyn. Trubachev argues that Florensky's interrogators expected him to write a tractate that would confirm his fascist sympathies. Instead, he shrewdly used his words to advance a vision of government that seemed sympathetic to the communist regime, yet implicitly challenged it. See Andronik Trubachev "Predislovie" [Foreword], in Pavel Florenskii, *Predpolagaemoe gosudarstvennoe ustroistvo v budushchem* [A proposal for the construction of a future government], ed. Andronik Trubachev (Sergiev Posad: Gorodets, 2009).

writings are in the process of translation. Secondary literature is quickly growing.

In this book, I have suggested why Florensky deserves our attention today: his vision of God's light, the "other" world, shining in and through the things of this world; his understanding of the symbolic and revelatory character of the creation; and his insight into how the cult—ritual and prayer—makes culture possible and sacralizes it. These themes resonate powerfully with many of us in a time of environmental degradation and social fragmentation.

Florensky's thought, like the European Romanticism of the nineteenth century, may be overly dismissive of industrial, secular "civilization" and its "rationality," but Florensky rightly challenges the scientism that is still too much with us. The proponents of Marxism-Leninism promised to construct a new, harmonious society on the basis of objective, scientific principles.[14] The result was political totalitarianism and the gulag. Today, Western political and social leaders, while affirming democratic political structures, frequently justify their social programs by appealing to scientific-technological expertise. As with Marxism-Leninism, such a stance easily reduces the natural world and even human beings to inert objects that are to be analyzed and manipulated to achieve certain "desirable" social ends.[15]

Philosopher Bruce Foltz describes our situation as one in which the "world is not transparent ..., but rather solid and opaque and self-sufficient, an idol of science and Enlightenment philosophy—with no interior and no other side—with a density that absorbs all light. It is open to no illumination beyond our own projections." Foltz turns to Florensky—and to the Church Fathers, the nineteenth-century Romantic poets, and C. S. Lewis and J. R. R. Tolkien—to recover an "ontological symbolism ... of

14. See Arsenii Gulyga, *Tvortsy russkoi idei* [Makers of the Russian idea] (Moscow: Molodaia gvardiia, 2006), 249.

15. See my essay, "Blessing as the Ground of Morality: Pavel Florensky and Political Resistance," *Journal of the Society of Christian Ethics* 41/2 (Fall/Winter 2021): 279–96.

how all creation serves in its very being to participate in, and make manifest, the energies of higher [divine] realities."[16]

I would add that Florensky issues a highly needed challenge to the Christian churches. Their principal mission is not to conduct moralistic crusades, whether politically right or left, but rather to set forth ontological truth. To be a Christian is to grow in one's capacity to receive and set forth divine beauty and glory. One truly becomes a "new creation," emptied of one's own ego, in order to enter into the mystery and wonder of what is "other"—ultimately, into the other, divine life of Father, Son, and Holy Spirit. Moral activity flows out of a changed being; it cannot take its place. As Soviet philosopher Arsenii Gulyga insightfully wrote, "[For Florensky] truth acquires an ontological sense. Truth is life, given to us. It is not knowledge about life; rather, it is true life."[17]

Questioning Florensky

In this book, I have offered an appreciative, though not uncritical, assessment of Florensky's thought. However, it is important for anyone who wishes to delve further into Florensky to be aware of three major concerns that I have mentioned along the way but have not posed as sharply as some of his critics do: his inattention to biblical salvation history, his medievalism (and concomitant antimodernism and anti-Semitism), and his reliance on Western philosophy.

Biblical Salvation History The renowned church historian and Orthodox priest John Meyendorff raises the first concern in his review of Russian Silver Age religious philosophy.[18] Florensky,

16. Bruce (Seraphim) Foltz, "'His Tabernacle Was Around Him': Prolegomenon to a Symbolic Ontology of Creation," unpublished paper presented at the Paideia Conference, May 20, 2023, Antiochian Village, Pennsylvania.

17. Gulyga, *Tvortsy*, 246.

18. John Meyendorff, *Rome, Constantinople, Moscow: Historical and Theological Studies* (Crestwood, NY: St. Vladimir's Seminary Press, 1996), 153–64, 188.

following the thinking of Vladimir Solov'ev, takes the principal theological-philosophical problem to be how God and man—the eternal and the temporal, the infinite and the finite, the ideal and the empirical—can meet and relate, without an all-powerful God destroying mortal humanity.

I have argued that Florensky found an answer not because he first worked out a Christological theory from Orthodox dogma, but rather because he had a personal and profound encounter with a living Christ. Florensky seems to have experienced a Christ who loved him unconditionally, and who in loving him brought together the two poles, the "other" world and this world, that Florensky could not reconcile on his own. This Christ was divine yet human, wholly beyond Florensky yet intimately near to him. Perhaps even more important to Florensky's subsequent thinking was his discovery of Christ's cross (and, more generally, of death, as in that of Fr. Isidore) as a place into which the light of eternity nevertheless shines, overcoming darkness and melancholy.

Nevertheless, Florensky's attention to the "vertical," the axis between heaven and earth that is constituted by a hierarchy of mediating agents, comes at the expense of the "horizontal." Florensky has little sense of a biblical history of salvation that begins in Eden, proceeds through the fall, continues in God's promises to Israel, and culminates in the life, death, resurrection, and return of Jesus Christ, the World Ruler. It is striking that the question of atonement—how Christ conquers sin by taking it upon himself and dying on a cross—plays no significant role in Florensky's thought.

While Florensky does see history developing toward an era of the Holy Spirit in which the world as a whole will become more transparent to God's glory, he pays remarkably little attention to the Christ who enters into history to heal the sick, cast out demons, interpret the Scriptures, and proclaim the kingdom. Nor does Florensky trace Christ's continuing work in the church's ministries to those who suffer injustice, disability, or trauma.

Meyendorff suggests that, in this respect, Florensky belongs more to the tradition of Origen than to that of Athanasius.

Nikolai Pavliuchenkov, one of contemporary Russian Orthodoxy's important interpreters of Florensky, has a similar assessment.[19] Florensky's metaphysics are problematic from an Orthodox dogmatic point of view. Basic to Florensky's worldview was his childhood experience of "another" world shining through the natural world. When Florensky later studied philosophy, he found that Plato and Solov'ev, influenced by Origen, gave him the categories by which to make sense of nature's revelatory character.

To be sure, upon entering seminary, Florensky stated an intention to "correct" Origen. Pavliuchenkov argues that he nevertheless failed. Ideas basic to Origen and Solov'ev remain dominant. Florensky does not have a clear doctrine of a creation *ex nihilo*, of a historical fall, or of a Christ who effects salvation in history. For Florensky, the creation, though ontologically different from God (he rejects pantheism), nevertheless retains an eternal, perfected existence in the mind of God. Similarly, the human fall affects only the empirical self (the "likeness" of God), not the ideal self (the "image" of God, which is already divinized). Christ's Incarnation and atonement are accessory but not essential to salvation, for history itself is an evolutionary process that eventually returns the world to its original condition.

Pavliuchenkov does not dispute that Florensky experienced a profound conversion to Christ and the life of the church. But as with his childhood experience of nature, Florensky relies primarily on Plato and Solov'ev to interpret Orthodox ritual and sacraments. Pavliuchenkov fears that at other points Florensky

19. Nikolai N. Pavliuchenkov, *Religiozno-filosofskoe nasledie sviashchennika Pavla Florenskogo: antropolicheskie aspekty* [The religious-philosophical legacy of Fr. Pavel Florensky: anthropological aspects] (Moscow: St. Tikhon's University Press, 2012); and Pavliuchenkov, "Bogoslovskie raboty i bogoslovie P. A. Florenskogo: 1902–1909" [The theological works and the theology of P. A. Florensky, 1902–1909], in P. A. Florenskii, *Bogoslovskie trudy: 1902–1909* [Theological works: 1902–1909] (Moscow: St. Tikhon's University Press, 2018), 7–35.

simply adopts occultist and popular folklorist ideas, as in his understanding of names. Moreover, Pavliuchenkov is struck by how little Florensky writes about a personal religious life. Indeed, in his memoirs for his children, he never mentions prayer or a personal sense of God's presence.

Where Pavliuchenkov finds Florensky more helpful is in his recovery of elements of Orthodox hesychasm with its confidence that one can experience God's energies (though not know his essence) directly through prayer (the Jesus Prayer, in particular) and ascetical practice. Florensky's interest in hesychasm and its defender, Gregory Palamas, is evident in his conviction that the divine light (energy) shines through the creation and the saints, especially Seraphim of Sarov. Florensky reminds us that the ultimate goal of the Christian is deification: to enter into the life, the energies, of God.

Medievalism This second issue—Florensky's medievalism, antimodernism, and anti-Semitism—has been carefully analyzed by the German scholar Michael Hagemeister.[20] Hagemeister argues that Florensky idealizes a medieval Russian, Platonic worldview, rejects (and caricatures) the Renaissance and Kant (along with modernity and its activist, humanistic spirit), and embraces a magical understanding of names, pictures (icons), and rituals.

Hagemeister documents Florensky's belief that an eschatological battle for world rule is taking place between Russia and the West. Florensky has a chauvinist Russian nationalism that is deeply anti-Semitic. In Hagemeister's (and Florensky's) words,

> Who are the dark powers of chaos, of levelling, of equality, of death? Who are the "enemies of humanity," enemies of culture, enemies of

20. Michael Hagemeister, "Wiederzauberung der Welt: Pavel Florenskij's Neues Mittelalter" [Reenchantment of the World: Pavel Florensky's New Middle Ages], in *Pavel Florenskij—Tradition und Moderne,* ed. Nobert Franz, Michael Hagemeister, and Frank Haney (Frankfurt am Main: Peter Lang, 2000), 21–41.

> the highest inheritance of mankind? Who are the opponents who play with salvation history, the allies of the antichrist? It is those … who preach the autonomy of the individual and of universal equality, and who put democracy and human rights in place of divine grace and obedience.… It is the Jews.

Hagemeister has persuasively demonstrated that Florensky anonymously authored several virulently anti-Semitic essays in the early 1910s. Florensky clearly shared popular Orthodox accusations that Jews had committed ritual killing of Christian children. He asserted that Jews had a mystical drive to have "blood." In response, Christians need to "beat up Israel, so that it comes to its senses and renounces its vileness."[21]

Avril Pyman, who has written the definitive English-language biography of Florensky, counters that "nowhere" in Florensky's writings are there "traces of anti-Semitism."[22] She notes Florensky's untroubled speculations that he might have Semitic roots on his mother's side. According to Pyman, Florensky simply used the common vocabulary of his time ("blood," "seed") to talk about ethnic and national identity. If these terms have in the meantime become thoroughly discredited, it is because of how the Nazis used them. Today, we have replaced them with the language (perhaps equally problematic) of genes and DNA.

My own reading of Florensky further complicates the question of his anti-Semitism. As I have noted, Florensky could get carried away by his curiosity. In his letters and occasional writings, he sometimes employs impulsive, ill-considered language. When he and Rozanov engage each other, Rozanov eggs him on to speculate wildly about Jewish blood and seed, and Florensky takes the bait.

After 1915, however, Florensky pays little attention to Israel or Judaism. What he does say simply reflects the widespread and

21. Hagemeister, "Wiederzauberung," 30.

22. Pyman, *Florensky*, 106.

unfortunate Christian supersessionism of that time. In *Salt of the Earth*, Florensky reports that Fr. Isidore "loves" Jews, because he is hoping to convert them. In *Pillar and Ground*, Judaism's monotheism functions as a foil to Christianity's trinitarianism. Whatever we make of Florensky's anti-Semitism, it is clear that he never offers a positive assessment of Judaism and the Jews—in contrast to Solov'ev, who in so many other respects influenced him.[23]

Florensky regularly caricatures not only Judaism but also other religions. He unhelpfully reduces Catholicism to scholasticism, papal authority, and theocracy; Protestantism, to rationality and private interpretation of Scripture. At the same time, however, Florensky does approvingly report Fr. Isidore's hope for uniting the Catholic and Orthodox Churches, a cause that Solov'ev had supported.[24]

Florensky's "chauvinistic nationalism" also requires qualification. To be sure, Florensky believes that Russians are a chosen (Orthodox) people who have been given unique insight into divine truth. Nevertheless, in *Pillar and Ground*, he warns that nationalism cannot bring about true social unity. What is needed, instead, is a kenotic love by which one person reaches out to another. Moreover, in his "Notes about Orthodoxy" (1923, but not published until the 1990s), Florensky laments how the Russian people have distorted their divine commission to the world; they have made a god out of their peoplehood, and instead of repenting of their sins they have regarded themselves as superior to other peoples.[25]

Hagemeister rightly warns us against admiring Florensky's "medieval" worldview uncritically. It includes too much "baggage" that

23. For Solov'ev's position, see Paul Valliere, *Modern Russian Theology: Bukharev, Soloviev, Bulgakov* (Grand Rapids, MI: Eerdmans, 2000), 192–203.

24. See my chapter 3. For Solov'ev, see Valliere, *Modern Russian Theology*, 178–92.

25. Pavel Florenskii, "Zapiski o Pravoslavii," in Pavel Florenskii, *Sochineniia v chetyrech tomakh* [Collected works in four volumes], vol. 2, ed. Andronik Trubachev et al. (Moscow: Mysl', 1996), 544–46. My thanks to Dr. Christoph Schneider for bringing this essay to my attention.

is truly troubling. Florensky's contemporary, Nicolas Berdyaev, had similar reservations. While acknowledging Florensky's brilliance, he regarded him as standing "for all the things" that Berdyaev himself "held in abomination: [Florensky] glorified … a rigid Byzantinism … [and] substituted Sophia for the living person of Christ and cosmic order for the freedom of man."[26] He was a "reactionary" aesthete.[27]

Nevertheless, in criticizing Florensky's view of the Renaissance and the Enlightenment, we need not caricature his "medievalism" in return. Florensky believed that the medieval worldview expressed genuine Christian truths. Medieval Christians were attuned to the world's symbolic, revelatory character. Today, some thoughtful Russian intellectuals, such as novelist Eugene Vodolazkin, believe that a postmodern world is leading us into a new Middle Ages. We will no longer experience history as a sequence of impersonal causes and effects but rather as a series of unique, divinely inspired moments, each of which opens us to moral self-improvement and deeper concern for others.[28]

Western Philosophy The third objection to Florensky has been expressed especially strongly by Fr. Georges Florovsky.[29] Florovsky championed a "neo-patristic synthesis" that would rescue Orthodox thinking from its captivity to Western philosophy and return it to its original biblical and patristic foundations.[30] He regarded Solov'ev and his followers, especially Florensky and Bulgakov

26. Nicolas Berdyaev, *Dream and Reality: An Essay in Autobiography* (New York: Macmillan, 1951), 166.

27. Nicolas Berdyaev, *The Russian Idea* (New York: Macmillan, 1948), 238.

28. See Gary Saul Morson, "Living Outside of Time," *New York Review of Books* (January 19, 2023): 48–50; and Eugene Vodolazkin, "The New Middle Ages," *First Things* (August 2016), https://www.firstthings.com/article/2016/08/the-new-middle-ages.

29. Georges Florovsky, *Ways of Russian Theology*, part 2, trans. Robert L. Nichols (Vaduz, Liechtenstein: Büchervertriebsanstalt, 1987), 276–81.

30. See Paul L. Gavrilyuk, "Florovsky's Neopatristic Synthesis and the Future Ways of Orthodox Theology," in *Orthodox Constructions of the West*, ed. George E. Demacopoulos and Aristotle Papanikolaou (New York: Fordham University Press, 2013), 102–24.

(in the latter's early theological work), as abandoning Orthodoxy for Schelling, Neoplatonism, and other Western thinkers. Florovsky's criticisms of Florensky are especially sharp:

> Florenskii did not proceed from the depths of Orthodoxy. In the Orthodox world he remained a stranger. The inner spirit of [*Pillar and Ground*] is western, having been written by a westerner seeking salvation in the East through dreams and esthetics. The romantic tragedy of western culture was closer and more intelligible to Florenskii than the problematics of Orthodox culture. It is highly characteristic that in his work he reverted past Christianity to Platonism and ancient religions. He became sidetracked in the study of occultism and magic.

Florovsky echoes Meyendorff and Pavliuchenkov: "Florenskii had no sense for history. He neither lived in history nor possessed an historical perspective." "He neither sensed nor left any room for the absolute character of the epiphany of God in the New Testament." "Florenskii's 'theodicy' contains no Savior—the world is somehow 'justified' without Him." "The 'experiment in Orthodox theodicy' is somehow carried out without Christ." "Florenskii has surprisingly little to say . . . about the sacraments."[31]

Florovsky's own theological commitments prejudice him against Florensky from the outset. Florovsky ignores Florensky's admission in *Pillar and Ground* that he could not address questions of Christology "without going beyond the bounds set for my work, whose object is a theodicy, not an anthropodicy. . . . If this is not taken into account, I risk being seen as a Christian without Christ."[32] Nor does Florovsky acknowledge Florensky's words "To the Reader" that one knows Orthodoxy only by experiencing it and entering into the life of the church.

31. Florovsky, *Russian Theology*, 277, 280.

32. Florensky, *Pillar and Ground*, 452 n. 68. See Florenskii, *Stolp i utverzhdenie*, 630 n. 66.

Florovsky seems to have known Florensky's thinking only in *Pillar and Ground*. Had he read *Philosophy of the Cult*, he could not have accused Florensky of ignoring either Christ or the sacraments. Florovsky fails to see how deeply devoted Florensky was to Orthodox ritual and the church's liturgy.

Where Florovsky is more helpful is in reminding us that Florensky mixes together, not always successfully, a wide variety of theological and philosophical resources. Alexander Schmemann, the great American Orthodox theologian, makes the point more clearly: "No one [other than Florensky] reflects better the peculiar combination of spirituality and aestheticism, mysticism and scientific preoccupation, traditionalism and modernism that were typical of that time."[33] Florensky does not ignore the Church Fathers, but he more often uses them to confirm his thinking than to ground it in them.

In Place of a Conclusion

Of the Russian religious philosophers of the early twentieth century, Bulgakov and Berdyaev have received the most attention in the West; Florensky, I believe, has a proper place alongside them. Although his works are not for the beginner, they do promise rich rewards to anyone who seeks a deeper appreciation of Orthodoxy's vision of the God who enters into the world and transforms it.

There is a second important reason to study Florensky today. He helps us recognize and assess historic currents of Russian thinking that regularly reassert themselves—and that too often have been tragically used for narrow nationalistic purposes. Florensky represents these themes in his unique way: the centrality of Orthodoxy to Russian national identity; the special mission of the Russian people to preserve Orthodoxy; and the distinctive presence within Russia of a divine beauty and glory that radiate

33. Alexander Schmemann, *Ultimate Questions: An Anthology of Modern Russian Religious Thought* (New York: Holt, Reinhart and Winston, 1965), 135.

through the very landscape, whose churches and monasteries on the horizon give Russia such a different "look" from the West's. What Dostoevsky expresses so powerfully in his novels finds lyrical philosophical formulation in Florensky's writings.

Florensky's dramatic life history, culminating in his death in the gulag, calls forth deep respect. Indeed, some admirers believe that he should be canonized as a saint. Notwithstanding his personal courage, assessments of Florensky the thinker will necessarily vary. We do best neither to idealize nor to discount his worldview. Whatever history's final judgment about his "orthodoxy," we can share his confidence that if there was anything good and valuable in his thinking, it will not be lost; it will live on and help us better know both God and ourselves.

Many of us today, in both East and West, long for a deeper sense of divine presence in a disenchanted world. Florensky has remarkable insight into the possibilities and perils of a way ahead.

BIBLIOGRAPHY

Florensky Texts in Russian

Florenskii, Pavel. *Bogoslovskie trudy, 1902–1909* [Theological works, 1902–1909]. Edited by N. N. Pavliuchenkov. Moscow: St. Tikhon's University Press, 2018.

———. *Detiam moim* [To my children]. Moscow: Moskovskii rabochii, 1992.

———. *Filosofiia kul'ta* [Philosophy of the cult]. Moscow: Akademicheskii proekt, 2018.

———. *Istoriia i filosofiia iskusstva* [History and philosophy of art]. Moscow: Akademicheskii proekt, 2017.

———. *Predpolagaemoe gosudarstvennoe ustroistvo v budushchem* [A proposal for the construction of a future government]. Edited by Andronik Trubachev. Sergiev Posad: Gorodets, 2009.

———. *Sochineniia v chetyrekh tomakh* [Collected essays in four volumes]. Vol. 2. Moscow: Mysl', 1996.

———. *Stolp i utverzhdenie istinny* [The pillar and ground of the truth]. 2nd ed. Moscow: Akademicheskii proekt, 2017.

———. *Vse Dumy—o Vas* [All my thoughts are about you]. St. Petersburg: Satis'/Derzhava, 2004.

Rozanov, V. V. *Literaturnye izgnanniki* [Literary exiles]. Vol. 2. Moscow: Respublika, 2010.

Trubachev, Igumen Andronik. *Put' k Bogu: lichnost', zhizn' i tvorchestvo sviashchennika Pavla Florenskogo* [The way to God: the person, life, and work of the priest Pavel Florensky]. 5 vols. Sergiev Posad: Gorodets, 2012–2018.

Florensky Texts in English Translation

Florensky, Pavel. *At the Crossroads of Science and Mysticism*. Translated by Boris Jakim. Kettering, OH: Semantron Press, 2014.

———. *Beyond Vision: Essays on the Perception of Art*. Edited by Nicoletta Misler. Translated by Wendy Salmond. London: Reaktion Books, 2002.

———. *Early Religious Writings, 1902–1909*. Translated by Boris Jakim. Grand Rapids, MI: Eerdmans, 2017.

———. *Iconostasis*. Translated by Donald Sheehan and Olga Andrejev. Crestwood, NY: St. Vladimir's Seminary Press, 1996.

———. *The Pillar and Ground of the Truth*. Translated by Boris Jakim. Princeton, NJ: Princeton University Press, 1997.

———. *Ultimate Questions: An Anthology of Modern Russian Religious Thought*. Edited by Alexander Schmemann. New York: Holt, Reinhart and Winston, 1965.

Secondary Literature in Russian on Florensky and His Context

Basinskii, Pavel. *Sviatoi protiv L'va: Ioann Kronstadtskii i Lev Tol'stoi, istoriia odnoi vrazhdy* [The holy man versus the Lion: John of Kronstadt and Lev Tolstoy, the history of an enmity]. Moscow: ACT, 2016.

Bul'gakov, S.N. "Sviashchennik o. Pavel Florenskii" [The priest Fr. Pavel Florensky]. In Bul'gakov, *Sochhineniia v dvukh tomakh: filosofiia khoziaistva/tragediia filosofii* [Essays in two volumes: philosophy of economy and the tragedy of philosophy], vol. 1, 538–47. Moscow: Nauka, 1993.

Burgess, John P. "Smysl zhizni v razgovorakh P.A. Florenskogo s det'mi po materialam perepisok" [The meaning of life as set forth in Pavel Florensky's correspondence with his children]. *Nauchnyi resul'tat: sotsialnye i gumanitarnye issledovaniia* [Research results: sociological and humanistic] 7, no. 1 (2021): 20–24.

———. "Sviatost' i svoboda: vzgliad Pavla Florenskogo" [Holiness and freedom: the view of Pavel Florensky]. *Nauchnyi resul'tat: sotsialnye i gumanitarnye issledovaniia* [Research results: sociological and humanistic] 5, no. 2 (2019): 55–59.

———. "Starets kak dukhovnyi rukovoditel': vzgliad Pavla Florenskogo" [Holy elder as spiritual director: the view of Pavel Florensky]. *Trudy Kurskoi dukhovnoi seminarii* [Works of the Kursk Theological Seminary] 1, no. 1 (2019): 25–30.

———. "Tainstvennye sviazi, soediniaiushchie vsiu zhizn': perepiska Florenskogo i Rozanova v 1908–1911 gg." [The secret bonds uniting all of life: the correspondence of Pavel Florensky and Vasilii Rozanov, 1908–1911]. In *Evangelie v kontekste sovremennoi kul'tury* [The gospel in the context of contemporary culture], edited by T. I. Lipich et al., 6–8. Belgorod: Epitsentr, 2020.

Chetverikov, S. I. *Optina Pustyn'*. Paris: YMCA Press, 1926.

El'chaninov, A. V. "Iz vstrechi s P. A. Florenskim" [From an encounter with P. A. Florensky]. *Vestnik* 142, no. 3 (1984): 68–78.

Florenskii, P. V. "Sviashchennik, ne sniavshii s sebia sana" [A priest who never renounced his ordination]. In Sviashchennik Pavel Florenskii, *Vse Dumy—o Vas*, 509–33. St. Petersburg: Satis'/Derzhava, 2004.

Gefsimanskii skit i peshchery pri nem [The Gethsemane skete and its caves]. Sergiev Posad: Sviato–Troitskaia Sergieva Lavra, 1899.

Gulyga, Arsenii. *Tvortsy russkoi idei* [Makers of the Russian idea]. Moscow: Molodaia gvardiia, 2006.

"Instruktsiia S.–Peterburgskoi Dukhovnoi Akademii" [Rules and Regulations of the St. Petersburg Theological Academy] (1894). Reprinted from the Archives of Americans of Russian Descent in Minnesota.

Mazyrin, A. "'Sergievskaia' ('Samarinskaia') tserkovnaia gruppa i Patriarshii mestobliusitel' mitropolit Petr (Polianskii) v 1925 g." [The Sergiev (Samarin) church group and the patriarchal locums tenens metropolitan Petr (Polianskii)]. In *Podvigom dobrym podvizalsia* [Having attained spiritual victory by means of spiritual achievement], edited by S. N. Chernyshev and Dimitrii Sazonov, 162–76. Kostroma: Kostroma Metropolia, 2017, http://bibl-kostroma.ru/wp-content/uploads/2018/07/Podvigom-dobrym_block-2017-web.pdf.

"Moskovskii starets Aleksei Mechev" [The Moscow holy elder Aleksei Mechev]. *Al'fa and Omega* 23, no. 1 (2000), http://aliom.orthodoxy.ru/arch/023/023-mechev.htm.

Pavliuchenkov, Nikolai N. *Religiozno-filosofskoe nasledie sviashchennika Pavla Florenskogo: antropolicheskie aspekty* [The religious-philosophical legacy of Fr. Pavel Florensky: anthropological aspects]. Moscow: St. Tikhon's University Press, 2012.

———. "Bogoslovskie raboty i bogoslovie P. A. Florenskogo: 1902–1909" [The theological works and the theology of P. A. Florensky, 1902–1909]. In P. A. Florenskii, *Bogoslovskie trudy: 1902–1909*, 7–36. Moscow: St. Tikhon's University Press, 2018.

Seraphim (Chichagov), *Zhitie prepodobnogo Serafima, Sarovskogo chudotvortsa* [The life of Saint Seraphim, the Sarov miracle-worker] (1903).

Shentalinskii, Vitalii. "Khranit' vechno" [Preserve eternally]. *Ogonek* 45 (November 1990): 23–27.

Smirnova, T. V. "… *pod pokrov Prepodobnogo": ocherki o nekotorykh izvestnykh sem'iakh zhivshikh v Sergievom Posade v 1920-e gody* [Beneath the protective veil of the Saint: notes about several famous families living in Sergiev Posad in the 1920s]. Sergiev Posad: Sviato–Troitskaia Sergieva Lavra, 2008.

Stepashkin, Valentin. *Serafim Sarovskii.* 2nd ed. Moscow: Molodaia gvardiia, 2019.

Trubachev, Igumen Andronik. "Filosofsko-politicheskie vzgliady sviashchennika Pavla Florenskogo" [The philosophical-religious views of the priest Pavel Florensky] and "Prilozhenie: khronologiia zhizni sviashchennika Pavla Florenskogo, 1918–1922 [Appendix: chronology of the life of Fr. Pavel Florensky, 1918–1922]. In Igumen Andronik Trubachev, *Put' k Bogu: lichnost', zhizn' i tvorchestvo sviashchennika Pavla Florenskogo*, vol. 4., 7–36, 371–678. Sergiev Posad: Gorodets, 2016.

———. "Istoriia sozdaniia tsikla 'Filosofiia kul'ta …'" [History of the composition of *Philosophy of the Cult*]. In Pavel A. Florenskii, *Filosofiia kul'ta*, 5–24. Moscow: Akademicheskii proekt, 2018.

———. "Predislovie" [Foreword]. In Pavel Florenskii, *Predpolagaemoe gosudarstvennoe ustroistvo v budushchem* [A proposal for the construction of a future government], edited by Andronik Trubachev, 5–6. Sergiev Posad: Gorodets, 2009.

———. "Prilozhenie: iz istorii sozdaniia knigi '*Stolp i utverzhdenie istinny: opyt pravoslavnoi teoditsei v dvenadtsakh pis'makh*'" [Appendix: the history of the composition of *The Pillar and Ground of the Truth: The Experience of an Orthodox Theodicy in Twelve Letters*]. In Pavel Florenskii, *Stolp i utverzhdenie istinny*, 2nd ed., 816–88. Moscow: Akademicheskii proekt, 2017.

———. "Primechaniia: Troitse-Sergieva lavra i Rossiia" [Notes: Trinity–Sergius Lavra and Russia]. In Pavel Florenskii, *Istoriia i filosofiia iskusstva*, 547–54. Moscow: Akademicheskii proekt, 2017.

Valentini, Natalino. *Pavel Florenskii.* Translated by Ol'ga Khmelevskaia. Moscow: Bibleisko-bogoslovskii institut sv. apostola Andreia, 2015. From the Italian: Natalino Valentini. *Pavel A. Florenskii.* Brescia: Morcelliana, 2004.

"Voskovaia skul'ptura Petra I: odin iz samych strannych eksponatov Ermitazha" [The wax sculpture of Peter I: one of the strangest exhibits in the Hermitage]. *Livejournal* (September 9, 2021), https://picturehistory.livejournal.com/6790935.html.

Other Secondary Literature on Florensky and His Context

Antonova, Clemena. *Visual Thought in Russian Religious Philosophy: Pavel Florensky's Theory of the Icon*. New York: Routledge, 2019.

Berdyaev, Nicolas. *Dream and Reality: An Essay in Autobiography*. New York: Macmillan, 1951.

———. *The Russian Idea*. New York: Macmillan, 1948.

Bethea, David M. "Florensky and Dante: Revelation, Orthodoxy, and Non-Euclidean Space." In *Russian Religious Thought*, edited by Judith Deutsch Kornblatt and Richard F. Gustafson, 112–31. Madison: University of Wisconsin Press, 1996.

Bois, Yve-Alain. "School." In *Revoliutsiia! Demonstratsiia! Soviet Art Put to the Test*, edited by Matthew S. Witkovsky and Devine Fore, 44–77. Chicago: Art Institute of Chicago, 2017.

Burgess, John P. "Blessing as the Ground of Morality: Pavel Florensky and Political Resistance." *Journal of the Society of Christian Ethics* 41, no. 2 (Fall/Winter 2021): 279–96.

Cassedy, Steven. "P. A. Florensky and the Celebration of Matter." In *Russian Religious Thought*, edited by Judith Deutsch Kornblatt and Richard F. Gustafson, 95–111. Madison: University of Wisconsin Press, 1996.

———. "Pavel Florenskii's Trinitarian Humanism." In *A History of Russian Philosophy, 1830–1930*, edited by G. M. Hamburg and Randall A. Poole, 190–204. New York: Cambridge University Press, 2010.

Emerson, Caryl. "Love as an Act of Rebellion: Orthodoxy and Literary Culture." *Christian History* 146: 21–25.

Fedotov, G. P. *A Treasury of Russian Spirituality*. London: Sheed & Ward, 1950.

Florovsky, Georges. *Ways of Russian Theology*. Part 2. Vaduz, Liechtenstein: Büchervertriebsanstalt, 1987.

Foltz, Bruce (Seraphim). "'His Tabernacle Was Around Him': Prolegomenon to a Symbolic Ontology of Creation." Unpublished paper presented at the Paideia Conference, May 20, 2023, Antiochian Village, Pennsylvania.

Gavrilyuk, Paul L. "Florovsky's Neopatristic Synthesis and the Future Ways of Orthodox Theology." In *Orthodox Constructions of the West*, edited by George E. Demacopoulos and Aristotle Papanikolaou, 102–24. New York: Fordham University Press, 2013.

Graham, Loren, and Jean-Michel Kantor. *Naming Infinity: A True Story of Religious Mysticism and Mathematical Creativity*. Cambridge: Harvard University Press, 2009.

Gustafson, Richard F. "Introduction." In Pavel Florensky, *The Pillar and Ground of the Truth*. Translated by Boris Jakim, ix–xxiii. Princeton, NJ: Princeton University Press, 1997.

Hagemeister, Michael. "Wiederzauberung der Welt: Pavel Florenskij's Neues Mittelalter" [Re-enchantment of the World: Pavel Florensky's New Middle Ages]. In *Pavel Florenskij, Tradition und Moderne*, edited by Norbert Franz, Michael Hagemeister, and Frank Haney, 21–41. Frankfurt am Main: Peter Lang, 2000.

Hagemeister, Michael, and Nina Kauchtschischwili, eds. *P. A. Florenskij e la cultura della sua epocha* [P. A. Florensky and the culture of his epoch]. Marburg: Blau Hörner Verlag, 1995.

Hosking, Geoffrey. "Foreword." In Avril Pyman, *Pavel Florensky: A Quiet Genius*, xv–xix. New York: Continuum, 2010.

Kenworthy, Scott. *The Heart of Russia: Trinity–Sergius, Monasticism, and Society after 1825*. New York: Oxford University Press, 2010.

———. "The Name-Glorifiers (*Imiaslavie*) Controversy." In *The Oxford Handbook of Russian Religious Thought*, edited by Caryl Emerson, George Pattison, and Randall A. Poole, 327–42. New York: Oxford University Press, 2020.

Kizenko, Nadieszda. *A Prodigal Saint: Father John of Kronstadt and the Russian People*. University Park, PA: Pennsylvania State University Press, 2000.

Kolsto, Pål. *Heretical Orthodoxy: Lev Tolstoi and the Russian Orthodox Church*. New York: Cambridge University Press, 2022.

Ladouceur, Paul, and Fr. Richard Rene. "Father Pavel Florensky, *Philia*, and Same-Sex Love." *Public Orthodoxy* (February 26, 2021), https://publicorthodoxy.org/2021/02/26/florensky-philia-same-sex-love/.

Louth, Andrew. *Modern Orthodox Thinkers: From the Philokalia to the Present*. Downers Grove, IL: InterVarsity Press, 2015.

Meyendorff, John. *Rome, Constantinople, Moscow: Historical and Theological Studies*. Crestwood, NY: St. Vladimir's Seminary Press, 1996.

———. *St. Gregory Palamas and Orthodox Spirituality*. Translated by Adele Fiske. Crestwood, NY: St. Vladimir's Seminary Press, 1974.

Misler, Nicoletta. "Pavel Florensky: A Biographical Sketch" and "Pavel Florensky as Art Historian." In Pavel Florensky, *Beyond Vision: Essays on the Perception of Art*, edited by Nicoletta Misler, translated by Wendy Salmond, 13–28, 29–93. London: Reaktion Books, 2002.

Paert, Irina. *Spiritual Elders: Charisma and Tradition in Russian Orthodoxy*. DeKalb, IL: Northern Illinois University Press, 2010.

Pyman, Avril. *Pavel Florensky: A Quiet Genius.* New York: Continuum, 2010.

Robson, Roy R. *Solovki.* New Haven, CT: Yale University Press, 2004.

Sanfillipo, Giacomo. "Conjugal Friendship," *Public Orthodoxy* (May 2, 2017), https://publicorthodoxy.org/2017/05/02/conjugal-friendship/.

Schneider, Christoph. "Pavel Florensky: At the Boundary of Immanence and Transcendence." In *The Oxford Handbook of Russian Religious Thought*, edited by Caryl Emerson, George Pattison, and Randall A. Poole, 293–308. New York: Oxford University Press, 2020.

Sheehan, Donald. "Introduction." In Pavel Florensky, *Iconostasis.* Translated by Donald Sheehan and Olga Andrejev, 5–29. Crestwood, NY: St. Vladimir's Seminary Press, 1996.

Sheredega, Natalya. "Andrei Rublev: Image of the Holy Trinity." *The Tretiakov Gallery Magazine* (2013), https://www.tretyakovgallerymagazine.com/articles/%E2%84%963-2013-40/andrei-rublev-image-holy-trinity.

Slesinski, Robert. *Pavel Florensky: A Metaphysics of Love.* Crestwood, NY: St. Vladimir's Seminary Press, 1984.

Solzhenitsyn, Aleksandr I. *The Gulag Archipelago.* Vol. III-IV. Translated by Thomas P. Whitney. New York: Harper and Row, 1975.

Valliere, Paul. *Modern Russian Theology: Bukharev, Soloviev, Bulgakov.* Grand Rapids, MI: Eerdmans, 2000.

———. "The Theology of Culture in Late Imperial Russia." In *Sacred Stories: Religion and Spirituality in Modern Russia*, edited by Mark D. Steinberg and Heather J. Coleman, 377–95. Bloomington: Indiana University Press, 2007.

Vasilevskaia, V. I. *Women of the Catacombs: Memoirs of the Church in Stalin's Russia.* Edited by Wallace L. Daniel. Ithaca, NY: Cornell University Press, 2021.

Yazykova, Irina. *Hidden and Triumphant: The Underground Struggle to Save Russian Iconography.* Translated by Paul Grenier. Brewster, MA: Paraclete Press, 2010.

Other Literature

Applebaum, Anne. *Gulag: A History.* New York: Doubleday, 2003.

Athanasius. *The Life of St. Antony and the Letter to Marcellinus.* Translated by Robert C. Gregg. Mahwah, NJ: Paulist Press, 1980.

Boswell, John. *Same-Sex Unions in Premodern Europe.* New York: Villard Books, 1994.

Brown, Peter. "The Rise and Function of the Holy Man in Late Antiquity." *Journal of Roman Studies* 61 (1971): 80–101.

Burgess, John P. *Holy Rus': The Rebirth of Orthodoxy in the New Russia.* New Haven, CT: Yale University Press, 2017.

———. "Iconography as Alternative Social-Religious Vision: Fr. Zinon (Teodor)." *Orthodox Arts Journal* (February 14, 2024), https://orthodoxartsjournal.org/iconography-as-alternative-social-religious-vision-fr-zinon-teodor/.

———. "A Visit to Fr. Zinon." *First Things* (January 2024): 47–52.

Carson, Rachel. *The Edge of the Sea.* New York: Houghton Mifflin, 1955.

Father Arseny, 1893–1973: Priest, Prisoner, Spiritual Father. Translated by Vera Bouteneff. Crestwood, NY: St. Vladimir's Seminary Press, 2002.

"The General Panikhida or Requiem Service." In *Service Book of the Holy Orthodox-Catholic Apostolic Church*, 7th ed., translated by Isabel Florence Hapgood, 564–69. Englewood, NJ: Antiochian Orthodox Christian Archdiocese, 1996.

Harnack, Adolf von. *Die Mission und Ausbreitung des Christentums in den ersten drei Jahrhunderten.* Leipzig: J.C. Hinrichs, 1902. English translation: *The Mission and Expansion of Christianity in the First Three Centuries.* New York: G.P. Putnam's Sons, 1908.

Heidegger, Martin. *Poetry, Language, Thought.* Translated by Albert Hofstadter. New York: Harper and Row, 1971.

Henel, Heinrich. Review of "The Mothers in 'Faust': The Myth of Time and Creativity by Harold Jantz." *Modern Philology* 69, no. 2 (November 1971): 175–78.

Hippisley, Anthony. *Emvlemy i simvoly (1788): The First Russian Emblem Book.* New York: Brill, 1989.

Humphrey, Edith. *Mediation and the Immediate God: Scriptures, the Church, and Knowing God.* Crestwood, NY: St. Vladimir's Seminary Press, 2023.

Kasper, Walter. *The Absolute in History: The Philosophy and Theology of History in Schelling's Late Philosophy.* Translated by Katherine E. Wolff. New York: Paulist Press, 2018.

Kenworthy, Scott M., and Alexander S. Agadjanian. *Understanding World Christianity: Russia.* Minneapolis: Fortress, 2021.

Kishkovsky, Sophia. "Putin Now Orders Return of Russia's Most Precious Icon to the Church." *The Art Newspaper* (May 18, 2023), https://www.theartnewspaper.com/2023/05/18/putin-now-orders-return-of-russias-most-precious-icon-to-the-church.

Morson, Gary Saul. "Living Outside of Time." *New York Review of Books* (January 19, 2023): 48–50.

Newman, John Henry. "Personal Influence: The Means of Propagating the Truth." In John Henry Newman, *Fifteen Sermons Preached before the University of Oxford*, 75–98. London: Longmans, Green, and Co., 1900.

Ouspensky, Leonid, "The Iconostasis" and "The Holy or Royal Door." In *The Meaning of Icons*, edited by Leonid Ouspensky and Vladimir Lossky, 59–65, 66–69. Crestwood, NY: St. Vladimir's Seminary Press, 1989.

Schmemann, Alexander. *For the Life of the World*. Crestwood, NY: St. Vladimir's Seminary Press, 1973.

———. *Introduction to Liturgical Theology*. Translated by Asheleigh E. Moorhouse. Crestwood, NY: St. Vladimir's Seminary Press, 1986.

Tillich, Paul. *Theology of Culture*. New York: Oxford University Press, 1959.

Todorov, Tzvetan. *Facing the Extreme: Moral Life in the Concentration Camps*. Translated by Arthur Denner and Abigail Pollak. New York: Henry Holt, 1996.

Viscuso, Patrick. "Failed Attempt to Rewrite History: Review of *Same-Sex Unions in Premodern Europe*." *New Oxford Review* (December 1994).

Vodolazkin, Eugene. "The New Middle Ages." *First Things* (August 2016), https://www.firstthings.com/article/2016/08/the-new-middle-ages.

Ware, Timothy. *The Orthodox Church*. New ed. New York: Penguin, 1993.

Zinon (Teodor), Arkhimandrit. *Besedy ikonopistsa* [Conversations with an iconographer]. St. Petersburg: Bibliopolis, 2017.

INDEX